WOODCARVER'S LIBRARY

WOODCARVER'S LIBRARY

FOUR VOLUMES IN ONE

Carving Faces and Figures in Wood

Carving Horses in Wood

Carving Wooden Animals

Relief Woodcarving

by E. J. Tangerman and Eric Zimmerman

Greenwich House

New York

Originally published in four separate volumes entitled:
Carving Wooden Animals by E.J. Tangerman, Copyright © 1980
by Sterling Publishing Co., Inc.
Relief Woodcarving by E.J. Tangerman, Copyright © 1981 by
Sterling Publishing Co., Inc.
Carving Faces and Figures in Wood by E.J. Tangerman,
Copyright © 1980 by Sterling Publishing Co., Inc.
Carving Horses in Wood by Eric Zimmerman, Copyright © 1983
by Sterling Publishing Co., Inc.

Photographs of Yugoslav art used in *Carving Faces and Figures in
Wood* courtesy of the Smithsonian Institution, Traveling
Exhibition Service, Washington, D.C. 20560.

This 1984 edition is published by Greenwich House, a division of
Arlington House, Inc., distributed by Crown Publishers, Inc., by
arrangement with Sterling Publishing Co., Inc.

Manufactured in the United States of America

Library of Congress Cataloging in Publication Data

Tangerman, E. J. (Elmer John), 1907–
  Woodcarver's library.

  Originally published in four separate volumes.
  Includes indexes.
  Contents: Carving wooden animals — Relief, woodcarving —
Carving horses in wood — Carving faces and figures in wood.
  1. Wood-carving — Technique. I. Zimmerman, Eric. II. Title
III. Title: Wood carver's library.
TT199.7.T377 1984   731.4'62   84-13482
ISBN 0-517-310910

h g f e d c b

Contents

Introduction

Recent years have seen a marked growth of interest in wood carving, particularly amongst home craftsmen. Whether it be carving as applied to furniture, the production of small individual items, or the sculpture of large statues or similar items in the round, more people are practising the craft than at any time during the last three or four decades.

The fact is that there is no other subject which combines so ideally craftsmanship with artistic expression. Taking the former, wood is an exacting material which, although responding kindly to proper treatment, rebels furiously against bad handling. Its strong grain characteristics have to be understood and allowed for if the work is to avoid the limbo of failures and half-finished mediocrity.

On the artistic side, an appreciation of form, proportion, and balance is essential – in fact it is true to say that no excellence of technique can make up for lack of artistic expression. This, in truth, can be a danger, in that a student, concentrating purely on perfection of technique, may lose sight of the necessity for good design.

If these two basic requirements seem too exacting, the reader will find it a comfort to know that ability in both can be developed tremendously. Of the two, technique is the more easily acquired. It is largely a matter of practice. As in all work, skill to do comes of doing, and in fact in the last resort to get on with the job is the only way of learning. However, there are certain fundamental things which have been learnt over the years, and to know these may save the reader many hours of frustration and disappointment.

Artistic appreciation comes more slowly, and one cannot do better than examine good work, either of the past or the present, and endeavour to recognise the qualities that give it life and excellence. There are plenty of examples of carving to be seen in museums, churches, and other buildings, and if an endeavour is made to carve something in the same style or spirit it will not be long before an appreciation of quality is developed. It is the old story that true recognition of merit does not come until one endeavours to do something of the sort oneself. It is only then that one comes to realise the skill which the gifted artist-craftsman has put into his work.

The examples of work given in this book have been chosen with a definite end in view, to help both the beginner and the man who has had a certain limited amount of experience. In most cases the designs are drawn out on a grid so that the reader with little drawing skill can copy them map fashion, but it is emphasised that it is better for him to take them only as a basis on which to found his work, and to attempt to originate his own design as far as possible.

W. Wheeler
C.H. Hayward

CARVING FACES
AND
FIGURES IN WOOD

E. J. Tangerman

Contents

Fig. 1. "Widows" was carved by Dorde Kreća, a Yugoslav carver. It shows two women seated back to back, and was carved from a single stump. It is 33¾ in (84 cm) tall. See Chapter IX.

You Can Carve the Human Figure

THE HUMAN FIGURE is probably what we know most intimately and think we know best. Other things around us—animals, flowers, man-made and other inanimate objects—impinge upon us and we know them after a fashion. We give them human attributes and describe human attributes with them interchangeably. Other elements—heat, cold, rain, distance, mountains, water, fire, etc.—affect our well-being, so we interpret or represent them in various ways, but basically we relate everything else to ourselves. This is particularly true of primitive artists.

It follows that the most interesting subject for a whittler or a woodcarver is the human figure. Many of the carvings pictured in this book are primitive, but they are basic as well. They show much more graphically than words the many approaches and attempted solutions to the problem we know best, yet never solve—ourselves. This book tries to provide answers, both by supplying basic proportions and techniques, as well as by showing how woodcarvers all over the world have solved the problem, or have tried to solve it.

We who have always had trouble carving the human form can take heart from the knowledge that we are not alone. A few of us, gifted with a second sight, are able to carve the human form or face with little difficulty. For the rest, it is a slow and painful process. But that is no reason to abandon the effort; the way to make a good human body, or a good human face, is to make one after another until they approach what our inner eye sees.

The content of this book is graded from relatively simple to complex. Both in-the-round and panel carving are included, with some step-by-step photographs and patterns for many of the figures discussed. Instructions and hints are as thorough as I could make them. Sizes range from miniature to heroic and figures vary widely in pose, dress, age and even emotion. I hope they will encourage you to try, and to keep on trying. You will find the effort as rewarding as I have.

E. J. Tangerman

CHAPTER I

How to Choose and Use Tools

IF YOU ARE JUST STARTING TO CARVE, you can't beat a knife and a piece of pine or basswood. The great convenience of the pocketknife or clasp knife is that you can take it with you and set up shop whenever you're so inclined. A knife with a fixed handle is safer for cutting (the blade won't snap shut on your finger) but a nuisance to carry; its edge must be protected against all things hard or soft. Its handle is bigger and more comfortable, but you need a sheath to carry it. The knife should be of good quality and have a carbon-steel blade, rather than stainless. It will rust if you don't keep it lightly oiled, but it will also hold an edge longer, which is important unless you long to carry a hone and a lap with you as well. As to blade shape and size, you'll find that you seldom need a blade longer than 1½ in (4 cm); a longer blade will bend and your hand is too far back to control it as well. A knife with one long blade with a sharp point (*saber* or *B-clip*) and a smaller one with a stubbier tip (*pen*) is the basic answer. It can have three blades, but shouldn't have more than that or the knife becomes too clumsy. I usually carry two knives—one with pen, spear, and B-clip, the other with pen and B-clip (Fig. 2). The three-bladed knife is larger and has wider blades, so will take heavier cuts; the small blade handles the delicate and hard-to-get-at spots and shallow concavities. The small blade is more likely to break and harder to control, as well as slower, but the big blades get in their own way on occasion.

Wood has grain and tends to splinter and split along it. It is much easier to cut with the grain than across it, of course (those long curling chips are cut with the grain), but a tree is a living thing and its grain may not be straight, or it may veer around damage or a knot. The first thing you must learn is to keep the grain in mind at all times. If you cut with it, it's easy; if you cut squarely across it, it's harder work but no problem with splitting; but watch out if you cut *into* the grain, because even the thin wedge of a knife blade may cause splitting and will certainly cause some roughness. The problem varies with the wood: basswood and white pine offer fewer problems

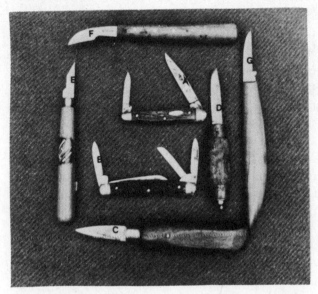

Fig. 2. Typical knives for woodcarving include: A, a penknife with pen and B-clip blades, and B, a slightly larger one with pen, spear, and cut-off pen. Both are German-made. Below them is C, an inexpensive fixed-blade knife, and to the right is a Swedish sloyd, D. The others are specialized shapes: E and F are used for chip carving; G is a German fixed-blade knife.

than ash or mahogany, teak less than walnut. You will learn about grain quickly and soon appreciate the necessity for cutting in the opposite direction on the into-grain side of even a slightly diagonal groove.

The standard cartoon of a whittler shows him paring off big chips with bold strokes going away from himself. That is very safe but produces only chips. The most important cut for the knife is exactly like that used by someone peeling a potato: the knife caught in the curve of the four fingers, the thumb on the work, and the cut made by closing the hand. That gives the greatest control because it is finger rather than arm muscle that does the work. (While you're learning this cut, be careful of your thumb.) Other frequent cuts are made with the thumb or the forefinger extended along the heel of the blade to provide added force just behind the cut itself. Or the knife may be gripped like a dagger and drawn or pushed to make a slice—this is an arm-muscle cut, so control is poorer. Another type of cut is that in which the point of the knife is pushed into the wood, then the knife is rocked or rotated, in the first case to make a triangular incision and in the second to make a cone-shaped depression.

Some cuts are better done by using the thumb or forefinger of the other hand to push and guide the blade. This is very helpful with harder woods and ivory because the actual cutting force can be so exactly controlled. The cut, in any case, is very short because the hand itself will be gripping or resting on the work.

7

Woodcarvers use more tools

BASIC TOOLS of the woodcarver are *chisels* with either flat or curved edges, pushed by hand or driven by *mallet*, depending upon the hardness of the wood and on personal preference. Chisels in general are shorter and lighter than carpenter's chisels of the same width and are available in many more degrees of curvature, of both edge and shank. They are often supplemented by *rasps* for rough work in soft woods and by *riffler files* (small, shaped files) for smoothing details.

The carver's flat chisel is called a *firmer* (*F*, Fig. 3), and differs from a carpenter's chisel in that it is sharpened from both sides, so it is less inclined to dig in. It can be obtained in widths from ¹⁄₁₆ to 2 in (1.6 to 50 mm). Edge is usually perpendicular to the side, but some have the edge at an angle and are called *skews* (*A*, Fig. 4). The skew is commonly used by European carvers much as we use a knife; they hold it by the blade rather than the handle for such work. Curved chisels are called *gouges* (*B*, *E*, Fig. 3), and can range from quite flat curves to a U-shape. The smallest U-shaped gouge, usually ¹⁄₁₆ in (1.6 mm) across the flat side, is called a *veiner* (*D*, Fig. 3), from the work it often does. The next size, ⅛ in (3.2 mm), is called a *fluter* —for the same reason. The very large ones are usually used for rough-shaping (up to 2½ in, or 6 cm, wide) although they can also smooth broad, curved surfaces in finishing. A modified firmer, called the *bullnose* (*G*, Fig. 3; *C*, Fig. 4), is being used increasingly by amateurs for shaping; it is simply a firmer with the corners rounded off, so that the edge is a flat arc.

There are a number of specially shaped chisel edges designed for particular jobs. Most familiar is the *parting*, or *V-tool*, shaped as its name implies (*C*, Fig. 3). It is used for outlining and for cutting accurate V-grooves, although one edge will tend to dig in and tear in diagonal cuts unless it is extremely sharp. Another is the *macaroni*, which cuts a channel that is flat on the bottom and square on the sides. Similar is the *fluteroni*, which cuts a smaller trench with arcuate corners.

Wide tools, and some narrower ones, are tapered down to the tang (which enters the handle). These are called *spades* or *fishtails* (*A*, Fig. 3; *B*, Fig. 4) and get into tight places better. The shank may also be forged into a long (*long-bent*) or a short (*short-bent*) curve near the blade (*A*, *C*, Fig. 5) to get into pockets or to undercut (the continuing problem of the woodcarver is clearance for his tools). There is also a *back-bent* tool shape, which is necessary, for example, to undercut individual grapes of a bunch, if you specialize in grapes. For small work there are shorter chisels with handles that

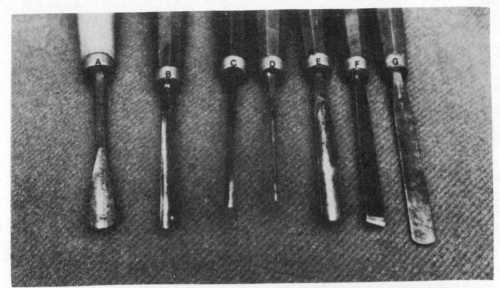

Fig. 3. Typical chisel shapes: A, 1-in (25.4-mm) #9 spade gouge; B, ½-in (12.7-mm) #10 gouge; C, ¼-in (6.3-mm) V-tool; D, veiner; E, ½-in (6.3-mm) #7 gouge; F, ½-in (12.7-mm) firmer; G, ⅝-in (16-mm) bullnose firmer.

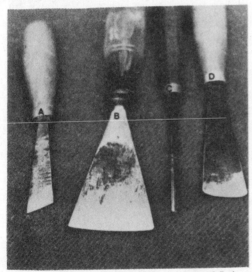

Fig. 4. Shorter tools include: A, 1-in (25.4-mm) skew firmer with homemade spade shank; B, 2½-in (6-cm) #5 spade gouge; C, ½-in (12.7-mm) bullnose #7 gouge; D, 1½-in (3-cm) #5 gouge.

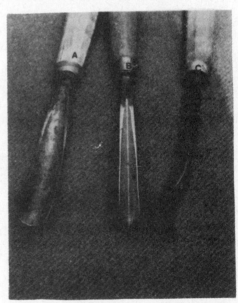

Fig. 5. Special shapes: A, 1-in (25.4-mm) long-bent #9 gouge; B, ¾-in (19-mm) spade V-tool; C, short-bent #5 gouge.

9

fit the palm of the hand, as does the shoemaker's awl or the engraver's burin. In modern days, most carvers stick to fairly low relief, so tools such as these specials are not necessary. The bent gouges, for example, have a tendency to spring and are hard to sharpen.

Carving tools are either held in one hand and struck with a mallet in the other, or pushed with one hand and guided and restrained with the other, so the work must be held or supported in some way. Oriental carvers put it in their laps and may lock a knee over a three-dimensional piece. Big panels will easily rest on a flat surface, while smaller ones can be set against a backboard, benchplate (Fig. 6), or wooden vee on a bench. It is also possible simply to nail (through waste wood) a panel to a surface, or to hold it in a vise. For 3-D pieces, however, European carvers long ago invented the *carver's screw*, which is screwed into the base of the work through a hole in the bench, then locked with a wingnut. (I have never found one necessary.)

Mallets were once shaped like wooden potato mashers (mine still are), but I've seen wood hammers, soft-faced hammers, and clubs of various sorts used. Nowadays, there are plastic-faced mallets, lead or babbit-metal mallets, rubber-faced mallets—whatever suits a particular carver's preferences. I use a light mallet for more exact control of many cuts. Other carvers do these by hand, but I have found that several weights of mallet will work as well.

What tools to buy is largely a matter of personal preference or availability when you start. As you learn, you will buy the tools you particularly need for what you prefer to do. I started with a kit of nine tools, several of which I have never used—or almost never. Authorities offer various lists, but these are based on their own teaching methods. Charles M. Sayer, who taught panel carving, suggests four initial tools: ½-in (12.7-mm), or ⅜- to ⅝-in (9.6 to 16-mm) No. 39 parting tool; ⅝-in (16 mm) No. 5 straight gouge; 1-in (25-mm) or ⅞-in (22.4-mm) No. 3 straight gouge; and ⅜-in (9.6-mm) No. 7 straight gouge. For relief carving, he adds a ⅜-in (9.6-mm) No. 3 straight gouge. H. M. Sutter, who has taught carving for the past 30 or 40 years, starts his students with five tools, plus an all-purpose carver's knife: ⅜-in (9.6-mm) No. 3 straight gouge; ⅝-in (16-mm) No. 5 straight gouge (these two preferably fishtail); ⅜-in (9.6-mm) No. 9 straight gouge; 1-mm or 1/32-in No. 11 veiner; and a ⅜-in (9.6-mm) No. 1 parting or V-tool. Note that neither suggests fancy shapes or skew chisels to start.

The numbers, by the way, refer to the so-called London system of identification in which a firmer is No. 1, a skew firmer 2, a flat gouge 3, and a

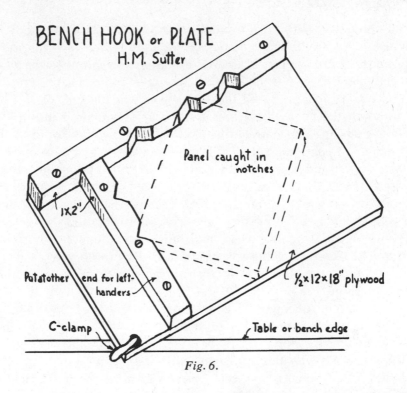

BENCH HOOK or PLATE
H. M. Sutter

Panel caught in notches

1×2"

Put another end for left-handers

C-clamp

½×12×18" plywood

Table or bench edge

Fig. 6.

U-shaped gouge 11 or 12, with the other arcs in between. Other numbers are used by certain suppliers for special tools or for their own catalog identification, but most also show a cross-section of the various sweeps or radii. Also, carving tools made on the Continent are sized in millimeters: 1, 2, 3, 4, 5, 6, 7, 8, 10, 12, 16, 20, 25, 30, 35 mm wide, etc. (1 mm = 0.039 in). The English system has tools from ⅟₁₆ to ⅜ in (1.6 to 3.2 mm) in sixteenths, then in larger steps up to the 2½-in (6 cm) maximum.

My best advice is to start with a limited set from a reputable supplier. Find out how they work, what you prefer to make, and what tools work best for you. You don't need a golfbag full of clubs to make a round. You'll need a flat gouge for roughing, shaping and cleaning up; a firmer for carving flat surfaces and angles; a veiner for outlining and emphasizing lines and/or a V-tool for similar purposes; as well as a gouge or two of varied sweeps for making concave curves. As you progress, add gouges and a skew chisel, but vary gouge size considerably; if you have a ⅜-in (9.6-mm), don't get a ½-in (12.2-mm) of the same sweep. For heavy work, carpenter's chisels and gouges are cheaper.

I find chisels easier to learn to use than the knife. The cutting edge is narrower and less versatile and it is pushed directly instead of being used in an arc by finger or arm power. If you use a mallet, you must obviously learn to watch the chisel edge, not the head of the mallet. You must learn to take it easy and not try to remove all the waste wood on the first pass. You must learn to adjust the angle of the tool as you cut so it doesn't run in and stick or run out and slip. You start cutting at an edge and work toward the middle; if you cut to an edge, the chisel will break out and tear the wood. Learn at once how to cut across grain with a gouge. Learn to be ambidextrous with the chisels. If you are planning a panel with a background, practice *setting in* or *bosting* before you try it on the panel. (First, you outline the background space with a veiner or V-tool, then you drive in firmers and flat gouges along this groove to limit the cut. Then, and only then, attempt to cut out wood with a gouge. These steps must be taken in order or you will gouge into the design, or the outlining firmer will crush surface fibres and mess up the sharp edge of the design.)

Your constant challenge will come from the grain of the wood. In any diagonal cut, for example, one edge of the gouge will cut cleanly, the other will drag and tear the wood slightly because it is cutting into the grain. You'll learn how to cope with this and soon will be adjusting automatically for it. The other major point is to keep your tools razor-sharp, particularly for cutting soft woods—so you'll have to learn how to sharpen. Makers of whetstones provide literature on the basics of this. (*See* Fig. 7 for typical sharpening equipment.)

Some general hints

WHEN YOU ARE USING either knife or chisel, try to avoid wedging out the chip; you may break the tool or split the wood. Obviously, tools are not to be used for cutting newspaper clippings, paring nails, or peeling electrical insulation; all these destroy the cutting edge. The old professionals laid their chisels out with the edges toward themselves, so they could select the right chisel easily. I find this hard to do because it requires reversal of the tool when you pick it up and when you lay it down. Some carvers put distinguishing marks on handles for rapid identification of frequently used tools.

Leave a light film of oil on the tools after use—it will reduce rusting. This is particularly true of pocketknives: sweat can be very corrosive. Keep tools very sharp. Store them out of reach of the curious, old and young, and keep the edges protected if you carry them about.

There are canvas and leather rolls available for carrying tools, or you can make them yourself. For storage, tools can be racked or placed in slots in a drawer. It is a good idea to hone a chisel after you've used it extensively, but do not strop it until you use it again; a stropped edge deteriorates rapidly, as any barber will tell you. Also, in sharpening, don't change the cutting angle without reason. Presumably, your tools were sharpened to the basic

Fig. 7. Sharpening equipment includes (clockwise from top): a round-edge roughing stone, an impregnated-rubber (flexible) fine-grit, two Arkansas slips, and a leather strop mounted on plywood.

15° angle when you got them. As you hone, you will probably widen that angle slightly because you tend to create a chisel edge. This is all right, but periodically it will be necessary to hone away metal from the entire cutting face to match the edge wear. Don't grind a tool unless you've chipped or broken the cutting edge or want to change it; grinding can draw temper or burn the cutting edge, among other drawbacks.

Lastly, if you nick yourself, protect the cut, because you may find you'll repeat the nicking. This is particularly true of the ball of the thumb when you make small carvings with paring cuts. It may be advisable to use a finger stall initially; stationery stores sell rubber ones that are used by people who sort papers.

The proper way to carve is to stand at a high bench or stand that is heavy enough so it doesn't shift under the mallet blows. Some sculptors have four-legged stands that are weighted with a rock toward the bottom, with the top adjustable for height, possibly even incorporating a lockable lazy Susan so it can be rotated. Panel carvers, like those who work on cuckoo-clock frames, have sloping tables with 2-in (5-cm) tops and pins to index and hold the work. I work on a trestle table on the terrace, a basement bench, or even on a bridge table. I sit down whenever possible. The main thing is to have a stable surface that will absorb mallet blows, with some sort of adjacent surface on which your tools may be placed. For any given job, you rarely need more than ten or a dozen tools. You can have whatever sort of bench or stand that suits your ego, and as many tools as you like, but a solid surface and good light, plus some air, suit me best.

Personally, I don't need a studio.

CHAPTER II

How to Choose the Wood

"WHAT WOOD SHOULD I USE?" is a common neophyte question, and one often asked by the sculptor undertaking work in wood as well, particularly if the sculpture is to be heroic in size. If you are a neophyte, you'd best start with basswood, soft white pine, or jelutong (now being imported from Indonesia). All are essentially similar in color and reaction to tools, although many whittlers prefer the basswood, if they can get it.

Here is a counter-question: "What sources of wood are available to me?" If it's only the local lumberyard, you have problems, because they probably don't stock basswood and their white pine may not be first grade. Also, thickness is likely to be 2 in (5 cm) at most, so you may have to glue up a laminated block for anything over that. Basswood may grow in your area and be known as *bee tree* (it's similar to European linden). It is soft, colorless, and doesn't split excessively. Ponderosa pine or sugar pine are almost as good. Avoid strongly colored pieces of the former. These woods are easy to work, but they don't hold detail very well and tend to break down if handled. Also, they are lifeless when finished in natural color, they're better painted or tinted. One caution: avoid yellow pine, which is hard, knotty, resinous, and tends to split.

Several other woods are commonly used for simple carvings, including poplar (bruises easily and tends to grip tools), cedar (its color may be a problem), and willow (watch out for splitting). Balsa may be good for models, but is unfit for carving. Old-time whittlers tended to use whatever was available, depending upon what they planned to make. (Some present-day carvers also scrounge.) In general, they tended to harder woods, particularly the fruits and nuts: pear, pecan, cherry, apple, walnut. All of these tend to check in large pieces, but they will take detail and finish more interestingly without color. Black walnut is without doubt the best American carving wood. It has a fine, tough grain, takes detail well, and doesn't have too much tendency to split. However, it is quite dark when finished.

If you can find them, butternut, red alder and myrtle are much softer than walnut and easier to carve. Redwood is quite soft and may alternate layers of hard and soft wood (winter and summer growth are at different rates); this makes trouble. Sweet or red gum is durable, but tends to warp and twist. I have carved ash with good results, although it is stringy. Cypress is good, particularly for large figures exposed to the air; it can be carved green because it has little tendency to shrink or check. Beech, hickory, sycamore and magnolia are all hard to cut and recommended only for shallow carving. Birch and rock or sugar maple are hard to carve and finish, but durable. Soft maple (commonly stocked by suppliers) is not a good carving wood. Eastern white oak is inherently strong and will take detail, but should be carved with tools. Swamp or red oak has a very prominent grain and coarse structure: avoid it. Dogwood is very dense and hard and can stand shock without splitting, but it is difficult to carve. Holly, our whitest wood, is hard and tends to check, but it holds detail well. In the Southwest, there are mesquite, ironwood and osage orange, all very hard, inclined to split and difficult to carve, but finish beautifully.

The imported woods, if you can get them, offer much more variety in color and figure or grain, but they tend to be as hard as walnut, or harder, so are not for the neophyte, the impatient, or the slapdash. Also, they are much easier to carve with chisels and in some cases with power equipment. The exception perhaps is mahogany, which is not one wood, but a whole series, some not even members of the same family. Quality and color vary with source and individual piece. Honduras mahogany is fine-grained and relatively soft; Cuban is dense and varies in hardness; South American likely to be grainy and splintery. Philippine mahogany has a reputation for coarseness, but can vary widely: I have samples ranging from white to dark red and coarse to dense; the heaviest is double the weight of the lightest. Other woods sold as mahogany include luanda. Primavera cuts like mahogany and can be stained to be indistinguishable from it. It is a white wood, hence is called white mahogany.

Teak, which comes from Burma or Thailand, is my favorite carving wood, particularly for panels. It is a warm brown, with little visible grain, and not subject to insect attack, warpage or dry rot. It does not vary or check to any degree and so is excellent for exposed carving. It is about like walnut to carve, but contains an oil that makes the tools slip through it easily, but do not be surprised to find that it dulls tools rapidly. This occurs because the wood grows in swamps and apparently draws up fine silica with the water—as our own holly draws up black dirt to become grey rather than white.

Chinese teak is not brown, but red and harsh-grained, which is why the Chinese enameled it black and most Americans think of teak as a shiny black wood, just as they assume that all black African carvings are ebony. (Many are now softer woods, stained or painted.) Ebony, which grows in Africa, India, Ceylon (now Sri Lanka), Indonesia, and South and Central America, varies in color from black (Gabon, from Africa) to dark brown with lighter striping (Macassar, from Indonesia, or Calamander, from Ceylon). Like lignum vitae and cocobola (lignum vitae in Mexico and Central America is guayacan), ebony is very hard and used primarily by sculptors willing to work hard per chip. Ebony, however, is the only black wood.

English sycamore (harewood) is like our holly and available in wider boards. Lacewood, satinwood, briar, sandal, purpleheart (heat it to make it purple), bubinga, vermilion (very crimson), and others will take fine detail but are very expensive—I use them for elements of mobiles and for pendants. They can be whittled, but you'd best know your stuff. Rosewood, which comes from many southern countries, varies from soft brown through dark red to red-brown and almost purple, with other colors thrown in (Mexico). This is a beautiful wood, but quite hard to carve and tends to give a heavy effect. Save it for pieces in which color and grain will not defeat your carving. Most expensive of woods is pink ivory, from Africa, once the private wood of Zulu kings. It is very hard, like ebony, and pinkish to red.

Finally, start with familiar and easy woods and work up to the others. The exotic woods make wonderful carvings, but take much in sweat, blood and tears. I have indicated, piece by piece, my choice of wood—or that of other carvers—throughout this book. Also, regardless of wood, avoid a blank with knots, flaws or checks if you can. Knots take the edge off tools and may fall out later. Both knots and flaws require some skill at finishing. Checks have a disconcerting way of opening and closing with humidity changes, and filling a check to hide it may cause pressure that will crack the piece later.

CHAPTER III

The Question of Size

How to decide it, and how to get a pattern to fit

USUALLY, THE SIZE of a figure carving is dictated by the size of the wood available, not so much its length, but its width or thickness. Lumber is 1 or 2 in thick (25.4 or 51 mm), which means a ⅞- or 1¾-in (22.4-or 44-mm) planed thickness. Widths are arbitrary 1, 2, 3 or 4 in, again reduced by planing. So, after you've selected the figure you want to carve, measure its maximum dimension and enlarge or reduce your drawing or photograph to fit the maximum dimension to the wood.

Generally, wood size is unimportant. If you are fortunate and can select, size is largely a matter of taste. If you are planning to sell the pieces, the larger it is, the more you can charge for it in general. Secondly, the larger the piece, the easier it is to carve detail and the less trouble you'll have with grain in complex areas, but also the more waste wood you'll have to remove. (Carving time really isn't reduced much by reducing size—as you approach a miniature, carving time will actually increase.) Thirdly, think of where and how the piece is to be displayed or used: big carvings soon fill all available space, and small carvings tend to be lost amid the larger decorations of a room. Fourth, a large carving tends to require less support because it has enough mass to resist even mallet blows; it does, however, require larger tools and a greater ability to get around it, and has a greater tendency to check. If you are whittling, you can't hold a large piece in your hand, and the whittling seems to go much more slowly as a result.

All in all, I would say that a figure 6 or 8 in tall (15.2 or 20.3 cm) is about right for whittling. It can be twice that size for carving with chisels. In this book most carvings are sketched at about half size, to provide some clue as to the taste (or wood availability) of the original maker. If you double the size of the drawings, you'll have the original size of the piece, unless a footnote specifies a different one (usually larger).

To convert the pattern to the desired size, the fastest method is to have the drawing photostatically enlarged. Most copying machines make only

Figs. 8 and 9. This shepherd from Oberammergau (above) is 6 in (15 cm) tall, but has a thin base—which looks good but is difficult to shape well. "Justice," an heroic 10-ft (3-m) figure, was carved of pine over a century ago to top a courthouse tower, and now is in the Shelburne (Vt.) Museum.

same-size copies, but there is probably a local commercial shop that does photostatting, and some of the newer copying machines can enlarge or reduce also. If you can take a photo of the drawing, you can blow it up in an enlarger and either print or copy to desired size, or you can project a transparency to any desired size and trace the image.

If none of these methods fits the situation, I customarily make a point-to-point outline sketch (*see* Fig. 10). I put top or base and side reference lines on the original at right angles to each other, and make all measurements from them. Similar base and side reference lines are put on the wood or another sheet of paper. Then I locate key points of the pattern by measuring from the base and side lines to that point on the original, multiplying the measurements by the enlargement or reduction factor, and locating the matching point on the copy. Obviously, it is easiest to double or triple the size, or to halve it; otherwise, the mathematics become too involved and the risk of error is great. If I'm doubling the size, for example, let's assume the point I am locating is 1½ in (3.8 cm) from the side and 4¼ in (10.8 cm) from the bottom. I measure 2 × 1½ = 3 in (7.6 cm) from the side and 2 × 4¼ = 8½ in (21.6 cm) from the bottom. When a number of such points have been located, lines of the proper shape are drawn to connect them.

POINT-to-POINT METHOD

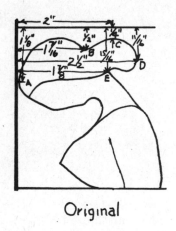

Original

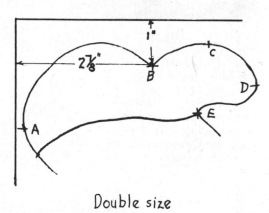

Double size

Fig. 10.

If you feel a bit shaky about the point-to-point method, use the method of squares (Fig. 11). On the original, or on a sheet of plastic, draw a grid of ⅛-in (3 mm) squares, big enough to cover the original, of course. On the wood, or on a sheet of paper, draw a corresponding grid of squares that gives you the desired enlargement (¼ in [6 mm] for double size, ⅜ in [9 mm] for triple size). Now copy the drawing square by square. It sounds slow and difficult, but is really quite fast and accurate, and the transparent template can be saved for reuse on other pieces.

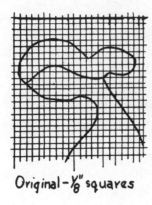

Original – ⅛" squares

Fig. 11.

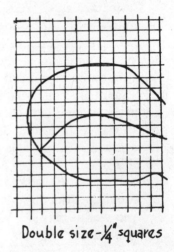

Double size – ¼" squares

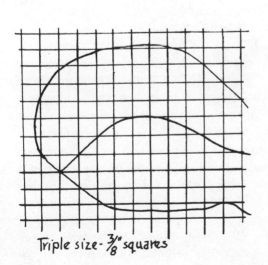

Triple size – ⅜" squares

METHOD of SQUARES

CHAPTER IV

How to Carve a Face – and Head

"How DO I CARVE A FACE?" is probably the most common question asked by woodcarvers intent upon improving their work. Unlike some other operations in the art, there is no simple answer here. This question leads to a question in reply: "What kind of a face do you want to carve?"

Caricature and "Western-style" carvings come closest to having a standard formula—most use a series of notches and surfaces to suggest facial contours. The competent caricaturist tends to develop his own style, often based upon his own countenance, and tends to repeat the head in the same position and with the same expression until it becomes a stereotype. Further, a great many such faces are not caricatures as much as three-dimensional cartoons or, more properly, grotesques—they rely for their humor upon a gross distortion of one facial feature, usually the nose. Such a face can be carved rapidly, with little practice, and its deficiencies in detail are compensated for by judicious touching up with paint or ink. To the serious carver, such a face eventually becomes trite. He seeks expression, likeness, normalcy, and comes to realize, as a sculptor friend remarked, "Caricature is a cop-out."

And well it may be. We all use the face as the most important recognition feature among humans. We establish race, mood, background, experience, state of health among strangers and identity among friends. We worry about the "face we present to the world." We know a great deal about the face, which we normally look at first and longest when we meet someone, so we set a higher standard for its proper reproduction. A carved figure can be misproportioned, awkwardly posed, or otherwise distorted and we are not particularly conscious of it, but we are immediately conscious of any error in a face, however small. What's more, we have memorized an endless number of stereotypes for races, for nationalities, for ages, and particularly for specific individuals. We have a catalog of images for historical figures based largely upon the face—for Jesus, Washington, Churchill, Lincoln, Jefferson, Napoleon, Franklin, and an endless number of other people—all from some particular portrait or traditional description.

The individual may, in point of fact, have differed markedly from the accepted facial image, but both his face (and his age!) are now fixed by convention. You can vary his body structure and even his clothing with some impunity and few are likely to notice, but change the face even slightly and even your friends will dismiss the carving as faulty.

There is, for most of us, a long and painful process before the achievement of good faces. No formula will help us beyond the initial stages. One can memorize facial proportions and a series of steps in carving and still not produce memorable faces for a very long time. This may be, in fact, one area in which there is no alternative for apprenticeship; that is, for long and painful practice. You must carve a thousand faces, as Michelangelo said, to carve one *good* face.

Initially, it is important to understand your goal and the steps towards it. What kind of face do you want to carve? Is it to be grotesque, caricature, formal face, or portrait (*see* Fig. 12)? Is it to be in the round or in low relief? If you are shooting at formal faces or portraits, endless carving of caricatures, for example, will be of little help. And once you abandon the profile depiction to carve faces at various angles, low-relief carving can be most difficult of all, because actual proportion must be replaced by a simulation of proportion in the third dimension. The smooth, well-rounded cheek may actually become almost angular in cross-section, and eyes and mouth are no longer uniform. The Egyptians, for example, spent centuries learning how to carve a relief head other than in profile.

The head is roughly like an egg set on its point on the neck which is half a head long in front for a male, thinner and longer for a female. The neck is like a tree growing out of the shoulders and leaning forward, so that the head is set forward, more so in the female than in the male. The face—forgetting for the moment any receding hairline—is the length of the hand and about two-thirds as wide as it is high. A most important fact is that the eyes are almost centered vertically—a very common mistake is to place them too high. Each eye is a fifth to a quarter of the width of the head, and they are normally about an eye-width apart. The tip of the nose is about halfway from the center line of the eye to the chin, and the mouth center one-third of the distance from nose tip to chin. Mouth width is 1½ to 2 times eye width, lip thickness (at center) a fifth of the distance from nose to chin. The ears are roughly as long as the nose and aligned with it front to back. They are just behind the center of the skull.

The most common mistake in face carving is to have the cheeks too far

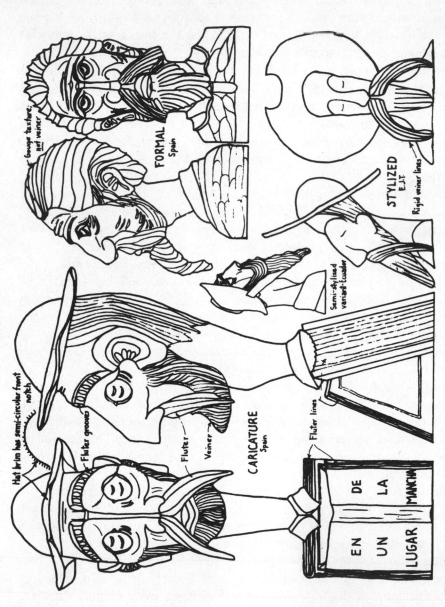

Fig. 12. Four versions of a popular subject, Don Quixote. Compare the simplification, streamlining, and lack of detail of the stylized version (lower right) with the detail of the others, which also put more stress on texturing. See also Figs. 13 and 14.

forward. The angle formed by nose tip and cheekbone is roughly 90° and the nose projects from the egg shape of the head when viewed in profile. The chin also projects from the same viewpoint, but not as much—only the classic witch has chin and nose tip aligned vertically, and even vertical alignment of brow and chin is rare (and makes for a very pugnacious face).

All of these ratios are averages, of course; any face varies from them. That's what makes us individuals. The face is not symmetrical, even if it looks that way; the small differences from side to side account for the abnormal look of a mirror image. Also, hairdos, beards, jowls and fleshiness tend to obliterate the egg shape, so the basic proportions are merely takeoff points for carving. (The Spanish caricature carver capitalized on this by making Don Quixote's face much longer than an egg shape and making Sancho Panza's almost pear-shaped—*see* Figs. 13 and 15.)

To me, there are two vital elements in making an in-the-round head in repose. One is the eye size, shape and positioning; the other the profile,

Figs. 13 and 14. Contemporary Spanish caricature of Don Quixote (left), with somewhat stylized eyes and nose. Formal head of the same subject is rough-finished and tinted, and also from Spain. Hair and beard variations are suggested by gouge cuts rather than the fine veiner lining of the first piece.

25

which includes brow, mouth and chin. The profile is particularly important in portraiture because it establishes the basic structure of the face to a considerable degree. (Typical profiles belonging to certain races or even tribes are being obliterated by intermarriage, particularly in the United States, so that children today often show decidedly mixed profiles. In countries where there has been a considerable period of such intermarriage, Mexico and Latin America for example, many mestizos are a mixture of Spanish or other European blood and one or more Indian tribes, and their precise origins are almost impossible to establish visually.)

The basic face, whatever its eyes and profile, is distorted by expression. Surprise shoots the eyebrows up, anger pulls them together and down, joy widens the mouth and lifts its outer ends, thus partially closing the lower eyelids, while pique and despair draw mouth corners down (tending to narrow the mouth). The face is also affected by age: vast networks of wrinkles, crow's-feet at eye corners, deep lines around the mouth, hollowing of cheeks,

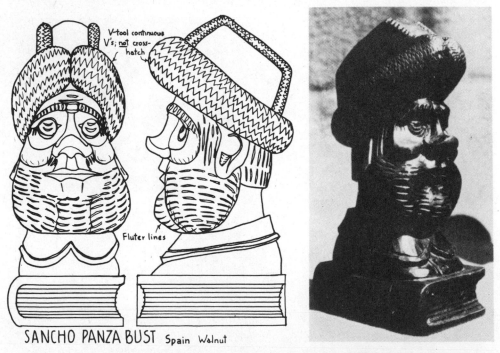

SANCHO PANZA BUST Spain Walnut

Fig. 15. This head of Sancho Panza is a companion-piece to the Don Quixote caricature (Fig. 13), and contrasts sharply with it in that it is stubby where Don Quixote is attenuated. Similarities in eye treatment identify them as products of the same sculptor.

26

bulging of the nose, possibly greater prominence of the chin from loss of teeth, sagging jowls. It is also affected by corpulence—the fat face is wider in the jowls and has few wrinkles. These are refinements of face carving, but are essential if the face is to be representative and alive, rather than static and frozen.

Fig. 16. Smiling conquistador (left) and dour Scot are two of the four caricatured faces on this four-way head carved in cedar and mounted on onyx. The other heads are Zapotec Indians. Such a carving provides excellent practice for carving faces.

You can practice all these elements by carving a four-way head or two. (*See* Fig. 16.) They're caricatures, of course, but they do place the nose on the corner of a block and the eyes midway of each side (in this case carved flat with the side). Or try a single head, starting with the nose at one corner of a squared stick. This automatically leaves wood for the ears and gives a reasonable slope to the cheeks, an idea which the Mayans used on cornice ends a thousand years ago.

27

Carve a step-by-step head

START WITH A SQUARED BLOCK. Mark off from one corner, both ways, a line down from the top 1½ times the width of the block; i.e., if the block is 1 in (25.4 mm) square, put the line 1½ in (38.1 mm) down from the top. This is the chin line (Step I, top left, in Fig. 17). Halve the distance from this line to the top and put in the eye line. Now, a third of the way down from nose to chin, put in the mouth line. (Some authorities make this two-fifths of the way; the difference is not too vital.) Now cut in perpendicularly across the corner at the chin and nose lines, and notch out wood from below so that you create a new sloping flat about a fourth the width of a side. Notch the corner at the eye line (Step II), cutting from both above and below. Also mark notch-outs for the ears, the bottom one in line with the bottom of the nose, the upper *above* the eye by an eye width. (It is convenient at this point to draw in a "reference eye" on the eye line, about a third of the block width in length and shaped like the oval of the complete eye, not just of the "open" part between the lids: Step II in sketch.)

Begin to round up the head on top, notching over the ears to make this easier, and splitting off the wood above the eye notch to flatten the brow (Step III). Also notch below the ears and rough-form the neck. Draw in eyebrow lines on the brow as arcs meeting at the center of the eye notch and rising to 1½ eye widths over the eye line at each side. Mark in a nose triangle with its apex in line with the *top* of the eyebrow arcs (so there is some width of nose at the eye line). Cut V-notches along the nose line to meet perpendicular notches cut in along the eyebrow line (also Step III). Mark in the mouth line again, and extend the lines on each side of the nose to the lower edge of the jaw. Cut a small notch to denote the mouth-center line, then cut away the sharp point of the chin and round the chin and mouth area to notches extending down from the nose.

Now begin to rough-shape the eye (Step IV), remembering that the eyeballs and lids are about an eye width apart and that each eye is about a fifth of the finished width of the head. Making these shapes involves deepening the grooves between eye and nose, and carving grooves between brow and eye, and eye and cheek.

This completes rough-forming, and you're ready for the shaping of Step V. Form the eyeball more accurately and slope the line below the brow. (Here we're carving an inset eye. Many people have eyes with folds or laps in this area, but let's leave that for a later head.) Rough-form the nostrils and fair off the cheeks next to them. Draw in a hairline to suit your fancy, then the

28

Fig. 17. Carving a head, step by step (I to VI).

ears and nose, and carve the shapes. Remember that there is a bulge along the brow line, particularly in males, so slope back from just above the eyebrow line to the hairline. Now you're ready for Step VI, finishing. Final-shape the ears and put in whatever convolutions you wish. Do the same for the nose and nostrils, as well as for the lips and chin. Normally the lower lip is shorter and fuller than the upper, and there is a definite groove between lower lip and chin—the chin is a fat oval bump, actually. Open the eyes by drawing in lid lines and hollowing out—*very* carefully—between them. Drill pupil holes and suggest the outline of the corneas by shallow V-notching. These latter steps determine the personality of the face, so they must be done carefully. Suggestions and ideas for carving the features are given in this chapter, including sketches. Study them! And good luck.

Carving the eyes—fine points

THE EYES are normally just above the median line of the head, but setting them at the median line is fairly accurate. There is an eye width between normal eyes, two eye widths between the pupil centers. There is one open-eye width between eye and eyebrow, and the eyebrow is highest and widest over the outer third of the eye. Eyes may be larger, or smaller, open wider or less, be wide apart or close. The forehead ends in the outer rim of the orbital (brow) circle.

All of these factors must be considered in laying out and carving eyes. Some other factors are sketched. These include: The upper lid normally covers the upper edge of the cornea; the lower lid is at its lower rim or below. (When the eye looks down, the upper lid lowers with it; the lower lid does not. When the eye looks up, the space between the lids is increased and usually the eyebrow is lifted as well.) The upper lid extends over or outside the lower at the outer edge, and the lower outer corner of the upper lid extends below the center of the globe of the eye. The *canthus major*, the eye muscle next to the nose, must be shown if eye shape is to be right. So must the bulge of the cornea and the bulge of the upper lid over it. Eye-cavity position and shape are very important; whether eyes bulge or are recessed, whether the line where brow meets nose is above or below the eye center, and the exact shape of the folds below the upper eyebrow, all are important if a likeness is to be obtained.

Most of the motion in the eyelids is made by the upper lid. In fact, a closed eye looks as if the upper lid had come down to cover the eyeball, an effect accentuated by the upper lashes, which cover the lower. Lowering the upper lid therefore creates a brooding or sleepy look; raising it can suggest, successively, attention, or alarm and fright. In this last emotion, the cornea may practically disappear upward.

A wink is not just a closed eye, unless the winker is an expert. The normal person winks by pulling up the cheek muscle below, so the whole side of the face, including the mouth, is pulled up. The crease between cheek and eye is intensified and the lower lid pushed up. Wrinkles radiate from the eye corners.

I begin an eye by shaping the oval of the eyeball, taking care to make it large enough to include the lids and allowing for any bulge between eye and brow or anything abnormal—like a puff—beneath it. The eyes may actually slope upward or downward slightly at their outer corners, and they may be slightly above or slightly below the normal eye line. (For rough purposes, the eye line is the center of the skull; actually, for most of us the eyes are just a bit above that, the skull center line running along the center of the lower lid.) Once the eyeball is shaped, be sure the eyeballs are roughly parallel with each other, because the eyeballs are basically in line from the side. The brow and the cheek slope back, so the eyeball is nearer the surface of the face at the outer edges.

Now lay out the lines for the upper and lower lids. The upper lid is normally up above center a bit more than the lower lid is below it, and the *canthus major* muscle at the inner edge points slightly downward toward the nose; this is actually a slight extension of the eye oval. Cut along the eyelid lines and bost or ground out wood between them, retaining the curvature of the ball (which isn't a ball but a long oval, as we see it). If you want to be accurate, carve the cornea as a slightly raised circle extending slightly under the upper lid. It is a circular shallow dome about a third of the width of the visible eye. The upper lid has a slight hump over it. Also, the upper lid extends just beyond the lower at the outer edge. In small figures the pupil can be just a hole drilled (again *very* carefully to avoid splitting off wood above and below) deep enough to appear black in normal light. Final shaping of the lids is the last operation, with perhaps a slight accenting of the cornea edge by V-grooving.

There are many simpler ways to make eyes, beginning with the rough V-notch and painted dot of quick caricatures. I have sketched a number of conventions; suit yourself, depending upon figure size and your abilities. If you really want to be meticulous, don't drill the pupil but carve it out, leaving a tiny regular or arcuate triangle at the top to simulate the "glint."

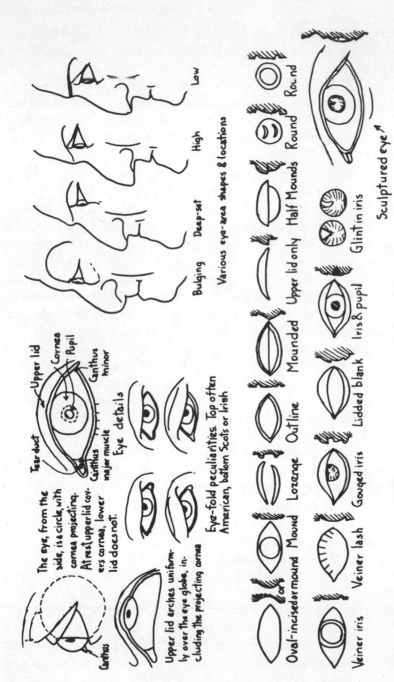

The eye, from the side, is a circle, with cornea projecting. At rest, upper lid covers cornea, lower lid does not.

Upper lid arches uniformly over the eye globe, including the projecting cornea

Canthus

Tear duct
Upper lid
Cornea
Pupil
Canthus minor
Canthus major muscle

Eye details

Eye-fold peculiarities. Top often American, bottom Scots or Irish

Bulging   Deep-set   High   Low

Various eye-area shapes & locations

Oval-incised or mound   Mound   Lozange   Outline   Mounded   Upper lid only   Half Mounds   Round   Round

Veiner iris   Veiner lash   Gouged iris   Lidded blank   Iris & pupil   Glint in iris

Sculptured eye

Fig. 18. Typical eye conventions: upper line simple, lower line more complex.

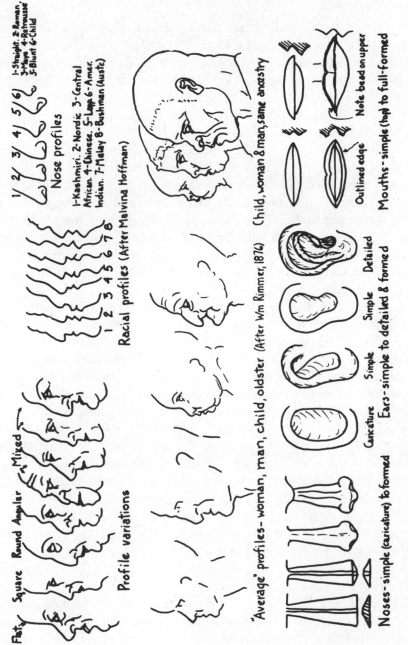

Flat, Square, Round, Angular, Mixed

Profile variations

Nose profiles

1-Straight. 2-Roman. 3-Maya. 4-Retroussé. 5-Blunt. 6-Child

1-Kashmiri. 2-Nordic. 3-Central African. 4-Chinese. 5-Lapp. 6-Amer. Indian. 7-Malay. 8-Bushman (Austr.)

1 2 3 4 5 6 7 8

Racial profiles (After Malvina Hoffman)

Child, woman & man, same ancestry

"Average" profiles - woman, man, child, oldster (After Wm Rimmer, 1874)

Noses - simple (caricature) to formed

Caricature   Simple   Simple   Detailed

Ears - simple to detailed & formed

Note bead on upper

Outlined edge

Mouths - simple (top) to full-formed

Fig. 19. Profiles and facial variations.

33

The nose and the profile

WHEN STATUES, ancient or modern, are damaged, it is always the nose that bears the brunt of it. The same can be said for prizefighters and caricatures. The nose is often considered to be a major factor in determining race and disposition. Nose shape is inherited, so we have Roman noses, Semitic noses, retroussé noses . . . you name it. Actually, much of the lore about noses is untrue. They have certain physical shapes, but to translate that into disposition and the like is folly.

Be that as it may, the nose is a key element in carving a face, and the shape it is given can be vital. Actually, the nose, forehead and chin are interrelated, and are based on the shape and structure of the skull. If the skull is rounded in front, the nose tends to be wide and flat, the forehead receding, and the mouth and chin profile both receding and longer than the norm. If the skull is squared off, the forehead and chin tend to line up in profile and we get the classic relationship of eyes at mid-head, with nose tip halfway down to the chin, and mouth centerline one-third to two-fifths of the distance from nose to chin.

The effect of all this is to make the nose very important in portraiture—more so than perhaps it deserves to be. But it is a very visible feature, particularly in profile, so all the details must be right, including the ridge line and overall height, as well as the spread of the nostrils, their shape and inclination, the meeting of nose and brow, its projection from the face, and so on. Miss the nose and you miss the portrait, and no mistake. As a matter of fact, make the nose genteel and you have a poor caricature, so the rules work both ways.

Nose width is primarily a frontal element, but it does influence nose shape and projection. A wide nose is usually flat, tilting the nostrils and making the flesh outside them appear wider than from the front. A retroussé nose makes the nostril openings more visible from the front and raises the nose tip above its base, making the septum more prominent. Also, there. is considerable variation in how the nose joins the brow. In some individuals, the brows meet in a V over the nose; in some there is a transverse wrinkle at the joining; in others, the nose actually runs up above the brow line or joins it without the declivity that most of us have.

The swell of puffy eyes, the shape of the lips and chin and the cheek profile are all much more visible in the silhouette than in the frontal view. So are many of the more subtle distinctions of race, sex and age. If the correct profile is achieved in a carving, much of the frontal forming of lips, chin and nose is simplified. Thus it pays to study the various profiles in which I have tried to show the variations, and perhaps have over-emphasized them slightly (Fig. 19).

The nose itself can be a simple tapered wedge in quick studies, but can be very detailed in faces expressing a particular emotion, or in a portrait. Even more important, however, in portraiture or emotion is the mouth, which actually is the biggest single element in expression. It is changed in shape to express an emotion, and the rest of the face must accommodate itself. Also, we have come to associate full lips with sensuousness, thin lips with severity, restraint, even parsimony. The mucous portions of a full mouth may occupy as much as two-fifths of the total distance from nose base to chin, particularly in female faces. The female is customarily carved with thicker lips than the male, perhaps because we have become accustomed to artificial widening if the lips are too thin. (Paradoxically, the brutish male face also has thicker, more protruding lips.) The hearty laugh is supposed to show teeth—which adds a carving problem. And so it goes.

There are an endless number of details about carving the mouth, including the amount of cupid's bow in the upper lip, the comparative "pouting" full-ness of the lower lip, the groove from upper-lip center to septum, whether or not to carve a bead along the top of the upper lip. (It is very rare in nature, but even the Egyptians knew it enhanced the face of Queen Nefertiti.) I always seem to have trouble with the subtle curves at the end of the mouth, and between it and the chin, because a slight change alters the expression so much.

The ears, once the amount of projection has been established, are basically also a matter of the silhouette. Many carvers give them a fairly standardized shape, with a few token gouge lines to suggest the convolutions inside. I have drawn, and usually carve, a somewhat more exact shape, because it is quite visible in the full head. Also, the jaw line comes up to meet the middle of the ear lobe. It can be quite prominent in a square-jawed male, almost indis-tinguishable in a soft-faced female, and shape varies widely with individuals. But it does establish the beginning of the neck, and the position of the Adam's apple in male necks with prominent ones. It also establishes the thinning of the head bulge behind the ears, which in turn has to do with the shaping of the back of the head. It must always be kept in mind, even when you carve a bushy-haired and bearded head.

Portrait faces

To MAKE A PORTRAIT—or a caricature—of an individual, you must identify and catalog the features that are unusual or abnormal, even if only slightly so. This is relatively easy with some individuals—witness the distinctive hair styles and moustaches of Hitler and Charlie Chaplin, the big ears of Clark Gable, the craggy face and mole of Lincoln, the square jaw and mouth of Washington (caused, I am told, by poorly fitted false teeth made of wood), the bushy hair and youthful face of Kennedy, the toothy grin of Carter, the specially shaped and prominent noses of Durante, Nixon, and Hope. Only when a face is near the norm—as in the case of Gerald Ford—is there a problem.

The men I mentioned above are public figures and have been cartooned so often that the eccentricities of their faces are well known. The cartoonist and the caricaturist accentuate these eccentricities, of course, but often so does the portraitist, although his accentuation is more subtle. Indeed, the line between portrait and caricature may be very hazy—one may be produced when the other is intended. I have a life-size portrait of myself in oil that my wife has never hung because the artist crossed that hazy line—at least in her opinion.

Some of us seem to have been born with the ability to distinguish and depict subtle differences in countenances. This is true of most portrait artists; the rest of us can approach portraiture only with much effort, time and difficulty. Also, the portrait artist seems to get some of the personality, the inner feelings, of his subject into his rendering. It may be a special position of the head, a quirk of an eyebrow or the lips, a "look" around the eyes. This is especially difficult to accomplish in wood because the material is solid and opaque, while flesh may vary subtly in tint or tone, even, occasionally, in translucence. Also, it is difficult in sculpture to reproduce the eye, to distinguish between pupil and iris, as well as to show the paleness of the eyeball around the iris, and the color and density of the eyelashes.

Another difficulty is to express the fleeting expression caused by muscle movement and the interrelationship of muscle, bone and skin. This is particularly hard when the subject is a child or a fleshy adult, because of the absence of the lines and wrinkles that personalize a mature face. In my own limited efforts at portraiture these elements have caused extreme difficulty, so it is with complete bewilderment that I watch portraitists capture a likeness. They have an inner "eye" which I do not, apparently, possess. I have had some success in working from photographs, which "freeze" an expression, particularly when they include strong light and shadow. (The usual frontal flash photos are almost useless because they flatten shadows.)

Portraitists have told me that they look for and record, either mentally or by quick sketches, the slight abnormalities we've been talking about, and then exaggerate them slightly in producing the portrait. It can be a lengthy process of trial and error, which is difficult when the base material is wood. Even the meticulous transfer of physical dimensions may not work, particularly if the wood has grain or imperfections, or is difficult to carve. This suggests walnut or mahogany, or teak if you can get it, all of which have enough inherent color to create an initial disadvantage. Maple and holly are better for color, but much more difficult to work. Pine or basswood are scarcely worth the time for anything but a quick caricature supported by tinting. And texturing—the development of tiny flat planes or an overall roughened surface, which delights the sculptor in clay and gives his work a personal touch—is doubly difficult in wood because such effects are usually obtained by appliquéing more base material upon an already well-sculptured likeness, and the woodcarver can't put material back that he has already cut away. All in all, if you attempt portraiture, I wish you luck. You'll need that, as well as skill and patience—both for yourself and your subject—because a fairly sure way of losing any likeness you may have achieved is to fiddle with it in the absence of the subject.

CHAPTER V

Carve a Caricature

Some types are standard, some are unique, but the viewer should smile

CARICATURES have undoubtedly brought pleasure and enjoyment to more people than formal carvings, whether it be to the carver or to the recipient. Until very recently, caricature has not been recognized as an art form because it violates a great many of the principles of formal art. Now it is an acknowledged folk art. Items can be made rapidly, thus sell at popular prices for the most part, and the quality does not have to meet some traditional standard. While we tend to think of caricature and whittling as knife products, caricaturists in Europe are much more likely to use chisels—because they have learned to carve that way. And American caricaturists with considerable experience supplement the knife with small gouges like the veiner and the fluter because they're so much faster and more convenient in producing concavities and fine lines.

Not all so-called caricatures *are* caricatures, of course; some are simply crude and some result from mistakes; some are simple and some quite sophisticated; some are original, while many are copies of traditional patterns. The line between realism and caricature is ill defined and caricature is often an unintended result. The carver is seeking to achieve more than a frozen, stick-like figure, or to suggest an emotion or idea that goes beyond physical characteristics. He must do this by providing expression, or by exaggerating a pose or physical characteristic, which is what an artist does when he achieves a portrait that is somewhat beyond a photograph of the subject. Over-exaggeration makes a likeness into a caricature, but where the line between them is, no one can say exactly.

Scandinavian carvers have for many years produced angular, blocky figures that are very well done. They are almost formulaic: three creases at elbow and knee, saggy breeches, wrinkled coats, slightly battered hats. Tyrolean carvers produce rounded, chubby figures. African carvers produced lampoons of the white men and women who bought them; these tended to attenuation, as do modern Haitian ones. Most of them show the subject with a smile or a grin, in many cases self-deprecating because of the smiler's dilapidated condition. We have developed a style similar to the Scandinavian in our so-called "Western," "mountain," or "Ozark" caricatures. The subjects are cowboys and Indians, tramps or workmen, but the stump or over-thin figure, the ill-fitting clothes and the V-notch wrinkles are characteristic. Better figures have strong planes, light or no tinting, and some emotion expressed in faces which are generated with relatively few lines.

In my first book, published over 40 years ago, I pictured an Italian band and provided the pattern for one member. Recently, a reader asked for patterns of the other members—he likes the band better than anything I've since provided, which is about 2,500 designs! (And these band figures are no longer carved in the Tyrol.) Just in case there are others who feel the same way, the original band is pictured here, with the patterns this time (Fig. 20). I have also included five caricatures from an unusual (at least to me) Scandinavian source, Denmark (Figs. 21 and 22). There are also two of a great series of figures being carved by a Michigan retiree in Florida, E. Kjellstrom, obviously of Scandinavian extraction (Fig. 23). He produces these at a rate of four a day, against standing orders. Most are male, seated or standing, with the characteristic face, and many have painted-on elements, such as the small picture on the breast of the birdwatcher, or the miniscule eyelashes on both. Mr. Kjellstrom is a skilled painter as well as a whittler. His designs can be carved rapidly with just the knife. Most are painted, but this is unnecessary because the blocky figure, detail, and strong lines will carry the carving. The figure is readily adaptable to whatever "props" the carver plans for that particular subject, and is unusual because of elements like the chair for the seated figure and the painting on the chest of the birdwatcher. (Elements like the bird, binoculars, and chair are carved separately and assembled, of course.)

Caricature carvers also tend to use themselves as models for facial expression—probably via a mirror—so the faces of their carvings tend to be their own, caricatured. (One American caricaturist, of Italian descent, makes a wide variety of caricatures, but all have his own distinctively shaped head and face, rounded like an olive, and all are sanded and rounded in finishing, like many Italian carvings.)

For contrast, I have included a jaeger (hunter) head from Oberammergau (Fig. 26). Compare the sophistication and detail of this carving with the simplicity of the others. This is *not* a caricature, but a study of an individual

39

Fig. 20. This street orchestra was commonly produced in the Tyrol of Austria about 50 years ago. The figures are tinted and stand about 6 in (15 cm) high.

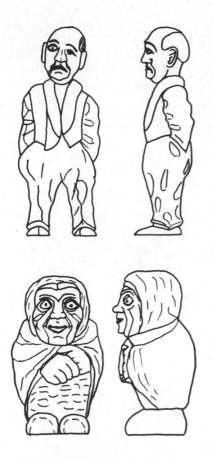

Fig. 21. These two Danish caricatures border on the grotesque. Note the strong lines and planes, the oversized heads, the droll expressions.

that shows his personality without lampooning him, yet it still expresses the humor for which a caricature strives. It is probably produced almost as swiftly as the cruder figures, but by a professional who has had extensive training, not only in carving but in anatomy as well, and who uses gouges to obtain subtle concavities. Compare this particularly·with the chimney sweep caricature and the seated couple from Denmark (Fig. 22), which have almost no modelling and relatively little detail, or even with Kjellstrom's figures, which have both carved and painted detail, yet appear primitive by comparison. The step from primitive to formal can be a very long one.

Slight variations in arm and hand positions make it possible for the same basic caricature to be engaged in a variety of pursuits, depending upon what is placed in the hand or how the figure is dressed. This can vastly reduce the amount of design and roughing time for a particular figure. Mr. Kjellstrom does this, as do many caricaturists who turn out figures of professionals: doctors, dentists, lawyers, or whatever. Also, certain faces are identified with certain individuals, as witness the Don Quixote and Sancho Panza visages shown here (Figs. 24 and 25) and in the preceding chapter on carving faces (Figs. 12–15.). I have sketched seven different caricatures of Don Quixote taken from five different countries (Fig. 25), some designs as much as a hundred years old, yet all the Quixote faces are thin and drawn and have the drooping moustachios and the goatee. Sancho Panza is always identified

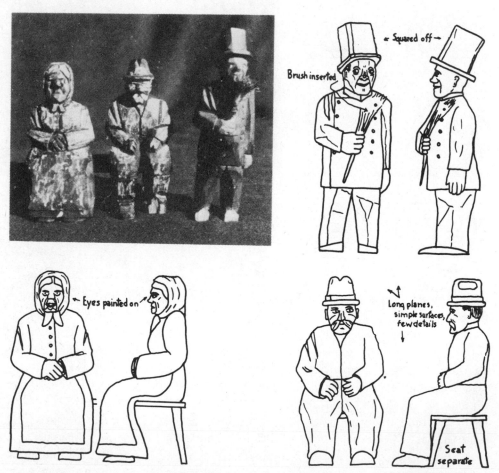

Fig. 22. Three old Danish caricatures of country people include a seated couple and a chimney sweep. Such figures were formerly carved by farmers as a wintertime occupation, and were usually colored with dull tints.

by a fatter, peasant face, usually with short moustache and beard and a hat on the back of the head. As can be seen from the sketches of Quixote, he can be wearing or carrying one of three kinds of hat, be in full or partial armor and armed in various ways, but the hat designs, the doublet or breast-plate, and the stripes around the upper legs are always the same—established by tradition. The same can (and has) been said about other historical figures, particularly if we have no precise portrait of them.

Fig. 23. Two basic figures, one seated, one standing, are hand-tinted and have painted additions, like that on the bird watcher's jacket. They are Scandinavian in form, and were carved by E. Kjellstrom, of Florida.

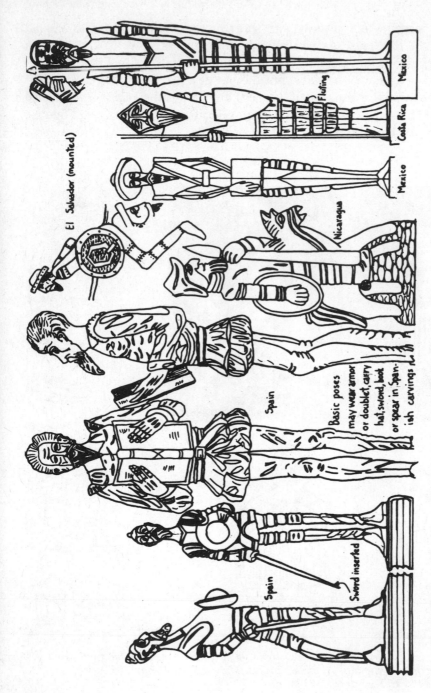

Fig. 24. Seven caricatures of Don Quixote, from five different countries, are sketched. Some of these figures are 100 years old.

44

Fig. 25. Don Quixote and Sancho Panza are the basic caricature subjects in Spanish-speaking countries. They are carved in endless variations, and their costumes and hand props vary as well.

Fig. 26. This small head of a jaeger (or huntsman) is very intricate, and is more of a portrait than a caricature. It was carved in Oberammergau and its back is flat, so it can be hung or mounted on a wall.

45

Fig. 27. This bass viol player is in jelutong and is a caricature of a friend. Personalizing inanimate objects is a common form of caricature and can be quite challenging.

It is possible to personalize an object in order to create a character from a particular calling or to suggest a personal characteristic. Thus, an identifiable caricatured human face can be put on the body of an animal or drawn within the outlines of an object such as a kettle, a pot, a bottle, or whatever. One example of this kind of caricature is the bass-fiddle player I carved in jelutong (Fig. 27). In point of fact, the possibilities in caricature are almost endless and there is little reason to repeat the same one, unless it is done for commercial reasons, as in the case of poor old Don Quixote.

CHAPTER VI

Who Took the "A" Train?

An assembly of various caricatures in various woods

MANY COMPLEX CARVINGS are made in parts and then assembled, for a variety of reasons. Individual figures made this way take advantage of grain, save wood, reduce the danger of checking. Also, these days it is hard to find large blocks of good wood, so large forms must of necessity be built up. Many carvers are basically whittlers who use the knife principally, and work best with relatively small pieces. This has led to the assembled carving, usually with each figure, or part of it, whittled individually. The so-called "Western-style" carvings are a good example: figures are assembled in a poker game, barroom, store, farrier's shed, ranch scene or other suitable background. Often, every detail is meticulously reproduced, even to the rungs on chairs and labels on miniature bottles, pips on cards, and all the rest. There are also adjustable assemblies in which a group of figures is included, but each figure can be placed separately at the whim of the owner. Examples of this are the Noah's ark, the Nativity scene, and, to stretch the definition a bit, the chessboard.

The virtue, and the complication, of such assemblies is that they can and should be viewed from many angles, so that they must be displayed, in most instances, on a pedestal in the open. I found that certain of my three-dimensional sculptures, like four-way and 12-way heads, a column of dolphins and the like, were constantly being picked up by viewers, so I customarily display them on a lazy Suzan—or even build one in if the figure is large enough. Such a carving is like a mobile in that it can present a great many separate "pictures," depending upon the viewing angle. This suggests carvings made like children's blocks, in which a scene may be varied by the way the blocks are stacked or placed. Figures might even have standard sides which could mate or interlock in the manner of a jigsaw puzzle.

These thoughts led me to the idea of a group of free-standing individuals which might be arranged in various ways, as they might occur in nature. I

47

Fig. 28. Mother with child and bundles is in cedar; Puerto Rican messenger with radio to his ear is in pecan. She sits on a non-existent seat; he grips a non-existent pole.

Fig. 29. The shape and dimensions of a subway seat are reproduced to scale in a template (right), so the figures have a uniform base. The grandmother with bundles and the newspaper reader are both in basswood and were later tinted.

Fig. 30. Two more standing figures: a portly businessman in mahogany and a black "dude" in walnut, with a separate birch cane whittled from a tongue depresser. The "dude" is leaning against an imaginary door.

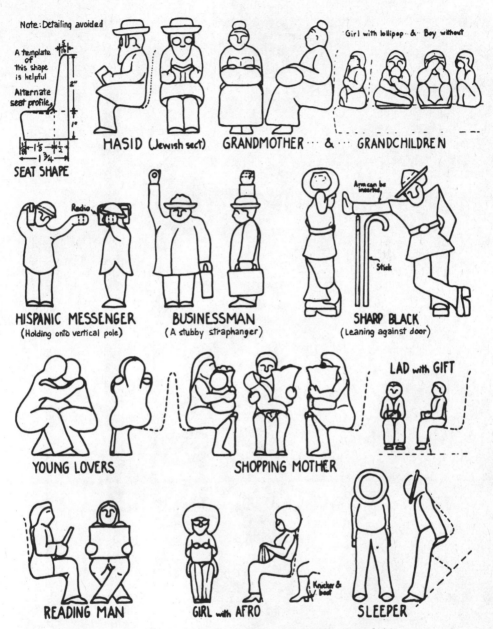

Note: Detailing avoided

A template of this shape is helpful

Alternate seat profile

SEAT SHAPE

HASID (Jewish sect)

GRANDMOTHER ··· & ··· GRANDCHILDREN

Girl with lollipop ·· & ·· Boy without

HISPANIC MESSENGER
(Holding onto vertical pole)

Radio

BUSINESSMAN
(A stubby straphanger)

SHARP BLACK
(Leaning against door)

Arm can be inserted.

Stick

YOUNG LOVERS

SHOPPING MOTHER

LAD with GIFT

READING MAN

GIRL with AFRO

Knucker & beef

SLEEPER

Fig. 31. Sketches of all the passengers, and of the seat template (top left).

49

Fig. 32. Near-faceless figures ride a non-existent subway car in this 13-figure group mounted on a 5×17-in (12.5×42.5-cm) cherry base. This piece provides good practice in whittling various woods and posing the human body. Similar figures can form other assemblies.

began with the idea of buildings of various shapes and sizes—a miniature village. Then I somehow got into the variety of people who take public transportation, their differences in life style, mode of dress, attitude, and all the rest. This led me, in turn, to a New York phenomenon—the subway, and the various characters who populate it at any time. (It might just as well have been a bus, a waiting room, a park.) Perhaps the greatest variation is on trains running up to Harlem and the Bronx, which include individuals of all races, ages, social levels, dimensions, and intentions. Thus began my "A Train," with a name borrowed from a Duke Ellington composition. It also appealed to me because I could use several varieties of wood, and because each figure could be a microcosm of humanity, intent upon his or her own pursuits and unrelated to other people on the train except by the coincidence of their being in the same place at the same time. (Authors have used this device for years in novels dealing with a disaster or important event.)

To begin with, the hardened subway rider scarcely notices other people—he is too preoccupied with his own problems, so he yields or pushes his way without conscious thought and his view of other people is hazy, at best. Therefore, I decided not to detail the features of the individuals or to carve much detail into their garb, but to concentrate on types and poses. Originally, I planned to have the figures seated in a row, but most subways have standees, leaners and sprawlers as well, so, as I made such figures, I found myself being pushed into a detailed background which, for me, would spoil the whole idea because there is a great deal of physical detail in a subway car (as there is in a bar, for example). This tends to take over, so that the viewer has difficulty focusing on the center of interest. First, I decided to simply have the seat, then I subtracted the back of the seat, eventually got rid of the seat and all detail; the background must be imagined.

It may be surprising for some carvers to learn that no one seems to have difficulty realizing that this is a scene in a subway car (or another kind of commuter transport somewhere else, although the characters elsewhere would probably be different), and the absence of a concrete "support"—or background—adds to the intrigue of the work.

I made the first several figures of basswood, assuming darker woods for the others, but, on assembly, I found that the white was too garish in contrast, so it was necessary to tone it; I used the German Beiz finishes (#1611 and #1614), which provide a greyed yellow or tan, darker in the indentations. The tall black is of walnut (Fig. 30), the straphanger of red mahogany, the woman with bundles is in cedar (Fig. 28), the messenger is of pecan

51

(Fig. 28), and the girl with the Afro is of butternut. Finish is Danish wood oil, which contains a little wax. The base is cherry and the figures are both glued and nailed to it with headless brads. Brads are also used to reinforce figures where they meet each other, so the assembly is no longer adjustable.

Most of these figures can be sawed out of wood that is 1⅝ in (4.2 cm) thick as planed. Because they are small, and because details of face and hands are not included (at least in mine), they can be whittled quite rapidly. The difficulty lies in avoiding over-precision and unnecessary detail. Unfortunately, people just don't see much detail in a subway car, and the carving should reflect that fact—it should be an accurate picture as a whole, not an assembly of accurate details.

To carry out the idea of undetailed figures, I left knife marks on the pieces and no finishing beyond that of the knife itself—no sanding or rasping or gouging of detail. I did, however, drill the straphanger's hand for the non-existent strap and the messenger's hand for the non-existent pole, and I provided all the figures with the hand props they would probably be carrying: radio, cane, bundles, lollipop, book, newspaper, glasses. These are as much a part of the individual as clothes. The figures are single pieces, except for the leaner, whose out thrust arm is set into a drilled hole, thus saving a considerable amount of good wood. Also, his cane is whittled from birch (a tongue depressor) and stained.

The base is ½-in (12.7-mm) cherry, 5¼ × 17¼ in (13.4 × 43.8 cm). There is no rigid requirement for this—it just happens to hold the figures in the order I chose. I was attempting contrasts: Hasid versus hippie, sprawling figure versus "all-business" man, and so on. Also, I assumed a central cross-bench to shorten the overall length; the group spread along one long seat is a bit too long. This leaves the children projecting interestingly in air, each being attached to the adjacent figure by glue and pin. (The two children, incidentally, were carved from a scrap of the grandmother, split in two.)

It still would be interesting to leave the figures so that they could be moved and rearranged, but that would require a real seat, perhaps even a real background, and the eventual arrangement turned out to be more fun, in my opinion, than the original idea.

CHAPTER VII

As We Carve Ourselves (Native Figures)

AMONG PRIMITIVE PEOPLES, the more imaginative carvers produce figures of their gods and the elements; the less imaginative produce miniatures of the familiar things around them. Among more sophisticated carvers, the highly skilled make figures of people; those less adept make figures of animals or objects. These are generalizations, of course, and do not always hold true. Regardless of skill, some of us are compelled, by ambition and competition, to attempt subjects that are well beyond us, and the result may be disproportion and unintended caricature. If someone is overweight, we carve him fat; if he has big ears or a big nose, we enlarge them or it. We produce, in effect, stereotypes—that is, caricatures or cartoons, whether we want to or not.

This is particularly true when someone attempts a portrait of an animal, or of a person of another race; we do not see the subtle differences which we distinguish in people "like us." All blacks, for example, do not have broad noses and thick lips; all Germans are not fat with close-cropped hair; Indians are not red, nor are Orientals slant-eyed. The fact is that the true racial or tribal figure is disappearing, so we must go back into the past to produce it.

It is only natural that any carver will picture local subjects; they are the most familiar. Mechanical and physical objects are measurable, animals and people much less so. Thus we rely on costume or environment to suggest identity. Western carvers do cowboys and Indians; Midwestern carvers do farmers, hunters or trappers; Eastern carvers make fishermen—all more recognizable by their garb and tools than by their faces (which are usually standard "American," lean and lined).

This is not an American peculiarity—carvers of other nations do the same thing. They too get some of the racial or tribal characteristics of their neighbors into their work, but they rely upon costume or appurtenances to distinguish occupation or geographical location. More important, any figure of a foreigner or of a person of another race we or they produce is likely to be a caricature.

In this chapter I have gathered together several examples from a number of countries to illustrate these points. All but two were produced by native carvers and they range from the simplest sort of depiction, like the Nicaraguan Indians (Fig. 33), to a sophisticated and stylized rendition of a Haitian woman (Fig. 34). They have one thing in common: they were produced for a regional likeness rather than for a price, so the work is painstaking. There are some caricatures, as well as more formal treatments. Among the group, there are surprisingly good renditions of two Chinese (Fig. 37); the carvers somehow caught a better likeness of their neighbors than did the other artists—at least in my opinion.

Some notes may be of interest. The man with the hand ax (Fig. 36) is from Spain and is not a crisp-edged carving but one in which the edges have been rounded intentionally. The lines of his clothes are accentuated by trenching along them (double lines in the sketch), and the entire figure is stained dark and brought to a gloss. The gloss and the rounding tend to defeat the carver's purpose, in my opinion, making the figure look like molded plastic. It is, however, a sturdy figure, a good pose, and shows more accurate observation, and more life, than the Zinconteco man from southern Mexico (Fig. 35). Each is carved from one piece of wood. In the Zinconteco figure, the carver has resurrected the large flat hat with many gaily colored ribbons (after a man marries, the number and brightness of the ribbons rapidly diminish), over-the-shoulder bag, scarf, distinctive huaraches, and shorts. (Nowadays, men of the tribe wear jeans, as do the men of another tribe in the area, who formerly wore loincloths done like a baby's diaper.)

Another Mexican excursion into the past is La Malinche (Fig. 38), by an Indian in San Martín Tilcajete, near Oaxaca, who drew almost entirely upon his imagination. She was a coastal Indian from far away, near Vera Cruz. (She was Cortez' mistress and interpreter.) This is a large figure, made for a gable decoration, 15½ in (39.4 cm) tall and painted in colors. She was, in a sense, a traitor to her own people, so the carver gave her a distorted, slightly hairy chin. He also provided modern dress coupled with an old elaborate headdress and rattles.

Also from Mexico is the figure of the rebel (Fig. 39)—a standard bearded face which could be Spanish or even Nordic (except for the cedar color). He is identifiable only by his dress and accoutrements. I have also included two of my own figures of Mexicans (Figs. 41 and 42), one of a woman offering a gift, the other a caricatured head. The woman praying is in holly and might well be an American—except that she is on her knees, wearing a shawl and offering a bowl. I carved the caricatured head from a piece of cedar bedpost, principally to practice the carving of rings—in nose, ears and around the clubbed hair. Rather idly, I made the nose an overly large Mayan shape and gave the figure the large and intense eyes of that race. It was not intended as a portrait at all, but my host immediately identified it as a likeness

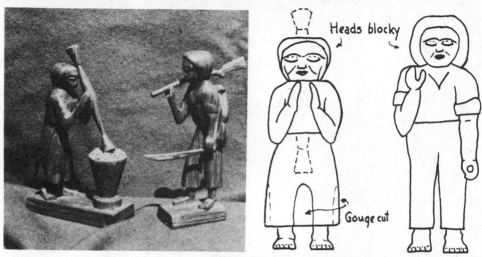

Fig. 33. *A rural couple, carved by a Nicaraguan Indian, is in mahogany and about 5 in (12.5 cm) tall.*

Fig. 34. *This stylized mahogany head is 15 in (37.5 cm) high. It emphasizes the Negroid features and is topped by a distinctive Haitian hairdo.*

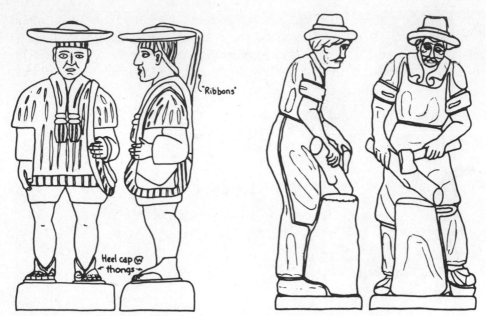

Figs. 35 and 36. A conventional cedar figure of a Zinconteco Indian (left), from the state of Chiapas in southern Mexico, is identifiable by his clothes. The figure of a carver or carpenter "axing a blank" is an older Spanish design, but shows professional skill and has a special finish.

of Benito Juarez, not realizing that it was at least as much a portrait of him, for he comes from the same Zapotec stock. (Neither, by the way, would be caught dead with earrings or clubbed hair.) The final Mexican example (Fig. 40) is a pleasant sun statue which I had to sketch without the use of a photograph. It is a delightful and imaginative composition, but exchange the rays for a robe and cowl and the figure becomes that of a monk.

The Haitian figures offer a sharp contrast to these diverse Mexican ones, particularly in their sophistication. Woodcarving is much more important in the Haitian economy than in the Mexican, which may account for this to a degree. Haitians have been exposed to French rather than Spanish influence, and to tourists, much more than have Mexican Indians. Oldest in style of the Haitian carvings, and probably the most truly local, is the itinerant (Fig. 45), identifiable by the stick and bundle which our own tramps used to carry as well. He has an excellent and sympathetically rendered face, so one feels he is likeable and human. Contrast him with the rather typical American carving of the "Old Timer" (Fig. 44).

Figs. 37 and 38. Two Chinese ivory miniatures (above), about 3 in (7.5 cm) tall. La Malinche (right), mistress of Cortes, was carved in Oaxaca. She is of copal, tinted, and 15½ in (29cm) tall.

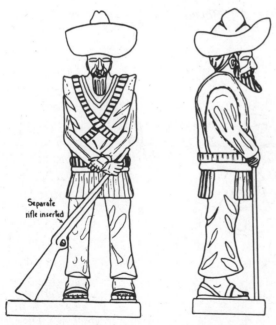

Separate
rifle inserted

Fig. 39. This bearded rebel, 10 in (25 cm) high, is in cedar and is identifiable by his "uniform."

The male and female busts (Fig. 46) on bookends are "standards"—less personalized renderings of typical Haitians. They contrast rather sharply with the caricatured figures of the man and woman (Fig. 43), and with the highly stylized female head. These latter three all exaggerate the Haitian Negro's facial characteristics, in one case with a humorous, in the other with an

Figs. 40 and 41. Mexican sun statue (left) is 2 ft (60 cm) tall. The kneeling woman in American holly is identifiable by her pose, her shawl, and her offering, all of which suggests a Central American derivation.

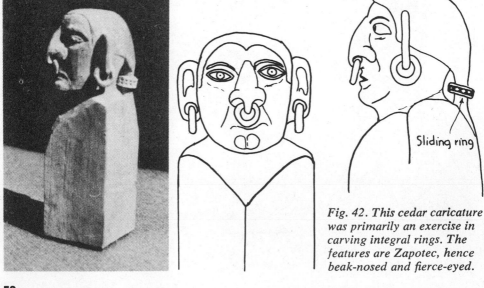

Fig. 42. This cedar caricature was primarily an exercise in carving integral rings. The features are Zapotec, hence beak-nosed and fierce-eyed.

understanding, hand. The caricatures were knocked out in short order, and to order; the others are much more deliberate and careful carvings. Detailing on the busts is particularly fine (as it is on the itinerant) and shows professional skill. The stylized girl has hair textured with small random gouge cuts and built into a bound pyramid; a variation curls the hair up into a high cornucopia. All of these figures, by the way, are in mahogany and finished with a low-gloss polish. The caricatures, by contrast, are in primavera (so-called "white mahogany") and finished with a shellac and alcohol mixture, or the equivalent, which gives an objectionable high gloss. The carver also used mahogany stain for color effects—and gets a cheapened look as a result.

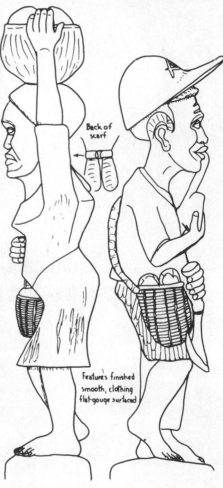

Back of scarf

Features finished smooth, clothing flat-gouge surfaced

Fig. 43. This caricatured couple, about 18 in (45 cm) high, is from Haiti and carved in primavera, stained for skin color. Their faces are individual, not standardized.

(The "Masonic" emblem on the baseball hat is startling, until one discovers that it is also a voodoo symbol.)

Even more sophisticated, and perhaps the result of more generations of fine carving, are the two Chinese ivories. At first glance they look alike and appear undeniably and typically Chinese. However, not only are the poses quite different (in the same general bulk), but so are the costumes and the accoutrements—and, most importantly, the faces. These are caricatures, too, but sophisticated ones. The faces are those of individuals rather than of types. Each is, in its own way, a little masterpiece.

Figs. 44-46. "Old Timer" (above left), an 8-in (20-cm) American figure in maple, suggests a Midwestern farmer. The musing figure of an itinerant (above, center and right), from Haiti, is in ebony and 20 in (50 cm) tall. The mahogany busts (lower left) have typical Haitian features, but are skilled portraits nonetheless, and make delightful bookends.

CHAPTER VIII

The South American Approach

IN SOUTH AMERICA, as on other continents, there are concentrations of wood-carvers. The largest, at present, is in a contiguous three-country area: southern Ecuador, northern Peru (which not too long ago was southern Ecuador, as the Tyrol was once part of Austria), and western Bolivia. This is a high-altitude, wooded region. Carvings, regardless of the country of origin, are generally similar in type and subject, well formed and well rounded, smoothly finished (in contrast, for example, with those of Argentina, which tend to be angular, rougher in finish and stained a fairly uniform black). These are not primitive carvings—they are obviously made by skilled carvers to familiar patterns and are designed for sale to tourists.

Ecuador is by far the most prolific producer of these carvings, with a wide range of both three-dimensional figures and panels, as well as a wide range of subject matter, from religious figures to animals, particularly the llama. Mahogany seems to be the preferred wood. There is evidence of a kind of mass production: the same figure will be available in several sizes, with larger sizes showing more detail. Exact duplication of form and detail suggests profiler roughing, although sellers insist this is not so.

Peruvian carvings are less regular and include a number of individual pieces made by Amazon Indians and other remote tribes. There is less of the Spanish and church influence in the work there, and still less in Bolivia, where favorite subjects appear to be the Indians themselves, although the technique and finish suggest considerable training and direction atop inherent skill. The Argentinean figures, on the other hand, lean heavily to gauchos and horses, but each figure differs in pose and other details from its fellows. In Chile, there is relatively little woodcarving, probably because much of the country is treeless or nearly so. The emphasis appears to be on the carving of other materials, except on Easter Island, which is Chilean only by agreement and treaty.

Most interesting of the carvings shown here, at least to me, are the Bolivian Indian busts (Fig. 47). They have similarly "fierce" faces, but they are

Fig. 47. These male and female heads of Bolivian Indians offer interesting contrasts despite having the same basic look. Note the wider eyebrows and thicker lips of the woman, and the prominent Adam's apple and stronger neck of the male, for example.

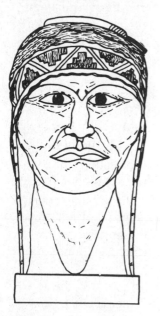

precise in facial detail, and I have tried to point out in my sketches some of the elements that distinguish the feminine head and face from the masculine one. They are superficially alike, but the subtle differences between the sexes are quite clear upon close inspection. How many times have you carved a face that somehow was of the wrong sex? (The cop-out is of course to put on a moustache or beard, or to rely upon the difference in hairdo to distinguish between them, but that's not sure-fire either.)

The Ecuadorian carvers do particularly well with a variety of traveller or mendicant figures. Three are shown (Figs. 48 and 49), each about 8 in (20 cm) tall with base, and made of the same dense medium-brown wood. Each is portrayed with an over-the-shoulder bag and two have begging bowls; all have a plaintive look about the face. The two shown together, however, were bought in Peru (and are officially from what has become northern Peru), while I bought the third (the hatless one) in Spain in a top-quality Madrid shop that preferred these imports to Spanish products. A somewhat similar figure is the piper from Bolivia (Fig. 50), again with the rather fierce face of the Andean Indian and the characteristic cap.

Fig. 48. Two Ecuadorian travellers, or mendicants, reveal an extreme attention to detail on the part of the carver. They seem overburdened and display a pleading look that was obtained by slightly tilting the head and making the eyes heavy-lidded.

63

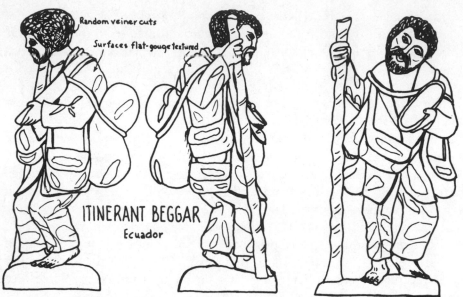

Random veiner cuts

Surfaces flat-gouge textured

ITINERANT BEGGAR
Ecuador

Fig. 49. This Ecuadorian mendicant was found in an exclusive Madrid shop. Note the details of the shoulder-load and begging bowl, features common to the other mendicants as well.

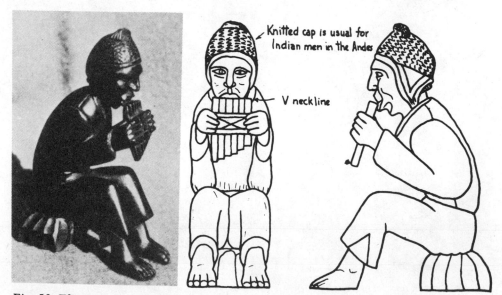

Knitted cap is usual for Indian men in the Andes

V neckline

Fig. 50. The Indian piper from Bolivia is a basic figure without crease lines in the costumes and other "standards"; he was kept simple to focus attention on the pipes.

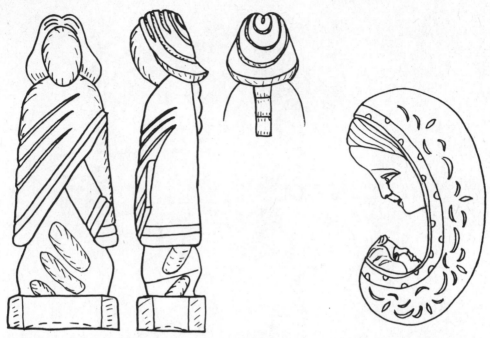

Figs. 51 and 52. The faceless, highly stylized girl (left) is, surprisingly, from Ecuador, as is "Madonna and Child," a simple treatment that is carved both left- and right-handed to be mounted in pairs.

Fig. 53. Caricature of Don Quixote is not a direct copy of Spanish versions. This one is from Ecuador and has a flow and unity that many caricatures often lack.

GAUCHO & GAUCHO BUST Argentine

Gauchos stained black & antiqued

GAUCHO & PONY Argentine

Hat separate.

COWBOY
Peru 150 yrs old
Originally painted

HUASO (Cowboy) Chile

Primitive...
carved by a
huaso

Fig. 54. South American versions of cowboys: "gaucho" in Argentina, "huaso" in Chile. They are unpretentious and powerful, and often primitive in design. See also Figs. 55, 56, and 57.

66

Figs. 55-57. The Argentine gaucho (left) is an obviously self-sufficient individual. The cowboy (center) was carved in Peru 150 years ago. The Brazilian cowboy is actually a modern copy, made from crude wood patterns and cast in rubber.

A number of designs in Ecuador were of the stylized sort, but they seem to be losing favor nowadays. A typical example is the girl with a simple oval replacing the features and a few major lines cut in the skirt and shawl (Fig. 51). She is in sharp contrast to the other figures and to the Madonna and Child panel (Fig. 52). The latter, about 4 in (100 cm) high, is made both left- and right-handed and meant to be used as a wall decoration. (Somewhat smaller ones are produced in Guatemala for pendants.)

Every Spanish-speaking country seems to have adopted Don Quixote as its own. In most cases, the carvings available seem to be copies of the familiar Spanish figures, essentially caricatures. The Ecuadorean one shown (Fig. 53), however, differs from the Spanish, although it is still readily recognizable.

In sharp contrast to all these figures are the rough-hewn carvings of gauchos from the Argentine (Figs. 54 and 55). They are strong and rather fierce in aspect and obviously the work of skilled carvers. Poses are limited, but details of dress and accoutrements vary widely from piece to piece, indicating

67

that they were individually made with only a basic pattern in mind. They are in a medium-weight wood and stained black all over, as if they were aged oak.

Some idea of what is available elsewhere is illustrated by the three cowboys, each from a different country. The Chilean huaso (Fig. 54) is a modern primitive, while the Peruvian one (Fig. 56) is a once-painted 150-year-old antique, but both are stiff and unnatural. The Brazilian cowboy on a horse isn't even wood, but a copy cast in rubber (Fig. 57)—the result of an all-day search for an example of figure carving in São Paulo by a friend who lives there.

Most of these figures were obviously done with chisel rather than the knife. The tendency in South America, as it is in Europe, is to use a skew chisel or firmer as a knife for carving detail. It has always seemed absurd to me when I see a European-trained carver gripping a chisel near the cutting edge with his finger tips to make it serve as a knife. To me, that kind of job can best be done with a knife, but carvers all over the world have a tendency to make do with the tools they have. Only in traditional European shops making traditional carvings do the carvers have an elaborate set of tools. In the rest of the world, many of the tools are home-made.

CHAPTER IX

Naive Art in Yugoslavia

FOLK OR PRIMITIVE ART occurs in all cultures and usually originates in rural areas. It is spontaneous, simple and unpretentious—most of the artists are self-taught and they draw ideas from their experience, their environment, their imagination. They treat their subjects, usually man and his environment, innocently and simply. Yet, on occasion, such works can be highly fanciful. Some of the work is done to decorate utilitarian objects, but most expresses religious feelings or simply the thoughts of the artist.

Unfortunately, the development of our industrial civilization has brought about a decline and debasement of primitive art. Rural artists migrated to cities to find more lucrative employment, or they became self-conscious of their spare-time carving. Others mass-produced what could be sold, suppressing their own creativity, and even adopting the ideas of other cultures. Thus we find Filipino carvers producing "native" art for Taiwan and Hawaii as well as their own, and the reverse—factories in Seattle producing carvings for Alaskan Eskimos to sell as *their* own. True folk art tends to weaken and die, as it has among the Maori, Balinese, Africans, and over most of Europe. (Interestingly, there is a revival of folk art in the United States—principally as a hobby.)

Most countries have belatedly recognized the value and uniqueness of their folk art and are now making frantic efforts to collect and preserve extant examples. The criterion is not whether the art is *good*, but whether it is *antique* (meaning, in the United States, over 100 years old). In some countries, efforts have been made to revive folk art through local groups, expositions, competitions, and state-sponsored schools or support, but many of these efforts are self-defeating; they tend to encourage the profit-minded rather than the inspired. Also, any training or exposure to others is likely to lead the individual away from primitivism—so folk art dies.

This has been particularly noticeable in Europe and New Zealand, where the state-run schools can no longer find apprentices. It is also beginning in the Far East and the Near East and Africa—industry provides quick money

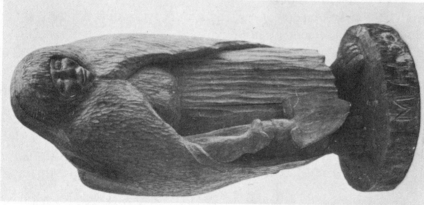

Figs. 58-60. "Butcher" (left) is a distorted piece that retains the shape of the log from which it was carved by Krešimir Trumbetaš. It is 28¾ in (71 cm) tall. "The Rain" (center), by Martin Hegedušić, is 15¾ in (38 cm) tall. The shawl is fine-textured to suggest raindrops; the skirt is vertically grooved. "Widows," by Petar Smajić, suggests a stark existence for both mother and children. It is 19 in (47.5 cm) tall and was carved from a plank.

Note veiner texturing: short & straight for body hair, random arcs for fur coat

Hands & feet crude & large body stubby.

Shallow transverse fluting

Fig. 61. "Prehistoric Man Digging," by Mijo Kuzman, makes effective use of veiner texturing.

Note stubby figure oversize hands

Oval base like original tree

Base is oval like original tree

Figs. 62 and 63. "Woman Washing" (left), by Dragica Belković, is a 24½-in (61-cm) stump figure with direct and simple outlines. Mato Generalić's "Newlyweds" has distorted proportions to reflect the naiveté of its rural subjects. Note the contrast in hand sizes and the oversized flower.

71

for less skill and effort. Thus it is rather surprising that a low-key effort to encourage folk art in Yugoslavia has been going on since the 1930s, originally among the artists themselves, and now with some museum and state support. This encouragement has resulted in a considerable body of work, of which some of the best are shown here. They were included in an extensive exhibit which toured the United States in 1977 under the sponsorship of the Smithsonian Institution Traveling Exhibition Service (SITES), which is also the source of all of the photographs reproduced here. The exhibit, incidentally, introduced another word for folk or primitive art—"naive," which like "tribal" may be more descriptive and less deprecating.

These pieces are not slavish copies of earlier masters, but typical of their own environment, distinctive and strong. They are often simple and obvious, and have some general characteristics—stump figures with oversize heads and feet, somewhat brutal features, a lack of decoration or elaboration. There is almost no "embroidery" in the Balinese, Maori, or Japanese manner. Even ordinary texturing of surfaces is relatively rare and is used only to enhance the basic idea, as in the primitive man (Fig. 61) or the woman in the rain (Fig. 59). Many of the pieces follow the outlines of the original wood, so proportions may be sacrificed. The result is a bold, powerful and readily understandable art—something that sophistication and training often kill. The preoccupation is with subject and idea, not with flow and finish. Thus these are excellent and unusual subjects for the neophyte *American* carver. They are, in the original, large enough to require chisels and mallet, and basic shape is more important than detail.

CHAPTER X

Flowing Figures from Bali

ALTHOUGH MOST WHITTLERS and woodcarvers make caricatures, very few distort the human figure to create a design. But the carvers of Bali have always been skilled in working the human body into a flowing design by lengthening or fattening the torso and/or twisting it into a sinuous pose that would be quite impossible to achieve in real life. The results are graceful and interesting carvings well worth emulating.

Most of the present-day carving in Bali is done for the tourist trade because of the chronically poor economy of the island. If a piece sells well, the carver reproduces it in quantity. However, older works were much more individualized, as some of the examples here show. The more unusual ones date from World War II and illustrate the extreme detail and intricacy which is still typical, plus considerable surface decoration and occasional painting of the softer woods. (Most modern figures are in hard woods and unpainted, the surface finish being smooth and reinforced with Kiwi shoe polish.)

Balinese subjects have typically tended to be people, foliage and birds, rather than animals, with religious overtones, because most of the population are pious Hindus given to the worship of Siva. Balinese ancestry is a mix of Indian and Javanese, so both of these influences affect their art, and their carving of wood is more intricate than that done in India, more flowing and less formal or repetitive. Further, their figures are not simply portraits, but are more like candid photographs, as if they were catching their subjects in the course of day-to-day activities.

The flute player, the head hunters and the girl with a flower (Figs. 65, 66 and 70), are the best examples of the human body attenuated into a design. The dancer (Fig. 67) is more typical, although it is also attenuated, and very delicate, particularly compared with the musician and the musing girl (Figs. 64 and 68), which are quite blocky in design.

One of the problems of creating a design with the figure is that it must be supported in position or it will be too fragile. (I know one American bird-carver who is forever repairing his egrets, cranes and shore birds because he

Figure is blocky, not fully modelled

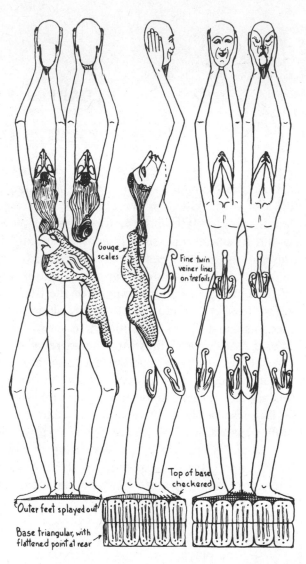

Gouge scales

Fine twin veiner lines on trefoils

Top of base checkered

Outer feet splayed out

Base triangular, with flattened point at rear

Figs. 64-66. Two flute players contrast sharply in design. The one above left is "blocky" for a female, sinuous but fairly heavy; the male musician (lower left) is more attenuated and detailed. Both are about 16 in (40 cm) tall. "Headhunter Dance" is quite unusual: rarely are two figures combined, and these are joined from heel to elbow. The assembly is 29 in (72.5 cm) high, and in sawa wood.

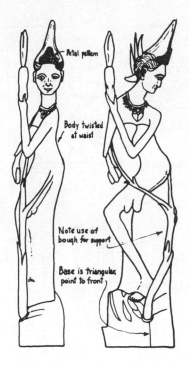

Aerial pattern

Body twisted at waist

Note use of bough for support

Base is triangular, point to front

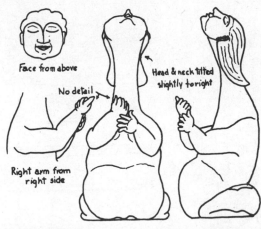

Face from above

No detail

Head & neck tilted slightly to right

Right arm from right side

Figs. 67-70. "Dancer" (above left) is a typical attenuated figure emphasizing vertical lines. The musing girl (above) is deliberately distorted and was carved by Bali's top carver, Ida Bagus Tilem. The old farmer (below right) is a 4-ft (1.2-m) piece and dates back about 40 years. The "Girl with Flower" is in ebony and stands 18 in (45 cm) high. See page 78 for photos.

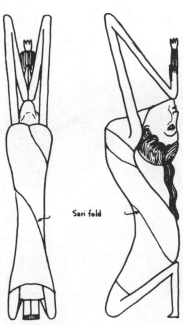

Sari fold

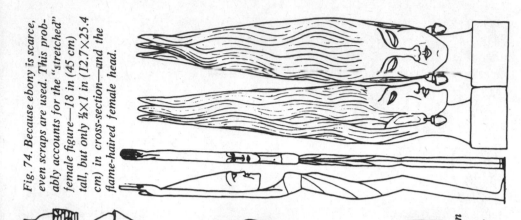

Fig. 74. Because ebony is scarce, even scraps are used. This probably accounts for the "stretched" female figure—18 in (45 cm) tall, but only ½×1 in (12.7×25.4 cm) in cross-section—and the flame-haired female head.

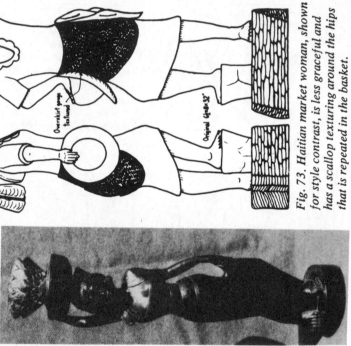

Fig. 73. Haitian market woman, shown for style contrast, is less graceful and has a scallop texturing around the hips that is repeated in the basket.

Fig. 72. Market woman of Bali is very graceful and has a flower-pattern texturing around the hips.

Fig. 71. Girl in feast costume is of ebony and wears a flower headdress. Note natural foot positions.

76

insists upon verisimilitude, so the heavy body is carried on extremely fragile legs.) Note that the girl with a flower has the long, thin arms supported by the chin and the dancer has arms and posterior supported by a somewhat artificial trimmed bush.

The willingness to distort a figure to achieve a design is shown quite dramatically by the attenuated female figure and the head with hair rising like flame shown with it in Fig. 74. (By making the face masculine and adding a beard, the latter can be made even taller. The Balinese make a sea god thus, with pebbled surface on upper lip and sideburns.) These suggest a similar treatment of American figures for the carver bold enough to try them; the "attenuated figure" can be made from scrap and is certainly not difficult, and the hair shape is not too difficult either because the long lines flow with the grain of the wood.

Bali and Haiti are interesting to compare because some of their carved figures almost look alike. Carvers of both countries do unusually well with the statuesque female or the wrinkled old man, but the Haitian figures seem to encourage a smile, while the Balinese figures are sober, almost sedate. Compare the Balinese figures of the girl in festive costume and the girl coming from market (Figs. 71 and 72) with the Haitian market woman (Fig. 73), for example, or the old farmer here (Fig. 69) with the resting itinerant from Haiti (Fig. 45). The Balinese emaciated male figure is particularly well done and suggests a willingness to spend time, which is rare in the Western world. The detail of the anatomy is also rather surprising from carvers who have had no formal art training; their understanding of musculature comes almost entirely from observation. The Balinese carver tends to use small tools and many light cuts; this is the secret of the delicate detail which he obtains. The wood is not whacked away initially, leaving it free of rough spots and incipient cracks and splits. Also, he supports the work on his knees or on a soft surface like the ground or a padded platform, so it does not absorb shocks from heavy tools and rigid clamping. Unfortunately, Westerners have never learned to squat like the Orientals and Eastern tailors, so their knees do not form as adequate a cradle. Also, worship of time and knowledge of glues and repairs is greater, so we can afford to risk damaging a carving, confident that we can repair it later.

These figures almost demand a hard, dense-grained wood, so they are not for the knife wielder or the basswood devotee. And they require an amount of time that makes them more suited to the amateur than to the professional, assuming equivalent skill.

The Balinese are also accomplished carvers of the human nude and the pierce-carved panel. They rarely, however, attempt a scenic panel, as the Haitians do. Haitian work, in general, is not as fine as Balinese, and includes many caricatures (probably for the tourist trade), but the two islands, on opposite sides of the world, make strangely similar flowing designs of the human figure.

The secret of carving figures like these is to begin at the top, roughing perhaps half the length, then shaping with small tools and many cuts, leaving details and prominent arms or similar frail elements supported or thick as long as possible. Don't cut at a great distance from the point of support. It is possible to lessen work by sawing the silhouette, but this must be done with care to avoid creating a slender section near the base. It may be helpful to support the piece, particularly in later stages, on a leather or chamois pillow filled with sand, so that the support can conform to the shape of the piece. During early stages, most pieces can be clamped in a vise, the clamp being moved down the piece as the work progresses. Most Balinese pieces are in Macassar ebony imported from the Celebes; this wood is dense enough to support the detail. It goes without saying that your duplicate should be in a similar wood: walnut, teak, cocobola, or ebony itself.

Figs. 75 and 76. "Dancer" (left) and "Girl with Flower." See page 75 for sketches.

CHAPTER XI

Base or No Base – Which?

WHETHER OR NOT a carving should have a base is superficially a matter of taste or circumstance. The human figure, like most mobile devices, tends to terminate in rather unstable bottom surfaces; if it is to stand firmly, it requires a base. Also, we have been trained to expect a base for any three-dimensional figure, just as we expect a frame for any picture. Thus the abstract sculptor finds a piece of beautiful and exotic wood upon which to mount his most recent glob, and the modern puts a pin in a block to support his assemblage of scrap iron.

To the whittler a base can be a problem, because it requires him to bore holes to separate the legs and to chew away wood across grain in order to create a surface which he must then texture in one way or another. The base will give his standing figure stability, but it often also detracts because of its size or rigid shape. On the other hand, a base provides the woodcarver with a means of holding the piece during carving. It offers him a choice between carver's screw and vise, and gives him the freedom to suggest rough or smooth ground, rocks, sea, or however he ultimately textures it. Of 50 small figures of people on my plate rail, 42 have bases.

From the owner's standpoint, the base makes life much simpler. It suggests the amount of space that must be allotted to the carving, gives evidence of one-piece construction in the cases where that is of importance, reduces the likelihood of injury to a leg, contrasts with the supporting surface, even gives a convenient place for a label and/or the carver's signature. But a massive base may check and split the carving, which of itself would adjust to humidity changes.

I have mixed emotions about bases, as the foregoing remarks may indicate. On good carvings—meaning that they take some time, effort and skill— I tend to include a base, but it may or may not be of the same wood as the original. Thus, for example, the squash player has a separate base and the self-made man grows out of one (*see* Chapters 17 and 18).

A base can, and should, be considered as either a help or a hindrance, depending upon the carving. If contact between figure and base is minimal, as in the squash player, an integral base is a constant nuisance during carving, but is essential for display, so it can be added later. For some figures, a base of contrasting or exotic wood can enhance the value of the carving. A rosewood base, for example, suggests that what's above is worthwhile. In a figure, the grain normally should be vertical and adding a horizontal-grained base may provide a pleasing contrast. But, in general, the thick, squared-off base for a light and lithe figure is anathema; the base should also be light and thin, or very tall, not just a block. If it is integral and massive, it should be hollowed out somewhat underneath to inhibit checking and rocking.

Balinese carvers show more imagination in the matter of bases than do most others. They often use a triangle, perhaps because they split wood in triangles from relatively small-diameter trees. (That makes as much sense as our using a rectangular base because the blank was a plank.) But a triangle provides one corner for each foot and a third for the base of a net, or a background stump, or a larger area to support the buttocks of a seated figure and a narrow one for extended feet. I don't advocate a triangle necessarily, but it is at least something different. An oval or a circle or a free-form shape can be as effective. I merely suggest that the base can contribute rather than confine.

The sides of the base can help as well, if properly treated. They can suggest the terrain or carry a simple design—anything to avoid a flat and uninteresting block, unless the carving is of itself so interesting that the block will not be noticed.

Lastly, there is the matter of base size. The conventional base is the size of the original block. That is faulty. If there is a base, it should look like it can and does support the figure, but not be so obtrusive that the figure dare not move off it. A larger base may give more solidity and save wood and time if added later; but often a figure is more dramatic if an elbow or foot projects over the base (increasing the risk of damage when displayed).

CHAPTER XII

How About Surface Texture?

WOODCARVERS are given to repeating the old, old saying that many carvings are ruined in the finishing. That is true, of course, because many carvers use whatever finish they have available or have used before, and their taste may be regrettably bad. Cheap carvings, particularly from underdeveloped countries, were frequently doused with shellac or cheap varnish, and some American carvings were (and are) finished the same way, making them shine like cheap furniture. This has encouraged purists to use no finish whatsoever, or simply oil and wax, although this combination is at times unsuitable as well, depending upon wood, exposure, humidity and occasional other factors, including insect infestation.

Some primitive carvers have felt their way into much more specialized finishes of many kinds, ranging from natural dyes to a "secret" formula used by a few carvers in Haiti and which gives a head or bust a smooth but slightly dusty surface exactly matching the complexion of some native women. What many of these carvers are actually striving for is not a finish, but a *texture* that somehow simulates or suggests the natural.

Quality wood sculptures commonly have one of two surface textures, either smooth and polished, which emphasizes the figure, color and grain of the wood; or tool marks, planes or surface patterns to emphasize the carving or the figure itself. The low-gloss finish is by far the most common, perhaps because the sculptor is more adept with sandpaper and riffler files than with sharp-edged tools, or because the wood proves recalcitrant. The textured surface may also be added after the carving, simply as an allover pattern of small scallops that catch the light without having any relationship to the strokes actually used in cutting and shaping.

Occasionally, artists break these patterns and strive for a surface that will have a dramatic look or feel or create a particular response of the figure to light, just as artists in other media apply pigments with a palette knife or leave the tool marks or fingermarks showing on a clay model. Some carvers actually develop a surface finish that eventually becomes a sort of personal

Figs. 77 and 78. Stylized "Mother and Child" (left) is in mahogany and about 12 in (30 cm) high. It was sandpapered smooth, and antiqued. "Old Man of the Sea" was carved in a greyed piece of driftwood. Hair and beard were textured with V-grooves blunted at the bottom to resemble fluter cuts.

trademark and others simply drift into coloring their work out of simple frustration.

These figures from Mexico, Bali, New Guinea and Haiti illustrate the point. "Mars," in carving the Haitian mother and child (Fig. 77), relied upon the silhouette for strength and design, so finished his piece smooth, with many of the lines fading into the body of the piece. He did not detail the features, the digits, or the musculature. He was striving for a smooth, flowing, harmonious shape, the result being reminiscent of many Balinese carvings.

In contrast, "Maurice" amplified the erosion of a piece of driftwood into a pattern of fillets which simultaneously produces the effect of hair and frames the face (Fig. 78). More than half the area is thus textured, so light tends to bring out the smooth surface of the face within a greyed or softer aureole of hair and beard. Pigments have been rubbed in to add a bit of color to lips, cheeks, teeth and eyes, but their effect is only to tint the grey wood slightly.

The two Mexican Virgins of Soledad (Figs. 79 and 80) are much more primitive than the preceding two figures. They have obviously been copied from earlier models, but have been stylized and interpreted as well. Crown, face, hands and flower are modelled, but the rest of the figure is primarily silhouette. The robe surface, however, is textured to suggest the opulent embroidery of the cloth robe. In one example, the irregular pattern is painstakingly produced with stamps—one a ⅜-in (9.6-mm) circle and the others a ⅜- and ⅛-in (9.6-and 3.2-mm) straight line. The wood, like pine, is soft and preserves the stamp pattern clearly. The figure, overall, is only 8½ in (21.6 cm) high. In the other figure, the pattern is incised.

Figs. 79 and 80. Two versions of the Virgin of Soledad (Mexico) are alike in the overall patterns in robe and skirt, although the one at left was textured with punches, the other with knife cuts.

The two dancers, carved in Mexico City a score of years before I acquired them, represent two of the traditional tribal dances of Mexico: one is the deer dance of Sonora (Fig. 81), the other the feather or plume dance of Oaxaca (Fig. 82). Both dancers are in animated poses, and the carver has contributed to their animation by giving them slightly blurred outlines and avoiding sharp detail, and, as a result, they appear to be caught in motion, particularly the plume dancer. The figures were rather carefully shaped, then the majority of each surface was textured—the deer dancer with parallel channeling by a small gouge, the plume dancer with scallops produced by a larger, flatter gouge. Neither face is detailed, although that of the deer dancer has a nose shape and a fortuitous placement of channels to suggest the mouth and eyes, both on the dancer and on the deer. Texturing covers most of the body surfaces of the dancers, except for the feet (which are presumably solidly supporting the figure), and a few other details. In the deer dancer, these are the ears and horns of the deer head (this is an assumption on my part because I had to replace missing parts) and the gourd rattles (maracas) in the hands. The gouge lines are not all parallel, but in some cases suggest lines of movement or of stress, as across the shoulders and the chest.

The plume dancer wears the familiar headdress, cape and apron, with the apron practically blended into the lines of the body. The cape, however, in real life ornately embroidered, is smoothed and patterned with stain. The headdress is regularly patterned with larger gouge scallops to suggest rows of feathers, but has an essentially smooth surface, while that of the real-life headdress is much rougher.

This particular carver, by the way, used a finishing technique that preserved, but partially obliterated, the lines of his carving. He apparently poured melted beeswax over the entire surface, so that it congealed and collected in all the hollows. Over the years, this clouded and collected dust, so it was necessary to scrape off larger accumulations, then alternately heat and wipe to get rid of most of it. No solvent available would dissolve this hard wax— as chemists who use hydrofluoric acid know, because they store it in wax bottles.

There are a number of other examples of surface texturing in other chapters. Each is mentioned as it occurs—like lining for hair, cross-hatching for roughness, and so on. They are worthy of a little thought and may give your work more real "polish" than can gloss varnish.

The pregnant woman from Iriana, New Guinea (Fig. 83), is somewhat Balinese in style and pose, particularly the head and hair, but differs sharply

Fig. 81. This "Deer Dancer" was surface-textured with gouge lines over a blocky silhouette. Texturing changes angle in stress areas. The only untextured areas are the antlers, rattles, and feet. The piece is 16 in (40 cm) tall.

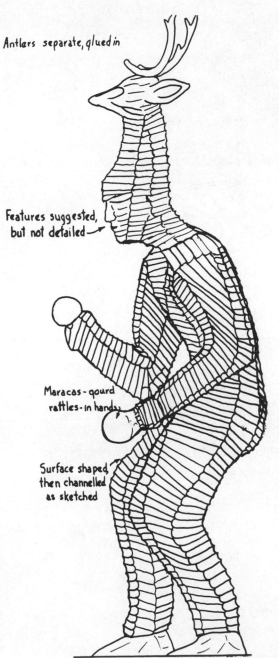

Antlers separate, glued in

Features suggested, but not detailed→

Maracas - gourd rattles - in hands

Surface shaped, then channelled as sketched

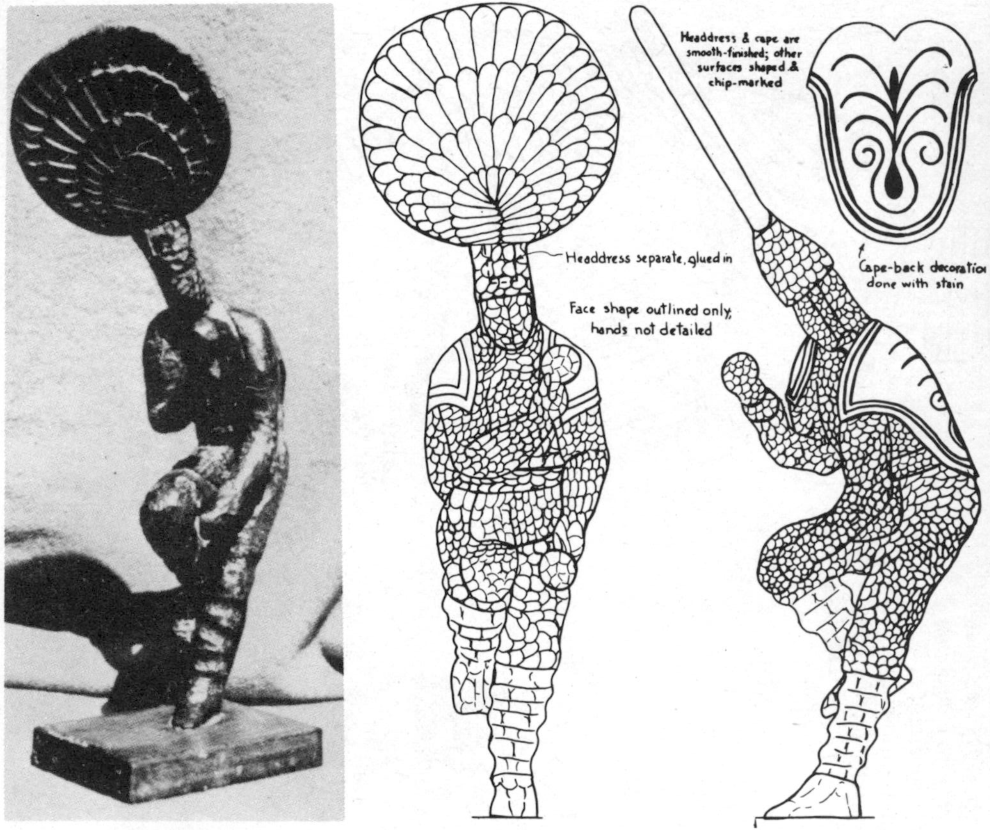
Headdress & cape are smooth-finished; other surfaces shaped & chip-marked
Headdress separate, glued in
Face shape outlined only; hands not detailed
Cape-back decoration done with stain

Fig. 82. "Feather Dancer" was carved by the same artist as Fig. 81, and in mahogany. Face and hands are not detailed, and all but the cape and feet are covered with small scallops.

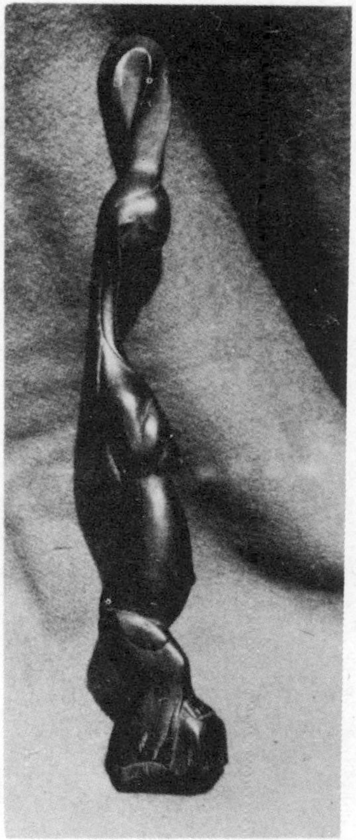

Fig. 83. Pregnant woman is from New Guinea and surprisingly sophisticated. It was finished smooth and stained black for a low-gloss effect.

in its arms, one of which is almost twice as long as the other. Also, the hands and feet are misproportioned, and the leg as short as the arm. The carver has accentuated the smooth curves of the figure by giving it a smooth, low-gloss surface as well. The base wood is light in color, so the figure was stained black, then rubbed lightly with grey or white pigment to give a dark-grey color. The only detailing of this primitive figure (which is surprisingly sophisticated in general design and treatment) is the veiner shading around the loincloth; otherwise tool marks and sharp edges have been removed. By contrast, a male figure from the same general area is primitive and blocky, with long gouge and firmer lines left in, as if the figure had been roughed out and then abandoned.

There are many other aspects of texturing, of course, including effects obtained by utilizing the figure or grain of the wood itself. In most cases, the carver positions his work, or modifies his design, to take advantage of surface irregularities or imperfections, like knots or color changes, or selects the piece of wood because its shape suggests the ultimate carving. In other cases, the carver must adapt his design to the shape of the available wood, so he makes a virtue of necessity.

The Japanese have long used the grain in still another way. They carve turtles, badgers, frogs, toads, goldfish and dragons in a cedar that has alternating hard (dark) and soft (lighter) stripes in the grain, and then erode the soft wood so that the surface has a series of ridges. The same technique has been used in this country on pine, redwood and cypress to create the effect of aging (we have done it by sandblasting), and has recently been "discovered" by tyro carvers. Another texturing technique is pyrography, used commonly by bird carvers to simulate the veining of feathers. A pyrographic needle can make the equivalent of veiner cuts with a dark-brown surface burned on, and can be quite dramatic in suggesting feathers, fur or long hair on light-colored wood figures.

CHAPTER XIII

Composites and Assemblies

MANY CARVED FIGURES, particularly large ones, are not single pieces, but composites of a number of pieces assembled by gluing, or with articulated joints, and many are made of more than one material, for one reason or another. Sometimes the composite is made because wood of the required shape and size is not available; because there is danger of checking or warping; because weight must be held down; because the pose develops problems with grain or wastes inordinate amounts of material; because the subject requires a material other than wood be incorporated to achieve a particular effect; because the figure must be posed; or simply because the carver expects to save time and effort by assembling components. In production operations, composites may make it possible for some components to be produced largely by machine or by less-skilled workers, leaving only the specialized work for the master carver. Sculptors have worked this way for centuries.

I have shown dozens of composite figures in this and previous books, some of them articulated toys, some rigid religious figures. The four shown here, however, are composite figures designed for a particular purpose. Although the Finnish man (Fig. 84) has head and hands as finely carved as any I have seen, the carver contented himself with those and the boots, while the body and clothes are of cloth. He demonstrated his skill in fine features (the lips have a slight curve at the left to accommodate a dangling cigarette) and detailed hands, but he was essentially producing a costume doll rather than a carving, and the cloth elements of the body provide the necessary flexibility for dressing and posing. Also, the body is covered anyway. . . . The right hand, however, is perfectly carved and tinted, even though it is thrust into a pocket.

This figure, probably the product of a family enterprise, is like a great many dolls of past centuries, which had wood or china heads and appendages, but bodies of cloth or leather, more or less realistically stuffed. With seams at joints, the figure was flexible enough to pose in a variety of positions.

The German doll (Fig. 86), drawn full scale, is a composite made almost entirely of wood. Her arms and legs are abnormally long and thin and she has no knee joints, but her arms and legs move quite realistically and her thin arms and legs make dress design and application easier. Only the head and appendages were enamelled in color. I replaced an arm and a leg for the doll, which is displayed in a local historical museum, and liked the design so well that I made my own of maple, using dowels for the arms and legs and modifying the connections inside to utilize modern screw eyes and wire links as sketched.

The form of the hip and elbow joints is, incidentally, the same as that used on a Chamula man and woman (Fig. 85), carved on the other side of the world, although the latter have fully carved bodies with integral legs and head, and articulation only in the elbows. Because the Chamulas are modern, the Indians used brads or short lengths of wire for the axles instead of the traditional thin wooden ones. There is less friction with them and they're stronger, if you're not a sentimentalist.

Fig. 84. This Finnish figure, 10 in (25 cm) high, has carefully detailed head, hands, and boots. The body is sewn cloth, topped by tailored clothes, and the hat can (and does) come off.

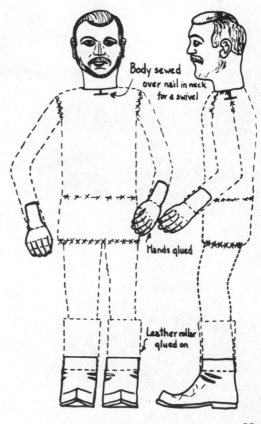

Body sewed over nail in neck for a swivel

Hands glued

Leather collar glued on

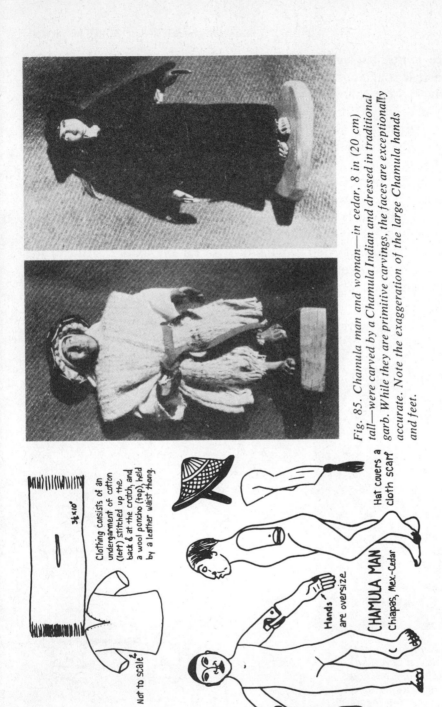

Fig. 85. Chamula man and woman—in cedar, 8 in (20 cm) tall—were carved by a Chamula Indian and dressed in traditional garb. While they are primitive carvings, the faces are exceptionally accurate. Note the exaggeration of the large Chamula hands and feet.

Clothing consists of an undergarment of cotton (left) stitched up the back & at the crotch, and a wool poncho (top) held by a leather waist thong.

Not to scale

Hat covers a cloth scarf

Hands are oversize

CHAMULA MAN
Chiapas, Mex.-Cedar

90

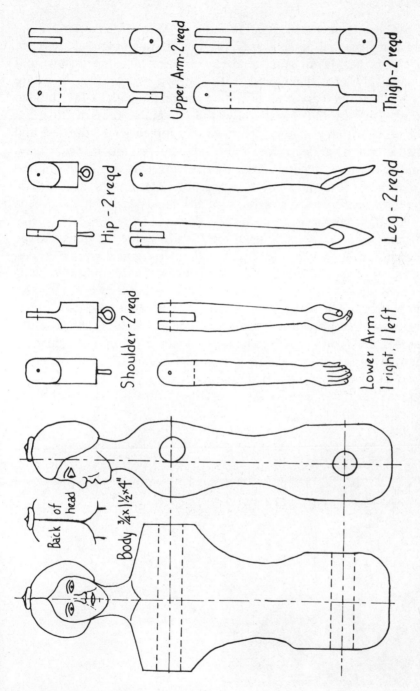

Upper Arm - 2 reqd

Thigh - 2 reqd

Hip - 2 reqd

Leg - 2 reqd

Shoulder - 2 reqd

Lower Arm
1 right, 1 left

Back of head

Body ¾ x 1½ x 4"

Fig. 86. This 19th-century stick doll is from Germany and was probably made thin of limb to facilitate dressing. Arms and legs were carved from dowels; the body and head are one piece. See photo on page 92.

The Chamula are, incidentally, a large tribe of Mayan derivation, living in and around San Cristóbal de las Casas, high in the mountains of southern Mexico. They have the Mayan nose, tend to be dark-skinned, are short and stocky, with relatively large hands and feet. The two figures from there are accurate averages, but the carver used female torsos for both, a fact hidden by the clothing. This, by the way, is how the Chamulas dressed 20 years ago and some still do today, though many have adopted jeans, dresses, and typical mestizo clothing, at least for town. The figures are in cedar, and represent some of the most accurate primitive carving I've seen. The uplifted foot on the man helps to avoid rigidity in the pose. Despite the accuracy of the faces, the figures are caricatures because the hands and feet have been overemphasized, thus making the forearms too short.

I still remember, after 40 years, a group of life-size statues of saints carved for a Catholic church in New Jersey. Because the parishioners were Negroes, the statues were negroid, the heads, arms and exposed body portions being of walnut, while the robes were in stainless steel. These figures were extremely dramatic composites, done with great skill and taste. It is also possible to combine various colors of wood in producing human figures, somewhat like three-dimensional marquetry, even to make low- or medium-relief plaques in this fashion, by assembling various colors and grains of wood in body-element-shaped blocks rather than in rectangular ones. The effect is closely akin to a jigsaw puzzle in assembly, and permits of no variation in outlines, but can be very dramatic.

Fig. 87. Nineteenth-century composite doll from Germany.

CHAPTER XIV

High Relief Permits Realistic Scenes

HIGH-RELIEF CARVING was, until perhaps 100 years ago, quite commonly done in Europe and Japan, and, by extension, in the United States. It was the common form of carved decoration in palaces and mansions, churches, temples and monasteries. Panels were incorporated in heavy furniture, such as chests and cabinets, applied in over-mantels, door frames and ceilings, even on walls. Much of the private decoration was composed of bucolic scenes involving people and animals with a background of trees and shrubbery, but in churches and monasteries it covered a wide range of religious subjects, from depictions of saints to the Stations of the Cross.

High-relief carvings usually incorporate a number of figures, often carved in the round, to depict a scene against a foreshortened background that serves as the equivalent of a stage setting (and which may include medium and/or low relief, as many museum dioramas do). Forced perspective is commonly employed. The most famous English carver, Grinling Gibbons, who commonly carved swags of flowers and fruit, was, in fact, criticized (and still is) for occasionally carving his subject in the round and appliquéing it to a panel. This permitted him to work from both back and front, and lessened the problem of how much undercutting was necessary—a problem which still plagues anyone who undertakes a high-relief carving. His favorite material was limewood, although he also worked in other woods, bronze and stone, and his work has never been surpassed in Europe. Some of his swags, in St. Paul's, London, and other English buildings, tremble at the slightest vibration—and have been trembling for almost 300 years.

The vulnerability of high-relief carving (both during and after carving) may be one of the factors that led to its decline. Others are: changing tastes in decoration, reduced availability of thick wood, and greater consciousness of time. In high-relief carving, a relatively enormous amount of wood must be cut away, unless frontal figures are appliquéd. Also, the completed work is fragile, a real dust-catcher, and has a tendency to appear florid and overdone by modern standards. Thus, high relief is relatively rare in the modern

93

world, perhaps unjustifiably so. It is quite easy to do, compared with medium or low relief, because the third dimension is more nearly correct. It offers a considerable challenge to the carver equipped with the necessary tools, time and skill, and is an interesting variation to the usual flat panels in which the third dimension must be subordinated, if not almost lost.

I am providing here four examples of high-relief carving, one an antique and the other three quite modern. It is interesting that the modern examples come from Spain, which is one of the few countries outside the United States where some high-relief carving of panels is still done. The older example is a panel carved in Austria after an 1869 painting by Franz DeFregger (1835-1921). Ken Evans, of Portland, Oregon, owns the unsigned carving (Fig. 88) and has made extensive inquiries about it. It is probably a copy of the painting, but the painter was originally a carver who didn't study painting until he was 25 years old, and the painting was made nine years later in Munich. (The painting is in the Tiroler Landesmuseum Ferdinandeum in Innsbruck, Austria.) Did DeFregger make the carving, then copy it later in oils, or did some unknown make the carving? Nobody knows, which is at least a minor argument in favor of signing carvings—something that European carver-craftsmen did not do often, because their work was often copied from paintings.

The subject of both painting and carving comes from an actual occurrence in 1809. Josef Speckbacher, the central figure, was a leader under the Tyrolean patriot, Andreas Hoffer. He was meeting with others at an inn when some of his men discovered that his eight-year-old son, Anderl, was actively participating in the fight for Tyrolean freedom against the French and Bavarians, obviously without the advice or consent of his father. In the picture, a Schutze (marksman) of the Freedom Fighters is returning the son to his father (Fig. 89). Note, in the carving, the almost free-standing figures, the complexity of the wall decorations, the detail in the "wall painting" of the Madonna and Child (Fig. 90) and the fully carved little wagon at upper right. Which was first, painting or carving? And who carved the panel? The carving is 4 × 24 × 20 in (10 × 61 × 51 cm), and weighs 37 lbs (16.6 kg) with its wide and elaborate frame (not shown). The wood is cembra pine. The carver shows textures on the deer horn and wrinkles on the faces, as well as defining hair and other details.

This is an excellent example of the use of high relief to tell a story, rather than being limited to the depiction of an individual or group, as a three-dimensional single figure normally is. It shows a familiar subject, and the

94

Figs. 88-90. The above carving is 4 in (10 cm) thick, roughly 20×24 in (50×60 cm), and includes every detail of the painting from which it was taken. Close-up (below right) of marksman and boy shows how the illusion of depth was obtained. Note the free-standing figures and perspective size-reduction. Other close-up shows detail of antlers and the low-relief miniature of the Madonna and Child.

95

Fig. 91. "Final Chapter," a 2 x 9 x 23½-in (5 x 22 x 35-cm) panel from Córdoba, Spain, depicts Cervantes writing at a desk, and the image of a dying Don Quixote and a grieving Sancho Panza above his head. Depth of the carving is 1½ in (38 mm) in deepest areas.

Back rounded to thin panel ends

Spain Chestnut(?)

Panza
profile

Arm & bed of Quixote

Cervantes profile

Quixote
profile

at end of
beard

at end of
rt. hand

Head of
Cervantes

carver was therefore able to base his work on fact—even if his "fact" is only a painting—and he wasn't forced to stylize because his knowledge did not extend to precise details.

As mentioned earlier, Spain is obsessed with the story of Don Quixote, and the story is quite familiar to the tourist world, so it is natural that many carvings depict at least the principal figures in the story. Thus, available three-dimensional figures in that country show Don Quixote and Sancho Panza in an endless variety of poses, afoot or on horseback. However, in Córdoba, I found a number of panels depicting scenes in the story, usually having to do with the battle with the windmill and Quixote's resulting discomfiture, but the one illustrated here (Fig. 91) was exceptional. It depicts Cervantes writing the last chapter of the book (or so I interpret it), the scene above showing Don Quixote dying with the ever-faithful Panza looking very concerned. It is thus a scene within a scene, perhaps similar to a cartoonist's drawing of a balloon depicting a thought over the head of the thinker. In any case, it provides a picture that no single 3-D figure could, and, from the constructional standpoint, includes faces in profile, full view and at an angle. What's more, in each case the face is expressing a particular emotion—and none is the stock caricature grin. The profiled face is by far the easiest pose to carve, regardless of depth of relief. Full face is somewhat more complicated because of the projecting nose and subtler differences in facial planes. Part-view or angle faces offer problems because curves must be modified; in this sculpture, even the professional had some problems with Panza's face.

The Moneylender panel represents a somewhat more conventional treatment of high relief (Figs. 92 and 93). It was produced as one of a series of subjects by the best-known of the Spanish carving factories, Ouro. It is actually a combination of various relief thicknesses, the central figure and the bookshelves being in low relief, the shelves with the pottery in medium relief —bringing them to the level of the outside "frame," about ½ in (12.7 mm) above the background—and the outer figures in high relief—about 1¼ in (31.7 mm) deep, or ¾ in (19 mm) outside the frame. These various heights can be distinguished in the angular view (Fig. 94).

In carving a panel, there is always the question of framing the subject. The Cervantes panel is allowed simply to "bleed" off the edges. The framing becomes whatever is behind it, and presumably of a contrasting tint or color. (The panel itself is quite dark.) Also, to avoid any feeling of massiveness or thickness, the carver has rounded off the top and bottom from the back, so the effect is one of lightness belying the basic 2-in (5-cm) thickness of the panel itself. Contrast this treatment with the more conventional self-framing of *The Moneylender*, or the partial silhouette of *Tryst* (Fig. 95), a quite modern handling. Most formal of all is the framing of the Austrian panel, which has a heavy and wide carved border to make the carving itself appear as if almost in a shadowbox, an effect accentuated by the forward-sloping floor, which makes it necessary to box the sides and the top of the finished carving to bring it up to framing level.

Thus we have four variations in framing—from nothing to a full box—although in three of the four subjects some part of the carving projects; even in *The Moneylender* panel, the self-frame is only about half the thickness of the two outer figures at their shoulders, as can be seen in the angled photograph (Fig. 94). The house wall provides a convenient background in *Tryst*, but it is broken by the recessed door and window, the projecting eave and the ground level below the suitor's feet. This helps create a feeling of reality from the shadows, regardless of where the panel is hung. On the Cervantes panel, the unframed treatment helps to create the illusion that each of the

*Fig. 92. "The Moneylender" is a carving-factory product from Spain. It is in chestnut,
1¾×9×15½ in (4.5×22×39 cm), with a background that is ½ in (12.7 mm) thick, and
an integral frame that is 1 in (25.7 mm) thick. See also Figs. 93 and 94.*

two scenes extends beyond the limits of the panel itself. If it were framed, it would be constricted and its unusual proportion of length to width might be displeasing.

Framing of a panel can be extremely important. A painting is, despite any effort at texturing by the artist, essentially flat, so its frame can enhance the third dimension. In a carving, the frame may constrict and inhibit the effect, as is evident in most old high-relief carvings. It is often much more effective to subordinate or eliminate the conventional frame, so that the carving itself is dominant and unconfined.

High-relief carving, of course, requires a great deal of roughing with gouges, and the dangers of splitting or over-cutting are constant. In most instances, the use of a router will save relatively little time. One way to reduce the time and cost of wood is to appliqué blocks in the areas which project

Figs. 93 and 94. "The Moneylender" panel (left): The central figure and bookshelves are in low relief; the pottery shelves are in medium relief. Angled photograph shows the various kinds of relief carving that were combined and reveals how much undercutting was done.

farthest, even to saw the blocks to the approximate silhouette before they are appliquéd. In work of this sort it is extremely important, of course, to make stop cuts across the grain first and to set in accurately. Templates of the various elements and even a sketch on transparent vellum will help in maintaining location, because guide lines are almost impossible to retain. Most important of all is to have a clear mental picture of the composition, so that you can remember to leave wood for such elements as the deer horns and Madonna picture on the background of the Austrian example, as well as to retain the various levels of the picture. In ivory carving, this problem is reduced by carving the scene in thin panels, then assembling them like a sandwich in a frame. This can also be done with wood, but the larger scale makes the trick evident in most instances.

Fig. 95. "Tryst" is an interesting high-relief composition from Spain. Its dimensions are 2×7¾×11 in (5×20×27.5 cm). Note that mother and daughter were carved in the round, as was the suitor, and all were undercut to make them stand out.

CHAPTER XV

Lower Relief and Modelling

IF HIGH-RELIEF CARVING is accompanied by problems in deciding how much undercutting is necessary, lower-relief carving brings similar problems in modelling.

Most present-day relief carving is quite shallow, with backgrounds sunk as little as ⅛ in (3.2 mm) on small plaques and ½ in (12.7 mm) or 1 in (25.4 mm) on larger ones. The illusion of greater depth is obtained by darkening or texturing the background, by pierce-carving, or by silhouetting the subject so that there is little or no background of the wood itself. This makes modelling and forced perspective extremely important; so important, in fact, that many carvers make mistakes and their panels have a "wooden" look (forgive the pun). Others are extremely intricate, containing so much detail, plus efforts to undercut, that they become fussy and over-detailed, losing their strength in more ways than one.

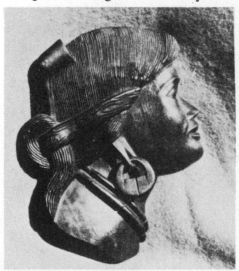

Figs. 96 and 97. Philippine women, in mahogany and 2 in (5 cm) thick, are almost half-relief. Each has an integral-carved earring. Because of the depth, modelling is relatively easy.

Here I have attempted to combine a great many widely differing subjects and techniques to provide a sort of index of low and medium relief, and of modelling, and to show how and where they differ from in-the-round, which is quite similar to high-relief carving. Consider, for example, the two silhouette panels in mahogany from the Philippines (Figs. 96 and 97), typical of the technique commonly in use there. Each is 10 × 13 in (25.4 × 33 cm), but carved from 2-in (5-cm) wood. This thickness, combined with the silhouetting and modelling, makes the carvings appear almost in-the-round, except for a flat back. The carver actually achieves considerable depth in modelling the face around the eyes and neck, which gives the face a natural look. Further, he carved the earrings free, using the old "chain trick" to achieve an effect.

Similar examples include the two women in Figure 98. The woman with child on the left is from Haiti, and the pregnant woman (with fetus outline pierce-carved in her abdomen) is from Costa Rica, yet they are strangely analogous, both in design and technique. The third dimension in both works is about half of actual size at the shoulders and hips; the effect is a double-sided medium-relief silhouette. Both are rather squared off as to torso; only the heads are modelled in the round, and neither details the face or arms. (For another photo of the Haitian woman, see Fig. 77, p. 82.)

The high modelling of medium relief is also obtained in the woman-and-child panel (Fig. 99) and the bullfighter panel from Ecuador (Fig. 101), as well as in the series of Indians and other figures from the Pátzcuaro area of Mexico (Fig. 102). The Mexican carver, or carvers, was not nearly so skilled in technique, but these figures have a crude strength, nonetheless. The carver let his imagination run free. Some of the full figures are 6 ft tall (1.8 m); all are at least 1 in (25.4 mm) thick, in soft wood. Sharply contrasting in size is the small head of a girl from Ecuador (Fig. 100), with its somewhat stylized face (accented nose and eyebrow outline), which is actually in the round in wood 1 in (25.4 mm) thick, framed by the hair at the top and brought to a pointed and thin tress below to provide delicate, balanced support on the base.

In all of these carvings, modelling is not much of a problem because the third dimension is deep. The difficulties increase as thickness is reduced, so that planes and apparent relative elevations become increasingly important. Familiar handlings of this problem are depicted in the little Indian-head pendant from Peru (Fig. 103) and the copy of an antique candle sconce from Spain (Fig. 105). The Peruvian carver made use of a triangle of wood to get an approximate face silhouette—a technique also used by the Maya and the Celts before we reinvented it in recent years as a way of getting proper face modelling. Because he used the triangle, the face itself is actually low relief. In the case of the candle sconce, the original carver sloped the support back above the eyes, thus achieving a projecting nose in another way. (This figure is primitive, to be sure, but note the strong stylizing and consequent dramatic effect.)

Still lower relief is used in the next series of examples. In the ebony pendant of the Mayan head (Fig. 104), overall thickness is only about ⅛ in (3.2 mm), but I used stylizing to define the headdress, cheek and eye, and accentuated this by inlaying ivory for the eyeball and earring. The Haitian-head pendant has an inserted earring for similar contrast. Ruth Hawkins in Brasstown, North Carolina, contrasted her two angels in holly (Fig. 106) by mounting them on a strongly patterned cross-section of branch, which ties the composition together and silhouettes the figures.

Robert Gurend of Haiti, who carved the vase (Figs. 107 and 108), is a street artist, working largely with two tools, a firmer and a V-tool, with a club serving as a mallet. He starts with rough-turned shapes of soft wood and holds them on his knees, so he can carry his shop in a shopping bag. His work is consistently strong because he understands the importance of having a single center of interest, accented by the carving technique. Thus the base and rim of this vase, as well as the minor collar, are decorated with simple V-tool patterns and the lower bulge with a floral design also done with the V-tool. This simply separates it from the uncarved base itself. The neck of the vase, however, is deeply carved and modelled, albeit primitive and stylized. The woman and the burro are the center of interest and stand out from the background, an effect accentuated by trenching or grooving the background around them. The trees and basket serve merely to fill out the perimeter of the band and can be amplified or reduced as necessary. This, by the way, provides a good example of how to adjust a design to fit a surface, a common problem in relief-carving of irregular objects. Gurend changes the design on each vase to avoid boredom.

In working out a design on a surface, or in carving shaped objects and plaques, it may be enough to use very little modelling, leaving much of the surface flat and undisturbed. An excellent case in point is a tabletop which, if carved at all, should have minimum-depth surface carving, so the stability of objects placed upon it will not be imperiled. Also, fewer crevices are thereby provided for the accumulation of dust and dirt. (This, of course, is

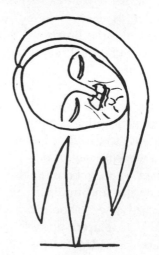

Figs. 98-101. A surprising coincidence (above):
The figure at left is from Haiti, that at right
from Costa Rica. Both are two-sided reliefs,
and only the heads are in-the-round.
Mahogany panel from Ecuador (above right)
is 11½ in (29 cm) tall, ¾ in (19 mm) thick. The
stylized head from Ecuador (below right) is
turned 90°, so hair is both frame and support.
Toreador and bull, also from Ecuador, was
pierced and silhouetted, and looks deeper than
it is.

DANCER† CAMPESINO† QUIXOTE†   MARDI GRAS FARMER

Note: Detail varies
as does design truth

Fig. 102. Sketches of primitive Mexican figures from Pátzcuaro.

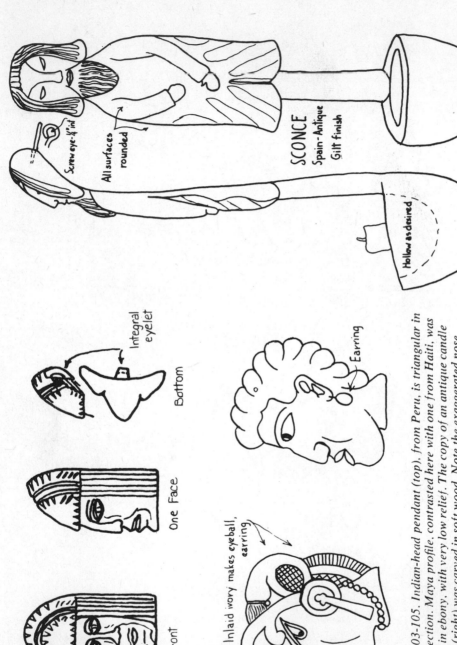

All surfaces rounded

Screw eye—¼"int

SCONCE
Spain–Antique
Gilt finish

Hollow as desired

Integral eyelet

Bottom

One Face

Front

Earring

Inlaid ivory makes eyeball, earring

Figs. 103-105. Indian-head pendant (top). from Peru, is triangular in cross-section. Maya profile. contrasted here with one from Haiti, was carved in ebony, with very low relief. The copy of an antique candle sconce (right) was carved in soft wood. Note the exaggerated nose and brow lines.

Fig. 106. These angels, carved in low relief in holly, would be lost as silhouettes unless placed against a contrasting back-ground.

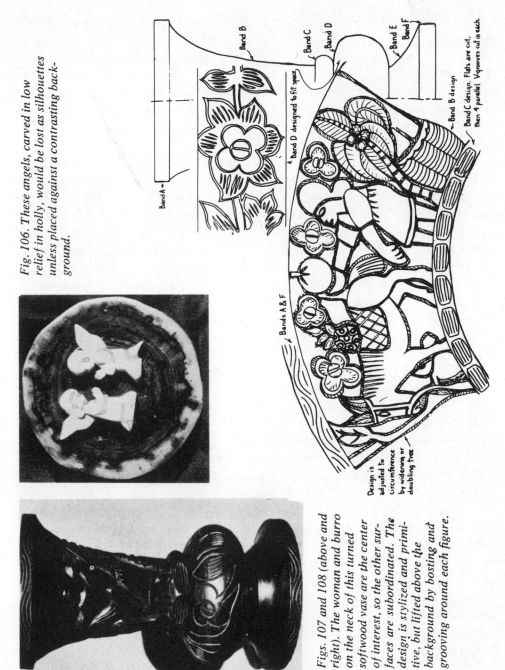

Band A

Band B

Band C

Band D

Band E

Band F

Band D designed to fit space

Bands A & F

Band B design

Band C design. Flats are cut, then 4 parallel V-grooves cut in each.

Design is adjusted to circumference by widening or doubling tree.

Figs. 107 and 108 (above and right). The woman and burro on the neck of this turned softwood vase are the center of interest, so the other sur-faces are subordinated. The design is stylized and primi-tive, but lifted above the background by bosting and grooving around each figure.

107

less important if the carving is to be covered with glass, but some compromise must be arrived at between the amount of wood surface there is to support the glass and its thickness.) The design should be worked out so that any complex or deep carving is away from the areas where stability is needed. A flat tabletop I saw in Bali had large and flat floral designs at the points where service and salad plates, saucers and centerpiece would normally be placed, while the rest of the surface was actually deep-relief and pierce-carved.

It is not always necessary to work over an entire surface and to blend all lines and model all contours; it may, in fact, be better on occasion *not* to do so. One factor is the grain of the wood. If it is strong and lovely of itself, carving should be subordinated or even omitted. Any effort to subdue a strong grain with even stronger carving usually ends in confusion for both carver and viewer. Again, if the wood is old and has a desirable patina, minimal carving will help to preserve the patina. If it is a chair back—or, worse still, a chair seat—minimal carving will be appreciated by any sitter.

In addition to the questions raised in the preceding paragraph, there are those having to do with technique. Should the design have crisp, sharp edges, or should it be modelled? Should it be trenched, leaving the background high around it, self-framed, or have the background bosted away? Should the lowered visual effect of shallow relief carving be compensated for by darkening the background or the lines of the carving itself as a scrimshander does? How much should line width be varied, groove-angle changed? Should surface texturing be used, and if so, should it be with veiner, V-tool or knife? Cross-hatched or gouge-scalloped?

Many of the answers to these questions depend upon personal taste, and I find myself varying from panel to panel, often simply to see what effect I can get. Any modelling or texturing breaks up impinging light and changes the apparent tone of what the observer sees. Thus, gouge-scalloping, cross-hatching or parallel-lining will make a surface appear darker because the reflected light isn't beamed as it is from a flat surface. Textured areas tend to sink back, an effect which can be enhanced by "antiquing" them—going over them with a slightly darker stain and immediately wiping most of it away, except in the deepest areas. (This is actually an "instant patina"— because true patina is merely the accumulation of dirt, grease, dust and such over a long period of time, and it is naturally heavier in the grooves and hollows.)

I find that irregular grooving tends to create the effect of slightly wavy

Figs. 109 and 110. Head of Tarahumara Indian (left), in cedar, was trench-carved and is self-bordered. The study of Benito Juarez is in mahogany and has various V-grooves detailing general features.

hair; regular and precise grooving suggests hair drawn tight to the scalp; fine veiner lines suggest fine hair (except on small figures, when *no* lines suggests even finer hair); and coarser lines suggest a pelt or coarse hair, as in a lion's mane. Tilting a V-tool away from one edge, thus lengthening the other side of the groove, tends to make the sharper side rise visually above the wider one. As the depth of relief is reduced, the effect of even slight variations in surface level and modelling becomes greater, so hollow cheeks and the like can be obtained with very shallow shaping. Also, with very shallow relief, crisp edges will stand out, rounded edges will disappear (an argument against sandpaper also). Trenching does not take away from the carving—see the Indian and Juarez (Figs. 109 and 110). It saves a lot of fussing over background and protects the carving itself. Framing is often confining and more trouble than it is worth.

The answers to others of the preceding questions, and perhaps additional ones, will become apparent by study of the shallow-carved panels. I carved the Tarahumara Indian (Fig. 109) from memory in Mexico, in a piece of cedar, using only a pocketknife. The high-set cheekbones are suggested by

109

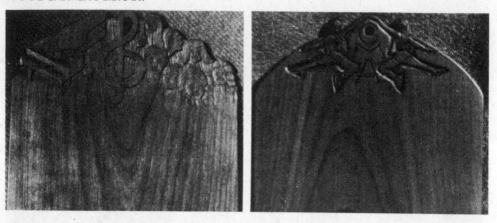

Figs. 111 and 112. Two breadboards, in cherry, are 7×11 in (17.5×27.5 cm). The one at left was made for a music teacher, the other for a skate dancer.

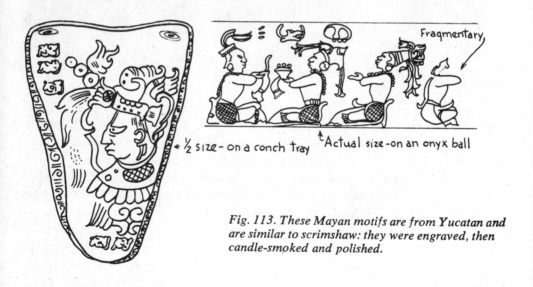

← ½ size – on a conch tray   ↑ Actual size – on an onyx ball

Fig. 113. These Mayan motifs are from Yucatan and are similar to scrimshaw: they were engraved, then candle-smoked and polished.

shallow hollowing beneath them, the deepset eyes by sharp brow lines above, the strong jaw and thick lips by the hollowing around them. It is less effective than the Indian by T. E. Haag (Fig. 115), which uses deepened relief. The

110

Figs. 114 and 115. Head of Napoleon (left) is in cherry; the background was bosted and darkened. The American Indian was carved by Ted Haag.

head of Juarez in mahogany (Fig. 110), also carved there, but from a Covarrubias sketch, is about 4 × 6 in (10 × 15 cm) and almost the equivalent of a pen-and-ink sketch. Sharp edges define the nose and eyes, the collar and hairdo. Tilted V-grooves raise the lapels above the jacket and project the lips forward from the lower cheek, as well as the hair in front of the forehead. The trench groove around the head is also tilted to give a wider outside edge and visually sets the portrait ahead of the background.

The psychological study of Napoleon (Fig. 114) was somewhat tricky to design but relatively simple to carve. The background was lowered to leave a heavy self-frame on top and sides and darkened to increase apparent depth. The tricorn hat somewhat disappears in the likeness of the imperial eagle; perhaps a little less antiquing of the eagle would have been better. The face itself is entirely made up of female nudes, each modelled somewhat, but not sufficiently to overcome the accent of his features. If nothing else, this is a good way to study anatomy and practice carving the nude.

The next example is a breadboard in cherry, carved for a music teacher (Fig. 111). The central clef masks a hanging hole, and the silhouette of the grand piano on the left is matched by a series of children's heads on the right.

111

To separate the figures from the background, and to control the visible grain to a degree, the background is lowered and textured with roughly parallel shallow gouge cuts. Another breadboard (Fig. 112), also of cherry, shows two skate dancers, slightly more modelled. Both examples approach outlining rather than relief carving at all.

Simplest of the lining techniques is an adaptation of the old art of lithography. This was usually done on stone, shell, or ivory, the resulting grooves being flooded with ink, the surface wiped dry, and the ink in the grooves transferred to paper by pressing the latter on the design. Scrimshaw, which is usually done on whale or shark teeth, or walrus ivory, is a variant of this technique, except that scrimshaw was often done with a pointed tool like a knife or awl, so the groove was simply scratched in, while in lithography the groove is cut with a burin, the solid chisel that jewelers use in engraving. In scrimshaw, the grooves are filled with India ink or a color and then the surface is cleaned with very fine sandpaper or steel wool. A similar technique can be used on wood, providing the wood is hard and dense and the grooves are actually cut, rather than torn, into the surface. (This is the old woodcut technique, actually, except that, like a scrimshawed piece, the design is produced for itself, not as a method of transferring the design to paper or cloth.)

The lithographed onyx and shell from Mérida, in the Yucatán (Fig. 113), are variations of scrimshaw. The lines, in these cases, are made with a burin, as in lithography, but they are filled by smoking with a candle, then wiping the surface clean. The onyx ball, probably a finial for an oil lamp or the like, is an antique, and the conch shell is quite modern, but they are both made in the same way.

The essential in any work like this is a steady and sure hand, as well as a clear and clean design, because every line will show in the finished piece. When used on wood, it becomes more difficult because of the wood grain. Also, because wood is likely to be dark, the filler color should be a white oil paint, which is applied in the lines as far as possible, then allowed to dry and sanded off. The problem with wood is that it has surface pores, so the pigment may fill them as well as the carved lines, and may tend to weaken the design.

CHAPTER XVI

How to Carve Nudes

THE TYPICAL whittled human figure turned out in the United States today is a male, often fairly mature and fully clothed, usually in ill-fitting garments at that. He has three wrinkles at each elbow and knee, a sagging seat, and a smirk. A major part of the reason for this is that most whittlers haven't taken the time to learn the proportions of the human figure, and it is difficult, anyhow, to work as the sculptor in clay does: making the figure in proper proportion, developing the musculature, then applying clothing or draperies. Such a procedure is difficult when one is working from the outside in. Nevertheless, any whittler or woodcarver who is familiar with proportion will turn out a better figure, as a sculptor must.

There are certain basic proportions for the figure, some of them dating back to Greece and Rome, including: an arm span equal to the height, the foot the same length as the head, and the face the same length as the hand. We also have developed a basic guide of measuring the body in "heads": the average male is 7½ heads tall, 2 heads wide just below the shoulders, 1½ heads wide at the hips, with arms 3 heads long below the armpit, and finger-'ips to elbow equalling 2 heads. The average female is somewhat shorter, with narrower shoulders and a broader, shallower pelvis, hence wider hips. The narrower shoulders combine with shorter and straighter collarbones to make the neck longer and more graceful, but puts more slope in the shoulders. Also, the female neck tends to have a greater forward angle, so there is a greater tendency to look round-shouldered, particularly in older women. The female has a shorter upper arm, hence a higher elbow location and shorter overall arm length.

The male body averages 2¾ heads for the neck and trunk (½ head for the neck, or less), and 3¾ heads for the legs and feet. The feet are a head long and half a head wide. From the ground to the crotch is roughly half the height, as is the distance from the pit of the throat to the tip of the outstretched middle finger. Upper and lower legs are equal in length. The distances from the sole to the top of the kneecap, from the kneecap to the point of the *iliac* (farthest forward part of the thigh bone), and from the pit of the throat to the lower line of the *rectus abdominus* (front abdominal muscle) are equal. Roughly speaking, the body can be divided into three parts: neck to hips, hips to knee, and knee to sole. The distance from the sole to just below the knee is a quarter of the height, and the distance from top of head to pit of throat multiplied by 5½ is the total height. In the male figure, the elbow is at the top of the hipbone and the fingertips are halfway between crotch and knee. The female torso is proportionally as long as the male, but the breastbone is shorter, so the abdomen is deeper and the legs are likely to be shorter. However, in females the leg length varies so greatly that it is difficult to estimate the standing height of a woman who is sitting or kneeling.

Proportions of the figure vary widely with age, of course. At birth the center of the figure is above the navel; at two years the navel is the center; but at three the center of the figure is the top of the hipbone. It moves down steadily as the child matures, until it is level with the pubic bone in an adult male and slightly above it in the female (because of her shorter leg length). The child of one to two years is about 4 heads high, at three years is 5 heads high and at six years, 5½ heads. The child of three is about half the adult height, of ten, about three-quarters adult height. The gain in height is about one head between ages 1 and 4, 4 and 9, and 9 and 14—and remember that the head is growing larger as well. The small child's head is almost round; it lengthens in proportion as the skull enlarges. Lack of knowledge of these relationships is the reason so many primitives carve a good Madonna but a very mature Child.

While only the stoop is commonly recognized, both male and female figures change with age and posture. The female figure tends to become broader and thicker through the abdomen and hips as a result of childbearing. Both sexes tend to develop a "pot," as well as the stoop, with advancing age. Women become noticeably round-shouldered as a result of added flesh between the shoulders. Compression of cartilage between the spine segments and between joints reduces overall height, and loss of muscle tone causes general sagging. The early-adult balance of the forward projection of the chest with the rearward projection of the buttocks is lost, allowing the chest to be less prominent and the buttocks more so.

In terms of planes, the male torso is a rough trapezoid from the line of the shoulders to the nipples, almost at right angles to the sides of the body. The abdominal plane extends downward from the nipples as a rough triangle sloping inward to the navel, where it meets a plane rising from the crotch to

Figs. 116 and 117. Companion mahogany busts from the Philippines show tribal hairdos and are each about 8½ in (21 cm) tall.

the navel. In back, the line of the shoulders forms the base of a triangle that extends downward and inward to the waist, where it meets a wider trapezoidal plane rising from the buttocks. The front planes tend to have a convex curve, the back ones a slightly concave one, which is divided centrally by the groove denoting the backbone.

The female figure is basically similar in structure, except that the plane of the shoulder extends farther outward to the nipples and meets the planes of the side in a gentler curve. The frontal planes are divided by the groove of the breastbone. Note that the breasts are set at an outward angle to the front of the torso because of the curvature of the breastbone and rib cage. In the female, also, the upper-back plane slopes outward more to the lower line of the shoulders, then inward to the waist, giving greater curvature to the backbone and a greater stoop to the shoulders. While the male neck is short and thick and rises firmly from the square shoulders, the female neck is longer, more slender and more graceful, and rises at a greater forward angle. Thus, in both sexes, the line of neck to head is not vertical, but slopes

115

forward. Also, the neck is not simply a cylinder. It tapers like a tree growing from the shoulders, more so in the male than in the female because of his normally greater shoulder-muscle development and heavier neck muscles. In addition, the male has the Adam's apple at the top. The female figure also commonly has a considerably greater outward slope to the planes. of the lower back, caused by the thicker thighs and more rounded abdomen, which creates a larger diameter at the buttocks and proportionally wider hips.

Greek and Roman artists glorified the male nude, but European artists since that time have preferred the female and considered it the ultimate in artistic achievement. Instincts aside, I find the female torso largely a series of harmonious curves, while the muscular male torso is much more difficult to carve. A slight change in pose alters muscle location and size, and smoothing the muscle curves tends to make a male torso look effeminate. The female torso is affected by change of position also, but the surface effects are not nearly so evident.

These comments, of course, are intended to apply to formal and properly proportioned, as well as somewhat idealized, youthful figures; older people are rarely depicted in the nude anyway.

Artists tell me that it is not possible to sculpt the human figure without a live model and some training in anatomy, but this is not necessarily true. It is possible to create creditable nudes without formal training, although working with models is a distinct help in locating muscle positions and the like. (One difficulty is that many models are nowhere near ideal in their proportions.)

The female nude panel (Fig. 119) was carved in Tualatin, Oregon, and I present it because it is *not* the product of a school-trained carver or professional artist, and because it shows greater variety in pose and technique than I have seen elsewhere. Ted Haag has worked in the round and in relief, large and small, both formal and stylized, and he has demonstrated imagination in mounting and finishing as well. He does not believe in sandpaper, preferring to finish surfaces entirely with the tools, but his nudes are an exception. He points out that viewers tend to stroke his figures and like a silky feel. This reinforces my earlier comments about the female nude: it should be largely an assemblage of smoothly faired curves.

Ted Haag's nudes are better than mine, and better than most I've seen or judged. He provides no information on models, but the proportions look good to my eye. I am reminded that Petty, who had quite a vogue some years back in drawing the "Petty Girl," eventually admitted that he used

Figs. 118 and 119. The modern Balinese nude at left is surprisingly stumpy. Note the oversized head. The shallow-relief nude at right is by Ted Haag and is about 3 ft (90 cm) tall.

several models, one girl for upper torso, one for arms and legs, one for heads and hands—and a male model for the buttocks! The man, he felt, provided a tauter posterior.

For contrast with Mr. Haag's females, I have provided two Balinese in-the-round nudes (Figs. 118 and 120) and a Filipino couple (Figs. 116 and 117). The tendency in Bali is to attenuate figures, as can be seen elsewhere in this book, so it is a bit surprising to see a stumpy and somewhat fleshy version in the standing nude. These are both in a wood that at least is colored like mahogany.

Nudes made as panels are quite difficult because the third dimension must be flattened, and there is the ever-present possibility that the figure will look

117

flat as a consequence. Meticulous care must be taken to produce continuous curves on surfaces. Also, the method of mounting is very important, unless the figure is a silhouette. Mr. Haag has done some experimenting in this regard with various degrees of relief for the same figure, and has also developed a shadowbox frame which is quite effective.

Fig. 120. Another modern Balinese nude, again with a head that is out of proportion with the body. It is, however, more graceful than the nude in Fig. 118.

CHAPTER XVII

An Action Sport Figure

MANY SCULPTURES are undistinguished and stiff, and so formal as to be almost unnatural. Even higher percentages of whittled pieces are similarly stiff and are misproportioned as well, so they are more caricature than statuette. Often the whittler has had no training in human proportion, had no suitable model available, was limited by a particular block shape, or was timid about cutting elements free. These may be excuses of the sculptor as well; the old Greeks often carved action figures with arms, feet or legs supported by unnatural columns, bushes, or just lumps of material.

There are subjects which can readily be spoiled if any of the preceding things are done—or mis-done. Sports figures are an excellent case in point, because the best poses involve an instantaneous freeze of a moment of supreme stress. The game of squash offers a good example because the play-

Figs. 121 and 122. Rough blanking (left) was done with a straight saw and chisels. Because the figure was small and easy to hold, whittling was the simplest method of fabrication.

ers are constantly in motion, and at about twice the speed of tennis. The player is frequently only slightly in contact with the playing surface, and his arms and legs are spread. Also, the racket represents a difficult sculptural element.

Thus, it was with some misgivings that I undertook a commission of and for a squash player, to be executed in mahogany. I had available an action snapshot that was taken from dead front, which of itself is rather difficult to find. (Squash courts have side walls, so most photos are taken from above, foreshortening the figure.) Because the player was obviously in contact with the floor only on the ball of one foot, with his body tilted well to the side in a turn, it seemed inadvisable to make figure and base integral. By making the base separate, I could gain both strength and contrast with the figure itself. Also, the racket projects so far across grain that it would be too fragile to withstand ordinary dusting. Thus, this figure is held to its base with a steel pin running up through the ankle at an angle designed to provide maximum support, and the racket was separately made and inserted.

A major problem was to provide a matching side view, because the legs are spread much wider than the frontal view suggests, and the elbow positions are not obvious either, nor is the twist in the back which makes the right shoulder appear narrower than the left in the front view. (This will not

Figs. 123 and 124. Rough blocking locates shoulders, hips, and limb position. Face, shoulders, feet, and hands are detailed, the right hand being shaped after the hole for the racket is drilled (right).

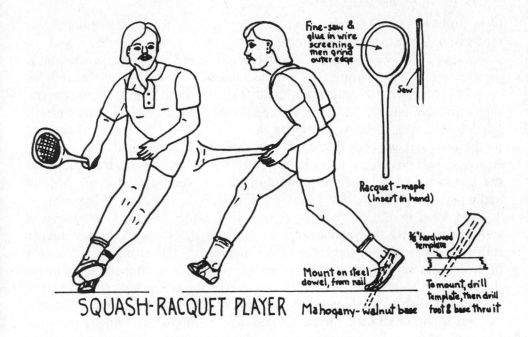

Fine-saw &
glue in wire
screening,
then grind
outer edge

Saw

Racquet - maple
(Insert in hand)

⅜" hardwood
template

SQUASH-RACQUET PLAYER

Mount on steel
dowel, from nail

Mahogany - walnut base

To mount, drill
template, then drill
foot & base thru it

*Fig. 125. Sketch and photo of finished
"Squash Player." The figure is 6 in (15 cm)
high over the base and was designed from a
frontal photo.*

be a problem for those who elect to duplicate this figure; I mention it for those who elect to depict some other sportsman in some other pose.)

Because there was no base, the entire silhouette could be sawed out to avoid a great deal of roughing. By the same token, the figure was difficult to hold in any conventional way while cutting was done, and I found it necessary to whittle much of it. Also, I made the figure somewhat heavier in build than the drawing, because the client, a squash player, is sturdy, in contrast to the thin and willowy Pakistanis who are the champions in this sport. It was obviously necessary to work carefully on the feet and arms because of the grain, and to be constantly aware of having wood available for the shirt and collar.

The racket is difficult, no matter how it is made. I elected to make it of some other wood than mahogany, to increase the strength. I used maple, stained to approximate the color of the mahogany. The stringing could have been done in several ways. The all-wood method is to thin the area within the rim, then to groove it with a veiner so that the string pattern is inverted. (Only a Balinese would attempt actual carving of the strings.) Another method would be to form the racket and drill its rim for stringing with mono-filament nylon or fine copper wire. However, I hit upon the idea of sawing the hollowed rim lengthwise with a fine-bladed jeweler's saw, then inserting a piece of aluminum fly-screen and gluing the assembly. After the glue set, the edge of the screen was ground away to leave an edge that looks very much like that of a strung racket.

CHAPTER XVIII

The Self-Made Man

A WOODCARVING OF A CARVER is quite rare. I recall only two among the thousands of designs I've seen. This is surprising, because the carver can be his own model and the material is a natural. Thus, I decided to make *Self-Made Man* from a section of 6-in (15.2-cm) walnut log and to follow the methods used by such eminent painters as Maxfield Parrish, Norman Rockwell and Andy Warhol: I took photographs from three sides to provide patterns. Further, I decided to add a fillip: I'd have me carving myself, with some of the log remaining to show the source.

The first step is to take the photographs. When the pose is selected, the photographer should focus on a level with the *center* of the subject and squarely to one side; this reduces distortion. Pictures from the front and other side should be taken at the *same* focus. Then the negatives or transparencies can be projected on paper at the desired size, and the pattern traced. (It is also possible to make photographic enlargements to the desired size, but there is usually a little distortion that makes tracing and adjustment of the various views necessary anyway.) Because of perspective and possible shifts in pose, such as a slight lowering or raising of the mallet, the patterns should be aligned, compared and adjusted before being traced on the wood.

If you are starting with a squared-up block, the views may be transferred with carbon paper; but if you start, as I did, with a log, it is necessary first to produce squared surfaces at the top and on three sides, at least (for the area of the carving only), so that the pattern can be traced. It is also advisable to square up the base at this point, so it can be used as a starting point for vertical measurement; the top will promptly be cut up. Squaring up will also reveal checks and flaws that may interfere with the carving. Small cracks can be reinforced immediately with thinned glue (like Elmer's, half and half with water), so they won't cause breaks during roughing out. Also, as you rough, any cracks revealed should be glued and/or filled before they cause trouble.

Figs. 126-129. Two of the three photos (above), taken 90° apart, that were the basis for the pattern. The photo without shirt was to show forearm musculature. The finished pattern is also the source of front and side working patterns and templates (below), cut from light but sturdy cardboard or plastic.

Figs. 130-133. First cuts are made at the top with hand saw and heavy chisels to clear the head and right arm; then the open area under the arm is roughed out. Removal of the waste wood between the arms is the next step, followed by a rough-shaping of the figure. The finished work is shown below right.

As usual, carving should begin at the top, with the base used for holding the piece. (On this particular log, the spongy growth-wood made clamping in a woodworking vise quite simple and flexible.) Waste wood can be cut away around the head and mallet of the figure with a cross-cut saw and flat chisel, then the back and far side are shaped. This work can be expedited by copying the drawing on heavy paper or cardboard and cutting out templates for front and side; I actually made my original sketch on heavy stock and used it (Figs. 128 and 129). Next, cut out the upper portion of the front, between the arm and head, and shape the head and the mallet for reference points for the rest of the carving. The body and arms can then be shaped. In carving the arms, be certain you retain proper lengths and proportions for the forearm and upper arm; obviously the carving will be more lifelike if the two arms match in actual length and the fists are the same size. Legs can also be rough-shaped at this point, and final decisions made about how much of the carver's body is to project from the log.

At this point, I got my nerve up to try the difficult portions of the carving —the right hand and the head, really the face—because if these two are not well done, the rest of the carving won't matter. The left hand is less important, but should be done next. This hand grips the chisel, which must be straight when viewed from its side, so it is essential to position the chisel on the leg and in the hand before the hand is finally shaped, otherwise you may have insufficient finger thickness on one side or the other. Also, it is difficult to produce a believable chip at the chisel end, particularly if the chisel is cutting at a slant into the grain, as it is in this pose. Further, the head must be tilted so that the eyes are watching, or appear to be watching, the cutting edge of the chisel—so chisel shape and position are quite important. (I found it necessary to vary a bit from my sketch at this point; you may, as well.)

Remember that, as you carve, you must leave wood for such things as the collar on the shirt, the eyeglasses and the hair, unless you plan to add them later. Shape the shirt and legs, using the photographs to locate the wrinkles in their proper places. Finish the face, carving the glasses in place and the hair (such as it is). The glasses, if you wear them, can be made separately from wire and installed; this makes carving of the face easier, but does add an element that is foreign and may cause dusting troubles later. If your figure is to have the cigar, the mouth and left cheek must be slightly distorted for it. It should be made separately and inserted in a drilled hole; otherwise it is across grain and will cause both carving and maintenance difficulties.

I chose to experiment with a different method of depicting hair, because mine is cut quite short and the usual veiner lines would suggest greater length. I put a thin layer of Elmer's glue in the major hair areas and sifted walnut sawdust on top of it until no more would stick. Then I added glue and more dust where needed. It worked out quite realistically, taking a slightly darker tone when finished.

A friend who, like several observers, missed the fact that the carver is carving himself, suggested the extension of the right leg. This was a happy thought, because it not only suggests that the figure is emerging from the log but also breaks the rigid line of the log edge. This edge can show chisel marks all around if you prefer; I showed them in front only, where he is obviously working, leaving the back of the figure quite rough in shape. (After all, how would he reach his back with the tools?)

Finish was several coats of spray matte varnish (satin) followed by two coats of wax. I had originally intended to remove the growth wood as a final operation, but decided to leave it, complete with nicks and wormholes, to strengthen the impression of a figure emerging from a log. As you probably know, the lighter growth-wood darkens when varnish is applied, so it is not disconcertingly light in the piece.

CARVING HORSES IN WOOD

Eric Zimmerman

This work is dedicated to my good friend,
E. J. Tangerman, who inspired the whole thing.

He who works with his hands is a laborer,
He who works with his hands and head is
an artisan,
He who works with his hands, his head and
his heart is an artist.
—————Author unknown

There is something about
the outside of a horse
That is good for the inside
of a man.
—————Liam O'Flaherty

CONTENTS

HOW IT BEGAN

In 1949, our community held a sesquicentennial celebration, and my company talked me into entering a Conestoga wagon and team of horses in a parade. During the restoration of the wagon, my interest increased to the extent that I made a scale model in full detail. When asked where the horses were, I set out to make a series of tracings for the individual units of the team and, after sawing out a profile of each, soon carved them into shapes to complete the set. Thus, a long series of carved horses was started, which covered a period of more than twenty years.

These first horses were in a quiet standing position, and the urge naturally arose to carve more active beasts. Having had a continual interest in horse motion, rhythm, conformation and general contour through studies involving both still and motion pictures, it naturally followed that some of this latent knowledge would serve as a basis for an unlimited series of designs. Over eighty-five models have been produced since.

The four horses were made of white pine, easy to cut. They were the first of many horses to be eventually cut. Note that each is slightly different, as to a leg or head position. The body shape is generally the same on each, but by tracing each one, I could alter the leg and head position to add interest. In several cases, wood was left between the feet.

The Conestoga wagon model is complete in every detail (Figs. 2 and 3), with small pinheads used as bolts; hinged wagon ends and tool-boxes; built-up wheels with hub, spokes and rims; removable tongue

Fig. 2. Conestoga
Wagon.

and double-tree and authentic top cover. The wagon bed is about 6½ inches long.

The axles were made from bicycle spokes, and the wheel nuts were made from the threaded insets which hold the spokes in the bicycle wheel rim. The prevailing motion of the wagon is forward, so the threading of the axles must be cut to turn the nut in a forward direction, and the wheel turning forward keeps the nut tightened. The metal hardware was made of ⅜-by-⅛-inch thin copper, drilled with a No. 64 bit. These were angles, brackets, and cleats. The top hoops were made from ⅛-inch-wide strips cut from a tongue depressor, which had been steamed for hours and bent to shape.

Fig. 3. The wagon chassis is complete and workable to scale. The brake assembly is fixed, but the front-wheel assembly can be disassembled; the tongue, double-tree and wagon-bed cradle can come apart.

133

The best way to build the wheels, I found, is to start with a good straight-grain hardwood (tongue depressors are perfect), then determine the diameter and multiply by pi (3.1416) to get the circumference. Then select a wheel to be copied, count the spokes and divide the linear measurement into equal spaces to accommodate the number of spokes. Plot the detail parts on paper. Make a hub with a hole for the axle rod and cut a groove around the center line of the hub. This is for the spokes which will be slightly tapered and fit tightly when assembled. Boiling the wagon rim strips, or giving them an alcohol treatment will make the wood pliable and able to bend into a complete circle for the tire. Taper each end to fit and glue in a slight overlap. You will learn from trial and error how to finally get a wheel made.

Fig. 4. Wagon with horses, shown as it might appear at a rest stop.

Figs. 5. & 6. Here are the original sketches from which the horses in Fig. 4 were carved. There were no difficulties with anatomy except for the one with its head turned.

Preliminary Studies

In my experience with horse carving, I learned early that some general and comparative knowledge was essential. Therefore, I took my cameras and notebook to the steeplechases and other horse shows and made stills and motion pictures (including slow-motion). I also acquired a few books on horses, from Frederic Remington to An'n Alcock. From the pictures I soon learned about breeds, characteristics, relative sizes and shapes, and background history.

The preliminary material shown here is not the complete story of the world of horses, but represents most of the basic elements of the family of horses that I have found useful in the work that I have done. A bibliography is also included to acknowledge the source of part of the

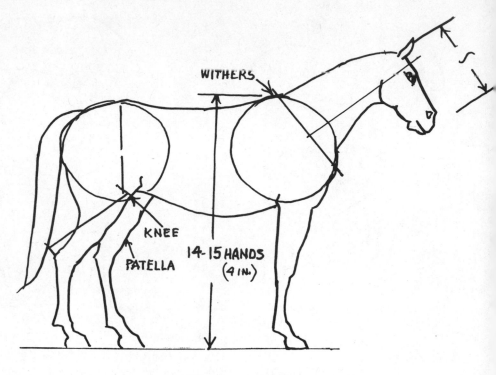

Fig. 7.

information I have accumulated. This material is intended for the carver who has some basic experience in cutting wood. There are many books written for the beginner.

General blocking-out and setting proportions are indicated in Figs. 7–10. Fig. 7 shows what is done over and over to begin some kind of silhouette for a standing horse, this horse is a thoroughbred. Note that most of the measurements of the horse's framework are based on the length of the head.

To measure the height of the horse, a reference is made to a number of hands. The average man's hand is four inches wide and this is the unit of measure for height. Example: 14 hands is 56 inches (measure to the top of his shoulder).

136

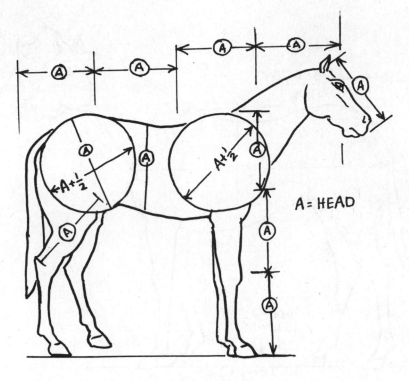

A = HEAD

Fig. 8.

Proportions

Every breed of horse has some variations in proportions and dimensions. Fig. 9 provides some guidance, especially in classes such as hunters and saddle horses. There is a great difference between sizes of horses, the tallest and largest being the Shire, and the smallest, outside of special breeding, is the Shetland. The Shire averages about 17 hands high and the Shetland averages about 30 inches or 7 hands + 2 inches.

Other general notes on proportions and characteristics are shown in Figs. 10–16. Here again Figs. 8 and 14 suggest a few practice exercises. Too many of these cannot be made to get the basic shape started.

137

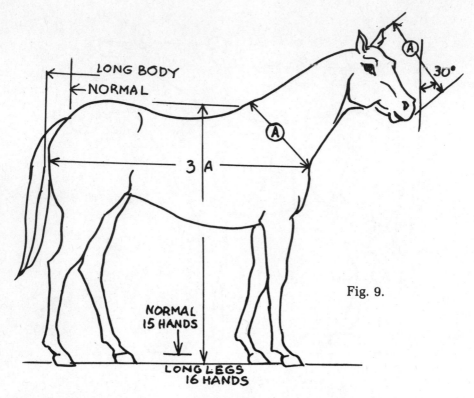

LONG BODY
NORMAL
3 A
A
A
30°
NORMAL
15 HANDS
LONG LEGS
16 HANDS

Fig. 9.

To the uninformed, all horses may look alike, but a little reading and a little study will soon reveal the distinct characteristics and relative shapes of various breeds and classes.

To someone who has looked through the various horsemen's magazines, it will be noted that most photographs of Quarter Horses are taken from behind at an angle. This is purposely done to show the muscular rear quarters. Most Thoroughbreds, Tennessee Walkers, and saddle horses have very trim rear quarters. The muscular rear quarters are the notable characteristic of the Quarter Horse, which enable it to make quick powerful starts. This is why they make great cutting horses on a ranch.

Another interesting point that is illustrated from these notes is the difference between the shape of the body at the chest and at the loin. The front of the chest carries the deepest portion of the rib cage and is

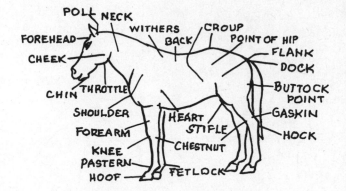

Fig. 10. Parts of the horse.

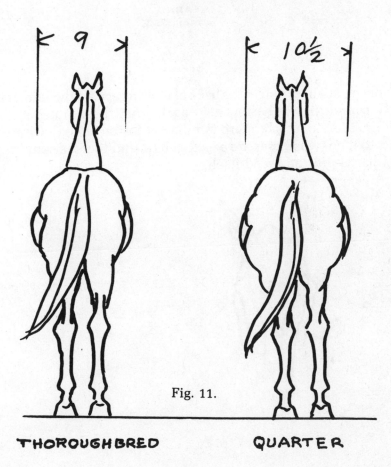

Fig. 11.

THOROUGHBRED   QUARTER

SADDLE
THOROUGHBRED
STANDARDBRED

ARAB
AKHAL TEKE

MORGAN
TENNESSEE

Fig. 12.

oval, or egg-shaped, and at the back of the rib cage, or the loin, it is more nearly round. It can be repeated again that these notes are merely guidelines. As one gets more familiar with the shape of horses, one learns that no two horses are exactly alike, and there is some variation of shape within the breed itself.

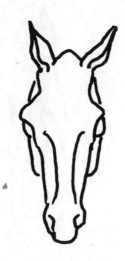

Fig. 13. Yearling.

Fig. 14.

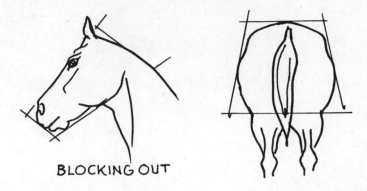

BLOCKING OUT

General proportions for the larger breeds are shown in Figs. 15, 16, and 17; the smaller breeds are shown in Figs. 18 and 19. More extensive descriptions of these will be found later in the section devoted to the various breeds.

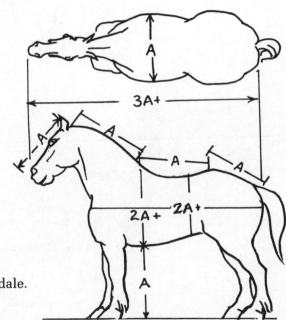

Fig. 15. Clydesdale.

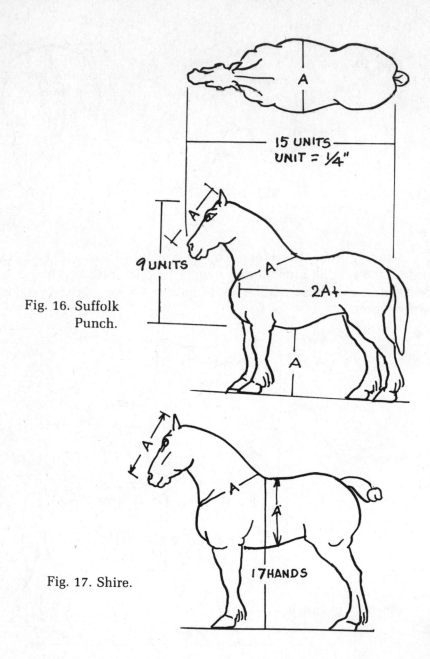

15 UNITS
UNIT = ¼"

9 UNITS

2A+

Fig. 16. Suffolk Punch.

17 HANDS

Fig. 17. Shire.

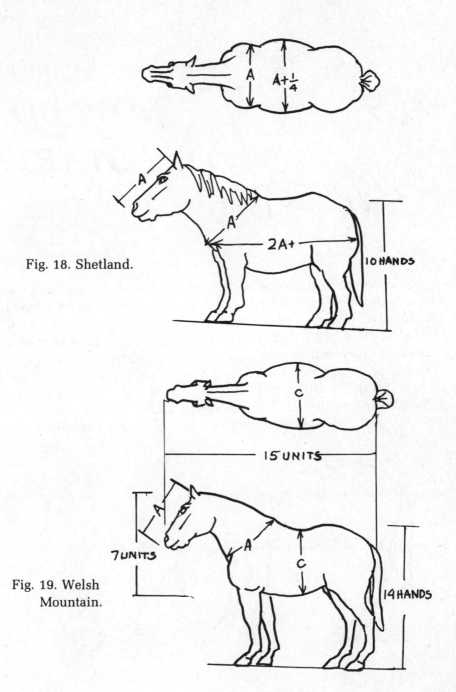

Fig. 18. Shetland.

Fig. 19. Welsh Mountain.

HOW DO YOU START?

You start at the beginning—with sketches and drawings. Not everybody is equipped with ability to draw and outline freehand. When this ability is lacking, try to trace something you like, and if it's too small or too large, get a photostatic copy which may be an enlargement or a reduction. At least, provide yourself with some kind of a profile drawing as Figs. 20 and 21. These are all preliminary to the model shown in Fig. 22. If it is not quite what you want, trace it and make some modifications which are closer to your requirements.

The next step is to trace or transfer this outline to the block of wood

Fig. 20.

144

Fig. 21.

and it is ready for the band saw or hacksaw to cut a wood profile of your model. Now you cut away all the material you don't need and you have a finished model. All the finished work in this book shows that I did just that.

The Completed Model

This very fine model (Fig. 22), a thoroughbred mare and foal, illustrates the quality of carving and finishing that is possible after considerable experience. The wood is cherry, and it was a joy to carve because of the

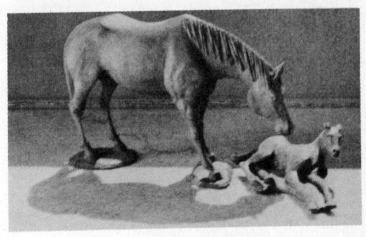

Fig. 22.

firmness of the close grain. Like most hardwoods, this one retained the sharp edges of hair, ears, feet and tail detail. The set required about 70 hours of almost symmetrical modelling. Most of the concentration was spent on producing good proportion and dignity of stance.

Copies and Tracings

When a print or photograph is to be copied for a full-round or bas-relief carving, it should be traced and transferred to the wood. Should enlargement or reduction be desired, the profile sketch should be blocked off in ¼-, ½-, or 1-inch squares and the corresponding enlarged or reduced squares should be prepared. Each section can then be pencilled in, reproducing the proportionate shape in each square. The finished job will be an enlargement of the original (Fig. 23). An easier way is to have a photostatic enlargement or reduction made and prepared for transfer to the wood.

I have made many by each method, but most of mine are development sketches, which started with some original idea, and were followed up with variations until the desired profile was produced.

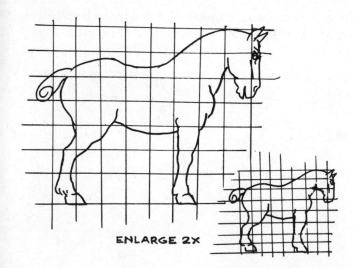

ENLARGE 2X   Fig. 23.

Typical of one of the methods of enlargement is the exercise shown in Fig. 23. This should be practiced on any number of outlines, and it can be enlarged three or four times, as desired. By doing it in reverse, a large image can be reduced.

Fig. 24 is an exact portrait. No originality was required, so it was traced from a photograph of a saddle horse, Capers. A good likeness was made from light mahogany in bas-relief. The carved model was mounted on plywood panelling wood and made up into a fine portrait. The composition of the ears and the vertical neck posture indicate that Capers was "acting up" and standing on his hind legs.

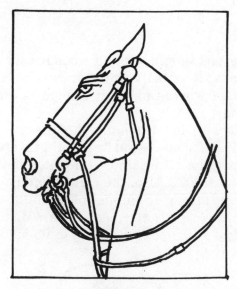

Fig. 24.

WOODS

Wood Has Character

One of the first things that should be understood in carving wood is the character of the various kinds. In the process of sharpening up on some knowledge of woods, I worked on most of them, from soft balsa to maple and walnut burl.

In working with balsa, one is reminded of the mushy, infirm and undecided nature of some people you deal with. Likewise, hard walnut or maple reminds one of the firm, straightforward and positive nature of some other people. Also, the cantankerous, unpredictable nature of marcel-waved buckeye reminds one of similar characteristics in still other people. Yes, woods, like people, have distinctive character, and you must deal with each according to its nature.

Fig. 25. Here are some faces I feel match the various types of wood.

White pine, balsa and soft mahogany are easy to cut, with no great resistance to the hand pressure. Some walnut, manzanita and maple are very hard and laborious during the rough cutting, but they are a real pleasure in the finishing stages. The firmness and smoothness of the grain and the even cellular structure graciously accept the sharp edge of the knife, giving up the small finishing chips with smooth integrity.

Preservations, or coatings, are limited to liquid wax for filling the pores and maintaining the original color, and oil, if a deeper richness is desired, as on Honduras mahogany, manzanita or teak. I like the wood itself and want no finish to come between the material and the observer.

Unusual Woods

An unusual piece of wood came from the butt end of a walnut tree that was quarter-sawn at the root structure. Some of my models were cut from this piece and had extreme contrasts of grain pattern and hardness. This provided some very intriguing cutting challenges and added interest to the finished appearance, Fig. 26.

Fig. 26.

Here is a good example of an Arabian horse (Figs. 26, 27, and 28), with arched neck, sensitive features and prancing feet. Fig. 27 is one of the profile drawings selected to transfer to wood for cutting. Note the selected angle of grain direction. The two free legs need all the strength available, of course, causing mostly cross-grain cutting of the main body contour. Most of the body and legs are completed before separating the free legs from the base. In finishing them, use the fingers gently to back up the ankle and hoof parts as well as for detailing fetlocks and shoes.

The slight forward motion causes the figure to take on the general shape of a parallelogram with unequal angles—a proportion of about 3.3:2.0.

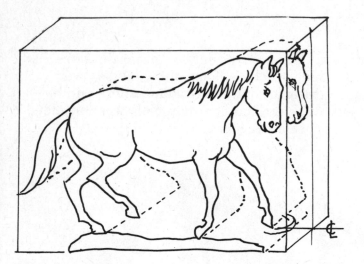

Fig. 27. After the outline of the desired shape is transferred to the block of wood the outline is sawed out with a band saw. The dotted lines indicate the resulting cut-out portion of wood to be carved, beginning with the shaping of the base on the center line.
The thickness of the wood should equal the widest part—the belly.

Fig. 28. Front.

Still another unusual piece of manzanita came from California. It isn't too different except for a deep red color when oiled. My big trouble came when a hind leg of a horse, which was in a cantering

Fig. 29.

motion, separated in three parts through the hoof and partway into the leg. Some internal disintegration, not noticed earlier, had caused the extraordinary situation. I wired the parts together, cut for a while, changed the position of the wrapped wire, and cut some more. When the three parts were glued together, all the long hours of work up to this point were salvaged. (See Figs. 29 and 30.)

Fig. 30.

On many models, a mistake often requires a slight change of contour or proportion to save the work.

The loping gait of the figure is typical of a Clydesdale whose weight prevents him from being too agile. He is an excellent workhorse and can be trained to clomp-clomp in a trot, drawing a brewery or dairy wagon, and seems to enjoy showing off to a crowd.

The Belgian farm horse, shown in Figs. 31, 32 and 33, was cut from an unusually curly buckeye, which was selected in an effort to produce

Fig. 31.

Fig. 32. Similar to Fig. 27. The desired outline is transferred to the block, the thickness should be about the same as the thickness of the horse's belly, and the shaping starts with the center line of the block.

Fig. 33. Front and rear views.

a model showing great strength and stamina. Powerful muscular contours give the effect of ability to move great loads. I had seen a picture of a similar workhorse with its head turned and decided that it would make an unusual model and would introduce some difficult cutting problems. Much of the cutting was across the grain because of the ornery habit of the curly, marcel-type grain to dip and skip, leaving pockmarks after each knife cut. It required great care and extra time. There is a risk of losing line edges when cutting tail and features.

Cutting between the turned head and body was tedious, difficult enough with normal grain. Several cuts to my left hand delayed this work, but this does happen. Turning the head reduces the proportion to an uninteresting, almost square shape, compensated for by an unusual position.

The curly, amber buckeye wood described was a gift from Ray Cottrell, a one time officer in the Wood Collectors' Society, which is international in its collecting activity. I'm sure Mr. Cottrell did not expect too much from this difficult wood. (What he does not know about wood is of no value at all; his lectures are extremely fascinating.)

A TEAM OF HORSES

I wanted to cut a team of four, matched, but with different leg positions, all running (Fig. 34). I had them hitched to a chariot, which places them as a team, four abreast. They are Arabians with the inherent desire of this breed to move fast with great agility when difficulty arises. The Arabian is very stylish with its fine facial features, its arched neck and its dainty pickup of feet when moving. To produce

Fig. 34. Chariot and horses.

variety in the team, I selected four different woods for color contrast—
walnut, white pine, Philippine mahogany, and Honduras mahogany.
Now, let us look at the problem of making four matched drawings.

This drawing had been made for another model with the rhythm of motion desired. I reduced it in size and used it for a starter.

Note that the main body line (heavy line) is about the same in all figures. Start moving the head position, change the leg position and swing the tail in a different line and you have it.

Again, tracing the body section, I find yet a different arrangement of the legs and a slightly different angle for the head.

This last one has the neck more extended, the front legs a variation of the top position, and hind legs similar to the top position. I kept tracing and changing slightly until I got what I wanted.

Figs. 35—38.

The extended legs, and the forward motion take on the shape of a parallelogram with unequal angles, with the proportion of 3.5:2.0. I gave myself some basic knowledge of horses in motion through many years of photographing races, steeplechases and hunter trials, normal and slow-motion. The advantage of this study is that many changes in the muscular contour are understood, when legs are extended and contracted. Another helpful thing was a study of the horse skeleton, noting the arrangement of various bones during the horse motion. These mini-models have good detail in the face, feet, hair and tail. They were fun to make, requiring about 100 hours.

TOOLS

Carving itself requires only a few square feet of space, and my toolbox can be carried in my hip pocket. Outside of the band saw for cutting the original profile, the only tools I use are shown here in Figs. 39 and 40.

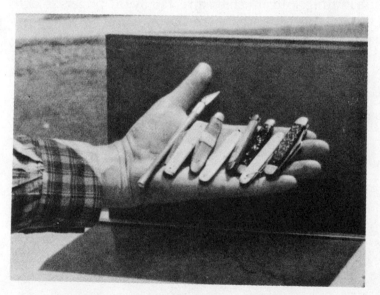

Fig. 39.

All the cutting, except for the fine grooving and details of facial features and hoofs, is outside contour shaping, and the hand knives are the only tools required. In feathering and detailing hair or tail

157

Fig. 40.

strands, I use a sharp point, and draw it along, taking a fine sliver at a time (Fig. 41). With care, some cutting can be done slightly against the grain, especially when forming a curved line.

With proper handling, knives can be directed by the fingers to cut some very fine things. It is the careless and overanxious moment in carving that opens the way for accidental cuts of the hand. One resolves to prevent a recurrence of these things but the drive to make progress overcomes these good intentions and you cut yourself *again*.

Fig. 41.

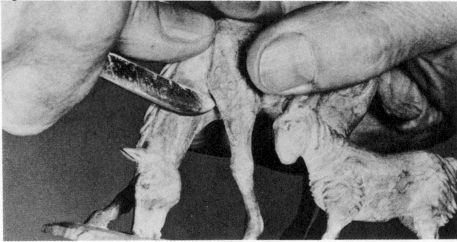

A heavy blade, several small pointed blades, and several large stub-end point blades are all that I need. The secret is keeping a sharp edge. Most of us are guilty of pushing a blade beyond its best cutting edge. As my horses are small, I use no other tools. My hand and fingers provide all the vise, clamps, and stops that I need. More detail on carving tools, types of auxiliary devices, and how to cut wood can be found in E. J. Tangerman's book, *Whittling and Woodcarving*.

Hazards of Whittling

I've often wondered how much the average carver butchers his fingers. It would seem that the person who does most of his work with a pen-knife will frequently put a pretty good nick in his hands, especially the thumb or a finger tip (Fig. 41). When working steadily, I have had my right thumb slit in many places. I've had some serious cuts, several that required dressing and stitching. This can be frustrating, especially if the blood stains a piece of blond wood with some little penetration. Then too, a bandage can create an awkward handling problem when the model is gripped with the left hand. Fig. 41 shows one of the cutting operations that, too frequently, produces cuts.

Fig. 42.

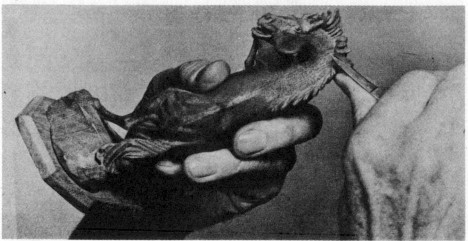

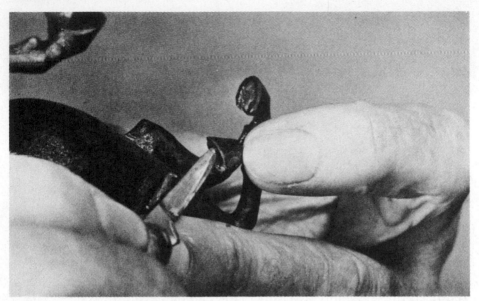

Fig. 43.

In some intricate models, the fingers can be trained to back up such delicate extended unsupported members, as a leg in motion or a flying tail, when the model is a horse. The body is held with the palm and a little finger or thumb, and the other fingers back up a protruding part for careful finishing and detailing (Fig. 42).

For many years, I was frequently in contact with an executive engineer who always inspected my right thumb and several other fingers for slits or scars, and if they were few or almost healed he complained about the inactivity. Once when I ran a large blade into my left hand, he observed the bandaged hand and was pleased, just like the students at Heidelberg University who recognized a scar on the cheek as a mark of honor.

These accidental cuts on the hands are more frequent in carving three-dimensional models. Rarely did I meet with an accident when cutting bas-relief. I have always felt that a cut on the finger or hand soon heals, but a wrong cut in the wood is permanent damage. That is why a dedicated carver takes an accidental cut in stride, especially if blessed with rapid coagulation.

THE HORSE IN MOTION

This model (Figs. 44, 45, and 46) shows a landing position which causes the rider to leave the saddle and fight for correct balance. It was an interesting model to shape because both rider and horse are in a slightly twisted position; the rider is connected at the boot contact with

Fig. 44.

Fig. 45.

one hand on the neck. The horse is actually on only one foot; the other is connected to wood for support. The wood is Philippine mahogany with a vertical grain which gives strength to the forelegs. The body and neck require cross-grain cutting, but mahogany is not difficult to cut.

Here is a good example of how to keep the forelegs in mind when cutting the hind legs. There is little symmetry in either horse or rider; the axes of shoulders and hips are not parallel. This horse is leading with the left foot. This is important. One must know just where the hind legs are when positioning the front legs. They seldom ever land in pairs.

The horse, in running or jumping, leads with either foot, in a trotting rhythm. The old Currier and Ives prints often show horses with both front and rear legs extended together. This is not accurate. It may seem to be this way when watching a horse race, but in actuality each hoof lands in a 1, 2, 3, 4 succession, usually front left, rear right, front right and rear left, in that order.

Fig. 46. Top and front views.

In planning a horse in motion, the first thing I study is the proper positioning of the feet. Once I have a general design in mind, I study photos and films that I have in order to have each hoof down or up the way they actually are.

After the profile of an animal is sawn out, you must visualize the widest points, such as the hips and belly, and if there is a rider, his or her shoulders and knees. Keeping the wood grain always in mind, start cutting away all the wood that is not needed. Begin with the legs, then thin down the neck and start rounding out the body.

Try to get some expression in the face. Cut in the eyelids and shape the nostrils. With a little experience you will get more than just a slit for eyes and a mere gouge for the nostril. Try to get some detail in the hair and tail. After a little experience, you will begin to cut some hair strands. To do this, take a small, sharp-pointed blade and draw it down time after time until you have a groove that is satisfactory.

Also pay attention to the detail of the hoofs and the fetlocks. These little details are the difference between an ordinary and a quality carving. Observe them in pictures you collect, and you will soon get the feeling of the movement and action of various parts when the horse is in motion.

Fig. 47.

Note that the arrangement takes the general shape of a diamond standing on a point, and must rock either way, in this case forward.

Figs. 47 and 48 show one of the first action models made of light mahogany. In this position the horse has jumped the timber, his forelegs are preparing to land and his hind legs are neatly picked up to clear the bar. He is supported by a pin through the bar.

The general shaping and detailing is not of the quality of later models. Eyes, nose and ears are rather crudely cut despite the graceful lines of body and legs.

Fig. 48.

Although the profile is all-important in producing a good flow of motion, these action poses demand careful attention to anatomic structure. I am my own severest critic. I have never completed a model that entirely satisfied me. In this case I soon discovered that muscular detail, facial expression and hair and tail lines could be improved. This is why I could not wait until the next one.

One of the most unusual grain patterns was found in this very stylish model made of walnut burl (Figs. 49 and 50). Generally the

Fig. 49.

Fig. 50.

grain runs horizontally to give strength to the extended legs; which were nearly as thin as matchsticks. Several degrees of hardness were found—from soft and even at the top of the head to hard and burly at the belly and legs. This model is well detailed, has good facial expression and is well muscled. Total time required was about 75 hours.

One of the most frequent questions asked by admirers of different models concerns the length of time required for the complete job. Unless one measures the time of each carving session, intense concentration, especially during the finishing stages, causes time to go by unnoticed until several hours have passed. Then a pause for reevaluation or relaxation may become necessary. I have found that when carving the hind legs of horses in motion I must keep an awareness of what the forelegs are doing, or are about to do. This is where some knowledge of body rhythm, conformation and coordination is essential. One part must always be kept in proportion to every other part.

Discounting the time required, the worth of a carved model can be judged by the kind of communication it makes with the eye of the beholder. All the fine detail, the well-executed knife-cutting and the elegant proportion of parts mean little to the person with a lack of sensitive judgment. I have seen people select models of lesser carving quality because something in the general appearance appealed to them.

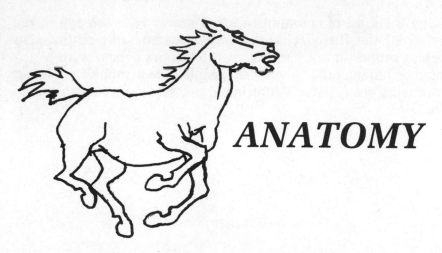

ANATOMY

When seriously carving horses as a specialty, it is impossible to spend too much time reviewing the basic frame structure. Among the devices I have used is a transparent do-it-yourself assembly that I put together some time ago (Fig. 51). It is a good scale model of bone and internal organ arrangement and serves as an excellent reference.

For centuries the horse has been the animal most admired by men. Thus it follows that the graceful motions of a horse in action ought to be

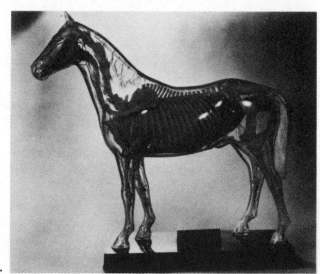

Fig. 51. This assembly kit, The Visible Horse by Revell provides an excellent means for learning horse anatomy.

understood. That is why anyone who takes a special fancy to horses should take some time and learn what happens to his framework when the horse is doing various things.

As stated earlier, many of the older lithographs and prints showing horses racing are not accurate. This was because of lack of observation and study of horse anatomy. In the horse book, *The Golden Book of Horses* by George McMillan, an account is given of the discovery of horse motion through a series of synchronized exposures from several cameras so that actual leg motions can be seen. Because no motion-picture equipment was in existence in 1872, this was the first and only set of pictures taken in series.

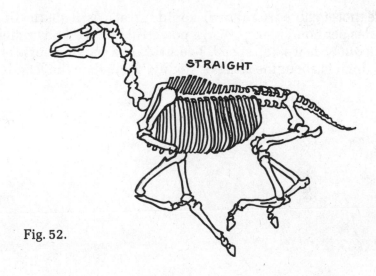

STRAIGHT

Fig. 52.

This exhibit of anatomy shows clearly how a horse's spine remains somewhat rigid and straight (Fig. 52) while he is running. The cat and dog families have spines that will curve, as in Fig. 53, and permit the rear legs to swing forward further, giving them a longer stride. The horse has more powerful rear legs which give him a greater thrust and still provide greater speed.

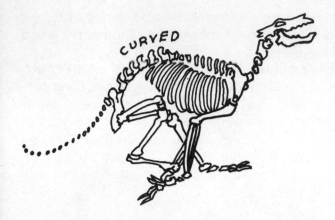

CURVED

Fig. 53.

The thoroughbred, Coaltown, could run at least a quarter of a mile at 49 miles per hour. Man o' War, a powerful winner, had tremendous stride, about 28 feet at top speed. The stride of a walking horse is about 7 feet, which is about the same or slightly more than the length of the body.

BREEDS

Hunter and Steeplechaser

Hunters and steeplechasers are said to be the result of a cross between a thoroughbred and a Percheron that took place long ago. They must be agile, obedient and strong enough to carry weight often for long distances, while clearing fences and obstacles.

This model (Fig. 54) required the most advanced planning and

Fig. 54.

sketching of any. The red mahogany block, 4 inches thick, was 75 percent wasted in the cutting. To show speed in the jumping horse, and a sudden jolting stop in the fallen one, I felt that one should be nearly symmetrical and the other very asymmetrical. Thus, the fallen horse was not at all in a formal posture. What do the hindquarters do when the body twists and lands on the left shoulder? The horse must be designed with many opposing lines, off parallel, to show violent action. The wood was even-grained and one has a desire to whack at it to get a chiselled look. This one, a real skull session, used up well over 100 hours.

Fig. 55.

Usually a pyramid design is static and quiet, yet this one shows how the action line of the jumping horse is suddenly stopped by the curved neck of the fallen horse. It is not recommended that the beginner try to do this model. There are far too many problems for the novice.

Fig. 56.

Mustang

The world of the mustang was always the open plains. The name is Spanish for "running wild." They were first tamed by the Spanish Moors and brought to Mexico by Captain Cortez in 1519, the first horses to land on the American continent. The Indians made use of them for working and fighting. Mustangs are usually shown in positions of violent action. (See Fig. 56.)

This most popular of all temperamental horses is shown trying to unload his rider (Figs. 57 and 58). It was one of my earliest horse-and-rider combinations and made of light mahogany. The man is attached to the horse by one hand, two knees and the boots. The grain runs vertically to gain strength in all but the right front leg, and this one must be carefully handled. To help this situation, the legs are not separated until the final stages. In finishing the right leg, one finger is used to back up the foot while cutting on it (Fig. 59). The fingers must be trained to back up cutting pressure on parts, with the same delicate touch as that of a piano or flute player. Note there is no saddle or harness shown.

Fig. 57.

Fig. 58.

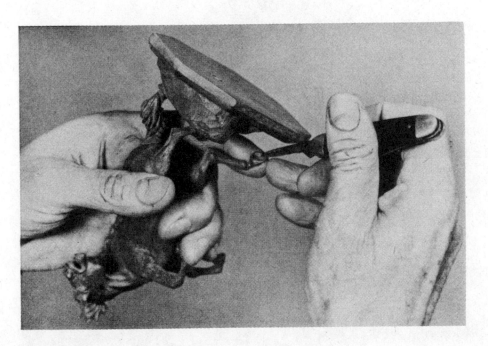

Fig. 59.

Again, here is an exciting and extremely active fellow (Figs. 60, 61, and 62) who is defiant of someone. Made of dark mahogany with grain running from extreme hind leg diagonally to the top of his head, the vulnerable parts during the cutting were the front legs and the tip of the tail. This one was full of bulging muscles because of the great tenseness and alertness of the body. With the head turned, we have a body that is not in any way symmetrical. Note that the hair flies out in a horizontal plain indicating the sweeping movement of the head. The whip of the tail, which adds to the horse's action, was a very fragile job that continually presented a challenge to keep in one piece. Here again, the

Fig. 60.

Fig. 61.

forelegs were the last to shape and detail, demanding great care and delicate gripping in order to prevent breakage when cutting. Over 90 hours of nerve-wracking work went into making it, but it was worth it.

It will be noted here that many of my more active models, especially mustangs, are supported on but two of their legs, indicating some

Fig. 62. Here and in Fig. 61 above are two views of the same excitable fellow.

Fig. 63.

kind of violent motion (Fig. 63). You have the immediate feeling that the other two, although raised, must come down and thus the motion is apparent. This one was among the earlier models, improved and more realistic in detail and construction. This fellow is leading with his left foot.

Here is shown the profile (Fig. 64), cut from red mahogany just

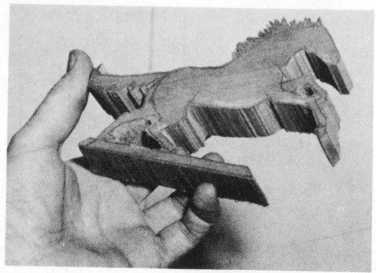

Fig. 64.

Fig. 65.

prior to carving. First the positions of the right and left legs are determined and cut away on opposite sides. The figure is quite symmetrical and the twist of the body action is no problem. This work required about 75 hours. The direction of the wood grain is here most important. The strength required in the two rear legs demanded that the grain runs with the position of the rear legs.

Since the subject is symmetrical, the modelling is normal. The importance of studying anatomy and muscle arrangement in order to get correct modelling contour cannot be stressed too much. When you understand the position of the skeletal bones, and the function and shape of the various muscles, you will be able to fashion the contour of the parts. Later in this book can be found some details on anatomy, particularly muscles.

A typical position of a mustang is to buck and kick (Figs. 65, 66, 67 and 68). This fellow, shown in Fig. 66, is made of a beautiful red cherry

Fig. 66.

wood, hard to cut in the rough stages, but enjoyable to finish. This one is among the best of my modelling jobs, and has a good swing and rhythm of motion. Here the grain runs diagonally from forefeet to tail, in order to gain strength in the supporting forelegs. The problem of cross-grain cutting requires great care in cutting the rear legs. Therefore, they will be the last to cut in the finishing stages.

Fig. 67.

Fig. 68. Note support between legs to protect them while detail is completed.

I actually started the cutting on the body and front section: head, neck and forelegs. Details of the hair and tail were left until the last.

One must always observe the rule "look at the rear legs when working on the front legs." This means that you must always be conscious of the shape and proportion of one part when working on another. If you become serious about making good horse models, get some facts on anatomy and continually study and refer to these details as you carve your horse. I cannot emphasize too strongly the value of basic knowledge.

One last detail about finishing. Rough-cut the rear legs to a general shape and finish the detailing of the hoof and fetlock assembly first. Then you can cut the shins and knee sections, working up to the body proper. As stated before, detail the hair and tail and eye parts last.

As you progress, you will commence to "feel" the proper proportion of the animal.

Some years ago I would visit the art exhibits in Carnegie Museum and spend an hour or two studying the priceless collection of ivory carvings. I would stand there and dream of how grand it would be to

Fig. 69.

Fig. 70.

have the ability to do something like that myself. I suppose that was the basis of my subsequent urge to carve. During my more productive years, I couldn't wait to get at my knife and a block of wood. Subconsciously a carving career had been germinating which, in later years, had sprouted and grown.

A very early model (Figs. 69 and 70) was cut from balsa wood in

Fig. 71. Front.   Fig. 72. Rear.

Fig. 73.

order to get a rough chiselled look. It was not shaved to a smooth surface as most others shown here were. This is not especially good modelling or detailing. (See also Figs. 71–78)

The drawings shown here were selected, from many that were used to cut the models shown on the preceding pages. Mustangs, even

Fig. 74.

Fig. 75.

when tamed, are active, jumpy and often contrary; thus, they should be designed with the busy, angular lines of motion.

The jumper in Fig. 74 was made from a very splintery deck mahog-

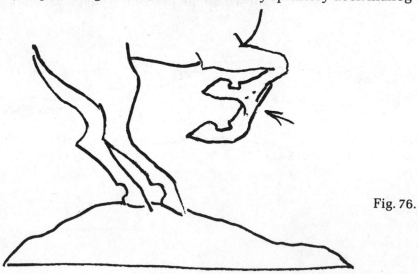

Fig. 76.

Fig. 77.

any and was relatively easy to cut. The front legs are out straight, but when landing, one will lead and touch down first. Figs. 75 and 76 show how good action can be found with the horse on two legs.

The mustang Indian pony (Figs. 78 and 79) is shown in a very springy canter, again supported on one leg, with the other rear leg connected by a raised section of wood. The front legs, the hair and the tail were cut across the grain. It is characteristic of a mustang bucking

Fig. 78.

and jumping. This is a most graceful flow of lines, with the positions of legs, neck and tail all indicating the rhythmic motion of the canter.

The rear and front legs were only roughly cut to finished dimension to maintain strength while working on the other parts, and fully detailed as the last part of the work. The head and body were completely detailed first. The rear legs were next and the forelegs were now completed. Eyes, hair detail and hoofs were the last to be done.

Polo Pony

Polo is an ancient game, possibly developed by the Hindus and the Persians centuries ago. The Indian name "pulu" became polo. The game further progressed in England where it became a sport for the rich, because they could afford the mounts for frequent substitution. The best polo horses are crossbred Thoroughbreds and cow ponies or Quarter Horses. They have been taught to move fast, stop, wheel and move rapidly in any direction. Horse and rider must cooperate perfectly. Here

Fig. 79.

are four of a team: The first (Fig. 79) is made of red mahogany, Fig. 80 was made of walnut, Fig. 81 is cherry, and Fig. 82 is light mahogany. In each one there is some delicate cross-grain cutting. Note that I do not try to detail too much harness or trappings, emphasis being on the coordinated action of horse and rider. Each model required about 65 hours.

Many times it will be apparent that a polo pony gets into a rocking motion when slowing up. The walnut model here tries to show that motion with each pair of feet moving almost together. This seldom produces good body rhythm. Note that the left rear foot is almost separated from the base. The drawing called for separation but it eventually appeared too risky. The grain runs diagonally with the lines of the rear leg. This required cross-grain cutting for the body and neck.

The delicate extremities such as a leg or tail of Figs. 83 and 84 can be backed up by a finger tip to absorb cutting pressure. This model required about 80 hours. Fig. 85 is a top view of Fig. 84.

Fig. 80.

Fig. 81.

Fig. 82.

Fig. 83.

Fig. 84.

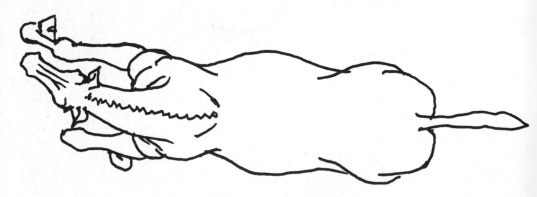

Fig. 85. Top view.

Fig. 86. Percheron and performer.

Percheron (Heavyweight)

Perhaps the most famous of this breed are found in the circus ring. They are sometimes known as "Rosinbacks" because of the rosin rubbed on their backs before they enter the ring. Originally brought from La Perche, France, they now are used for hauling and farm work, but their specialty is prancing around the circus ring. The center of Percheron breeding, today, is in Wayne, Illinois. They are mostly white or dappled grey and easily trained to trot to the waltz or two-step music of the circus band (Figs. 86, 87, 88 and 89).

Fig. 87.

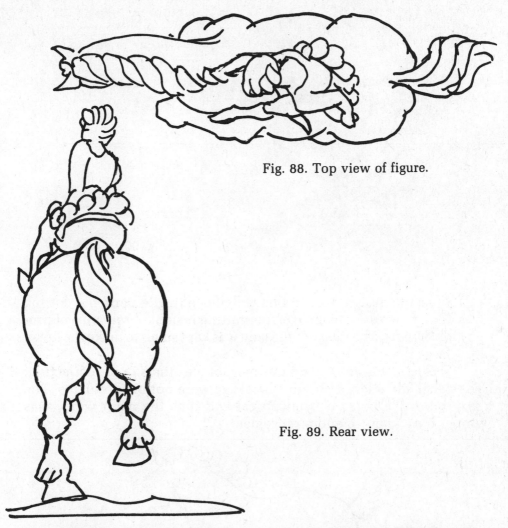

Fig. 88. Top view of figure.

Fig. 89. Rear view.

A good piece of straight-grain maple was used and difficult cutting produced the usual crop of finger blisters and cuts. The tight-grained wood held the minute edges well, and was a delight to finish. Continual shaving gave the whole model a smooth appearance. It would be a sin and a shame to use sandpaper. A two-tone appearance was caused by using wax on the body and rider and applying oil to the hair and tail and fetlocks. By balancing the horse on one toe, a rocking motion was indicated.

Fig. 90.

Since the design does not have delicate fragile parts the cutting was done progressively all over, permitting instant observance of proportion of parts. The figure of the lady was kept small to make the horse look larger.

This fellow is not as fragile as most of the others in my collection. The usual anxieties of possible breakage were not big problems. The position of the horse is symmetrical and thus the main worry was proper muscle bulge and arrangement.

Fig. 91.

An unusual pose (Figs. 90 and 91) and an unusual wood together add up to a fine example of rhythm in horse motion. Made of curly buckeye, it was a real challenge to cut into any kind of reasonable shape. Curly buckeye does not respond to carving strokes as an even-grain wood does. The grain has a deep marcel, which at any time takes a dip and leaves a wavy pattern. This means that careful cross-grain cutting is the only way to produce an intended surface. Every cut is a major operation. No one has faced real carving hazards until he has worked with curly buckeye. Four models similar to this one were made of this buckeye, each requiring about 80 hours.

Two models are shown (Figs. 92 and 93), both of which are stylized, not intended to be natural positions. Since they are both of

Fig. 92.

Fig. 93.

sturdy proportions, the cutting was progressively done, beginning with the body, and each leg and neck was cut a little here and a little there, and gradually the proportions of the parts could be evaluated. As said before, when cutting on one part, the eye should be aware of the relative shape of the others.

On these models, emphasis is placed on muscular shape, good detail of hoofs, fetlocks and fetlock "feathers"—the hair on the fetlocks. The eyes, nostrils, curving hair and tail should also be well detailed, adding to the excitement of the action.

Belgian

A compact animal (Figs. 94, 95 and 96), the Belgian has powerful hindquarters. Credit is often given to the humid soil of Belgium and the rich grass for his strength. Often used in the Middle Ages as a battle charger, the breed naturally became a farm horse, where it excels today in this country. This cherry model is swinging its short, heavy legs in a trot, which is top speed for its muscular body. Cherry takes longer, about 90 hours, but all the blisters and cuts are worth it when the finished animal is oiled to a deep red.

The cutting, starting with the profile cutout (Fig. 96), is slow, cherry being a tight-grained hardwood. Here again, the model should be progressively carved, keeping the eye on the progressive proportions of each part as the work develops. Too much cannot be said about the study of muscle action and anatomy in order to know what the outside contour should be.

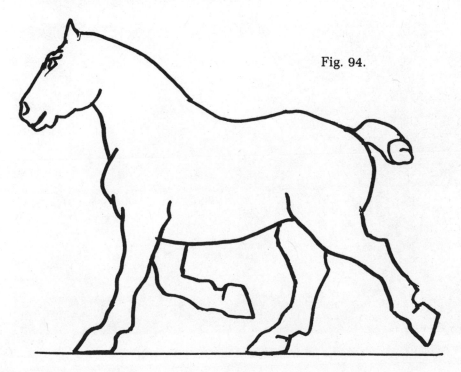

Fig. 94.

Fig. 95 (top) and Fig. 96 (bottom).

Shire

This is possibly the biggest and broadest horse known, weighing over a ton. (See Figs. 97 and 98.) The "feathers" on his legs were said to protect him from the sharp grass in the marshy fens of Lincolnshire, England. Largely used in early forests to drag logs and to pull great loads in western American grain belts, he has become a symbol of bigness on farms. This carving, too, was made of cherry, with the usual problems of this hardwood. The close grain holds detail well. Total time was about 70 hours.

The early stages of cutting cherry are rough when only knives are used, but the finishing is a joy, since cherry holds the edges of the grooves and contours.

Fig. 97.

Fig. 98.

Lipizzaners

A compact, powerful and exceedingly graceful animal, the Lipizzaner is often called "the ballet dancer." They are trained to perform a routine of difficult tricks, such as leaping, pirouetting and unusual kicking (Figs. 99 and 100 show the Capriole). A very old breed, they were originally crossbred from Arab stallions and Spanish mares and became pure white in color. The rider sits erect and his communication with the horse is not evident to the spectator. This breed was almost lost in World War II when the Nazis hid the whole Lipizzaner herd in Czechoslovakia, and General George S. Patton later provided a way of escape back to the American Zone in Austria.

Among the many Old World gavottes and mazurkas these white dancers perform are three more commonly known figures shown here. The first, the Capriole, is a springing leap which when complete finds all four legs stretched out like those of a flying Pegasus. This is one of the more sturdy models, made of dark walnut, and reflects the strength

Fig. 99.

of the animal. The hair and tail are arranged to indicate the jerky leaps being made. Also note the rigid posture of the rider, who may be communicating a signal to the horse, but no one can detect it. As usual, walnut is a very firm wood to detail.

Another well-known performance of the Lipizzaner is the Courbette, shown here in a drawing in Fig. 101. A model of this one was made of light mahogany and it, too, has the muscular look of the sturdy animal. To complete a Courbette, the horse is trained to balance on his hind legs and take successive leaps or hops. It takes a strong,

Fig. 100.

well-disciplined animal to do this, but the Lipizzaner is trained all of its life to perform these unusual movements. Fig. 101 is made of Honduras mahogany, a relatively easy wood to carve. The tail touching the ground provides a third support.

Fig. 101.

Another similar performance is the Levade, where the horse crouches on his hind legs very low and slowly raises his body to a 45 degree angle, not to a standing position. This cannot be done by any other horse, and the best of this breed cannot hold the pose longer than 10 to 15 seconds. A model was not made of this one.

Fig. 102.

Saddle Horse

Fig. 102 shows a very stylish four-gaited horse, made of dark mahogany, oiled to accentuate the dark red color of the wood. It was carved full-round, detailed from a desirable photograph, almost perfect as an illustration of slow gait. With cross-grain to contend with, the left front leg and the right rear leg were very carefully shaped. Here is a very good example of the importance of carefully placing your design on wood and allowing the grain to run in the direction where strength is needed.

These two legs are the last to be detailed. In this delicate cutting, back pressure is supplied by the forefinger, while the thumb and two middle fingers grip the solid parts of the body. Very frequently, cross-grain cutting is necessary for some of the parts of the model.

204

Fig. 103.

Fig. 104.

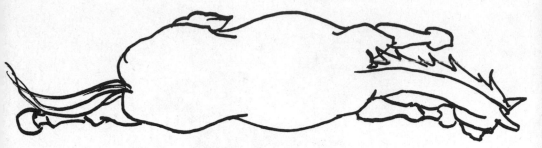

Fig. 105. Top view.

Tennessee Walker

One of the smoothest riding horses of any riding class, this horse gives his rider the feeling of being on a magic carpet (Figs. 103, 104 and 105). He has three gaits: the slow, flatfoot walk, the running walk and the faster rocking-chair canter. The origin of this breed is said to be a mixture of thoroughbreds, Morgans and standard breeds which were brought over the mountains to Tennessee by circuit riders, travelling preachers and other early adventurers from Virginia and the Carolinas. Long, rough-riding excursions developed a combination of stamina, easy strides and good manners from the original breeds which were the background of these walking horses from Tennessee.

The model shown here was made of a very hard walnut, and produced several of the worst cutting accidents to my left hand. For example, while undercutting the belly area, I ran about ½ inch of blade into the thumb side of my hand and later slashed the left forefinger fairly deeply. I am reminded of these and other cuts every time I look at this fellow.

Diagonal legs work in unison, with the left forefoot touching down slightly ahead of the right rear foot, and the rear foot coming down ahead of the forefoot point. These long strides are the secret of the smooth riding comfort. Note that the head is slightly turned, but the rest of the body is symmetrical. Emphasis is again placed on the necessity of studying the actual position of each hoof in the running or trotting movements of the horse. This model required about 95 hours to make.

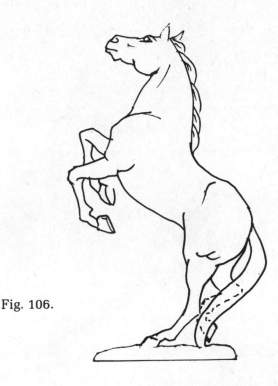

Fig. 106.

Thoroughbred

From Arab and Turk speed and stamina came the original stallion stock that was brought to England to become the fastest horse ever known. He is a very sensitive animal, a born racer with ancient Oriental ancestry (Fig. 106). He is credited with a stout heart and a stubborn desire to keep going in spite of trouble. About 1900, after Daniel Boone had promoted the breed in Kentucky, some American jockeys shortened the stirrups and rode high up on the horse's neck, providing the fast runner with even greater speed.

Figs. 106 and 107 show a typical jumpy pose of the breed when in defiance of something they do not understand or do not like. It was intended to be different than the average pose of a thoroughbred. It was cut from dark walnut, with a slight twist in the body which created some interesting problems of body balance. Note that he is actually standing on one hind leg, having some support from the end of the tail

Fig. 107.

Fig. 108.

and the tip of the left hind hoof. The grain runs vertically, causing some cross-grain cutting in the forelegs. In addition, some problems were caused by some hard burl patterns, which slowed up the job and made it require about 90 hours to finish.

Here is a running position (Figs. 108, 109 and 110) cut from light

Fig. 109. Because the grain of the wood does not run always with the position of the legs, it is important to keep a small portion of wood connecting the two legs until the hoof detail is complete.

209

mahogany. For interest, he also is resting on one leg with the lifted leg connected to the base and not quite fully separated. Flying rear legs became a problem to finish, and they were the last to detail. Here is a good swing to the action, showing the graceful movements of a fast animal. In each of my models, I try to introduce something other than a normal placid look. Some of the well-known thoroughbred champions are Man-o-War, Black Gold and War Admiral.

The drawing is one of the many preliminary sketches of a series. The grain runs diagonally from the head to the rear hoofs, and thus the body parts are all cross-grain cutting.

Fig. 110.

COLTS

It was inevitable that the small fry be a part of the collection, and here is a two-week-old foal who is all legs. I made several models over this pattern of light mahogany and walnut (Figs. 111, 112, 113 and 114). In Figs. 113 and 114 it is posed on one leg, and as usual problems are caused in cutting the free legs. It has the appearance of bouncing and awkwardly springing along. By placing it on one rear leg, it is evident that good motion is developed.

Fig. 111.

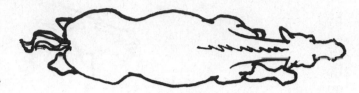

Fig. 112. Top view.

With a small amount of material in the finished model, great care must be used in developing good proportion. Mistakes can easily ruin the job, and I've made some, but my German ancestry has taught me to salvage everything possible.

The mini-model of two-day-old foals staggering (Figs. 115 and 116) is about as tiny as one can go with wood. They are about one inch

Fig. 113.

Fig. 114.

high, made of dark mahogany, and oiled to keep a dark color. Eyes, feet and hair cannot be too detailed, but the try gives one a better feeling for these details in larger models. The lariat hanging on the post is a short length of string, varnished to hold a rigid coil. Great care must be taken on these very small models.

Fig. 115.

Fig. 116.

MIXED GROUP

A yearling colt and a mascot goat (Figs. 117, 118 and 119) proved to be the most difficult of all the models in the collection: first, the problem of two animals from one block and second, the endless trouble with curly buckeye, mentioned previously. Positioning the front legs to allow the colt to graze required some observation. The leggy fellow makes a fitting companion for the short stubby goat. The wood and its

Fig. 117.

214

Fig. 118.

peculiarities are described earlier in this book. Needless to say, with the wood problems always a threat of disaster, the cutting required to separate the two animals was most tedious and seemingly endless. Here again, all finishing was done by carefully shaving the surface of the wood.

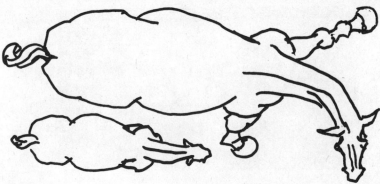

Fig. 119. Top view.

SPECIAL APPLICATIONS

This group of carvings represents a different technique of cutting. Here, the complete round of the model becomes more or less an outline for the profile, which is accented in depth by shadow lines and highlight areas. Most carvers use motor tools and chisels, but mine are cut with various blades of my hand knives. The first model (Figs. 120, 121 and 122) has been mounted in a frame, the picture part being basically dark mahogany. The lighter horse was cut from a laminated layer of white pine and the base part was cut from a laminated strip of dark

Fig. 120.

Fig. 121.

walnut. Fig. 122 shows the first stage—the basic cutting on mahogany. White pine was laminated above the right-hand horse. A base strip was later applied below the horses with walnut. Great care was used in preventing any undercuts because several porcelain castings were made from it and the slightest undercut will prevent the release of the plaster mould.

Fig. 122.

The graceful lines of Fig. 121 formed the basis for the carving that was cast later into a porcelain plaque. White pine, mahogany and walnut were laminated to produce a multi-color effect.

The horse-head plaque (Fig. 123) is a portrait of a famous Lipizzaner horse, Siglava Monterosa. He was copied from a picture found in Major Podhajsky's book, *The White Stallions of Vienna*. The cutting is not deep and it is suitable for moulding and porcelain- or plaster-casting. I keep these plaques waxed in order to apply a lubricant should a clay moulding be desired at any time. The wood was white pine.

Fig. 123.

The plaque in Fig. 124 was deeply cut and somewhat undercut for greater modelling. It is a deep red mahogany, oiled to keep the dark color. It would require a rubber mould if copies are ever made. A deep-set shadow-box frame was made to set off this deep relief and it was placed in the Admissions Office of Seton Hill College in Greensburg, Pennsylvania.

The horse-head drawing (Fig. 125) was carefully copied from a picture, and after several tracings were made this one was considered a fairly accurate portrait of a famous Lipizzaner horse. These horses are pure white, lending themselves to white pine or birch.

Fig. 124.

Fig. 125.

Fig. 126.

The drawing (Fig. 126) was one of many traced of a horse and rider to show the actual clearance of an obstacle, with the horse's hind legs touching the brush. When made in the wood, the rail was used and the horse is still rising to clear it.

The cowboy (Fig. 127) is an interesting arrangement that was cut on a diamond-shaped piece of light mahogany, with the bottom point supported on a suitable base, making it a free-standing plaque.

These two wild, exciting subjects made excellent plaques, having many angular and opposing lines of motion. The broncobuster in Fig.

Fig. 127.

128 was made into an outline, single-line cutting and Fig. 130 was a deep-cut relief in mahogany. Both were made entirely with knives, but rotary cutting equipment can be used on the outline. An interesting sketch (Fig. 129) could be made into a relief carving with some lively action and a lot of outline detail. White pine or mahogany is suggested.

Fig. 128.

Fig. 129.

Fig. 130.

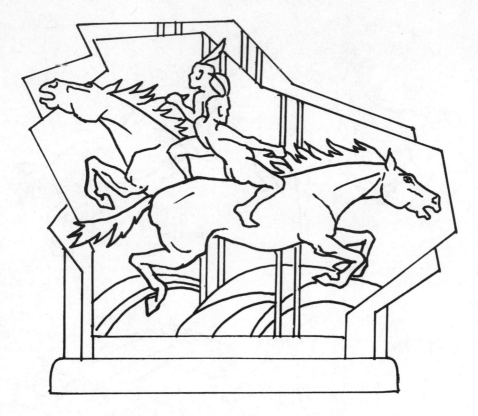

Fig. 131.

The Indian group in Fig. 131 was cut in red mahogany and oiled to keep the rich red color. The idea came from sketches made of a statue, but details are not available. Here is some really wild action. The two sketches in Figs. 132 and 133 are variations made up from sketches used in making up full-round models described elsewhere. They could be made up into bookends.

Ornaments

Of the many horse heads cut at one time or another the walnut model of Fig. 134 was developed further than any other. It was moulded and cast into bronze and aluminum, from both sand and match-plate moulds.

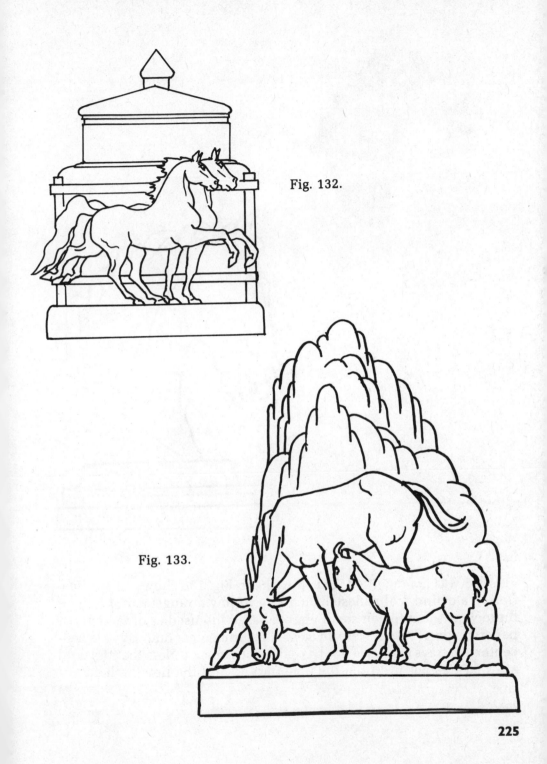

Fig. 132.

Fig. 133.

225

Fig. 135.

Fig. 135 was not moulded. The drawing in Fig. 136 shows an application to a cylindrical pedestal such as a trophy arrangement. Many of these were mounted on small marble bases and used as ornaments or paperweights. Others were suggested as ornaments on heavy, raised-center ash trays and some for box-cover ornaments. Note that the wild attitude was derived from the open mouth and the flowing hair.

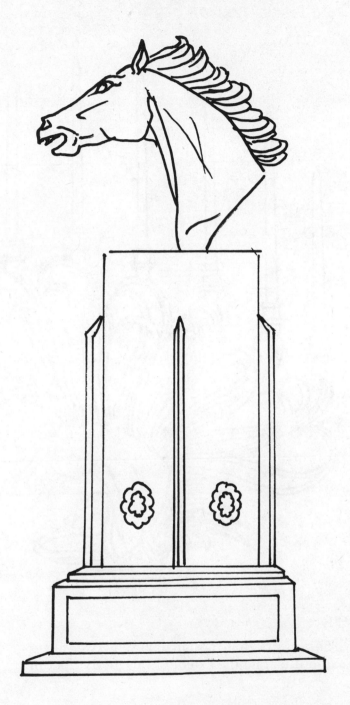

Fig. 136.

Fig. 137.

The very elaborate design of Fig. 137 was never made up, but it is shown to illustrate the extent of imaginary doodling.

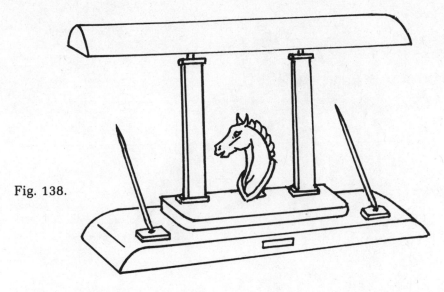

Fig. 138.

An interesting application of the horse head that is shown in Fig. 138 was this idea and several others that were made for suppliers of desk equipment.

The drawings shown in Figs. 139 and 140 are of patterns made up for door knockers. Fig. 139 was sand-moulded and cast in bronze, as was a similar arrangement. The arrangement of Fig. 140 was developed into a white pine pattern and has made an excellent and popular door knocker in bronze. The photo (Fig. 141) shows how the white pine model was cast into brass and used for many gifts.

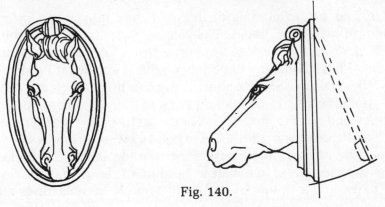

Fig. 139.

Fig. 140.

Fig. 141.

Bookends

An endless number of bookend designs can be made from sketches used in cutting full-round models (Fig. 142). A few are shown here, some in bas-relief and one full-round carved horse in white pine (Fig. 143). The latter is working hard at performing his task of holding up books.

In making up models of this sort, one must keep in mind the undercutting of the horse. The tendency is to try reproducing the finished article in bronze or porcelain. I did not mention epoxy because I have had little experience with it and what I did try turned out to be a failure. Some undercutting can be permitted if a rubber or fish-glue mould is to be made. I stick to clay moulding for porcelain castings and rubber moulds for brass casting (lost-wax process).

The Percheron in the model in Fig. 143 was cut and waxed without the upright against his knees as shown in the sketch. He looked much better with his knees in the clear, holding the book upright. Someday I will make a rubber mould and have some bronze castings made.

Fig. 142.

Again I wish to point out that no sandpaper or emery is ever used in the finishing of any kind of carving. Sometimes small cutting impressions are desirable to provide a textured look. If a more polished look is desirable, I carefully shave it a little smoother.

Fig. 143.

I've used many kinds of wood for the models and find that maple or cherry make up the best-looking finished models. The models in Figs. 144 and 146 were finished in a smooth-grain maple. One reason for this choice is that, when waxed, the grain hardly shows in any strong pattern, and I like these better that way.

Fig. 144.

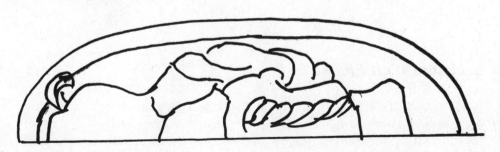

Fig. 145. Top view.

Fig. 146.

Sectional Wall Plaque

A more complicated project was a 22-inch-high mosaic-type bucking bronco and rider in a wild, jumping motion. Twenty-two pieces of various colored woods such as walnut, mahogany, white' pine and birch were used fo produce an interesting assembly shown in Fig. 147.

234

Fig. 147.   Fig. 148.

On the next few pages will be shown a few of the general arrangements and working drawings. The outline is an enlargement of the model described previously.

Each of the many pieces was first cut in profile and roughly shaped. Then they were fitted and carefully finished for joining. Each piece was dowelled horizontally and glued and allowed to dry. When all the pieces were together (Fig. 147) the complete assembly was screwed down to a dark walnut base which was made one inch wider than the general outline of the complete model. The completed model was then heavily varnished.

When the sectional parts for the mosaic are determined, each is numbered for individual cutting, fitting (Fig. 149), and developing in cross-sections of each. The model is visualized and the thickness of each piece established.

A general arrangement drawing of the horse and rider was used as a basis for all of the cross-sections and itemized sketches. The only material other than the several kinds of wood was the hemp rope snub rein, which was soaked in varnish to make it rigid when placed and allowed to dry.

235

Fig. 149.

Each of the cut pieces requires a marked-up sketch showing the thickness and kind of wood to be used. Outlines of each piece are traced on the required wood for cutting. After complete assembly, the

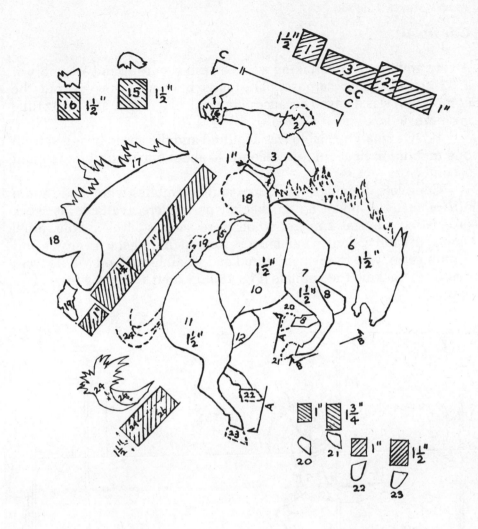

Fig. 150.

edges are rounded and detailing is completed, with many of the knife cuts left to provide a somewhat chiselled look. By using several kinds of wood, a color pattern can be established. Total cutting and mounting time is about 115 hours.

Carousel

A very ambitious undertaking was the design, cutting and assembly of a 22-inch-diameter carousel. The parts have all been cut, but the completion was delayed because of the lack of the right jive-waltz tune on a music box.

First, a small turntable was acquired and the speed changed from one revolution in about four seconds to about one revolution in eight seconds.

Complete drawings of all parts and assemblies were made and a bill of material made up so that all parts were available as work progressed. Several kinds of wood were used, such as maple, pine, mahogany and walnut; small mirrors were found; steel wire crown and pinion gears were formed and fitted and small hardwood rollers were made for tracking the animals (Fig. 150) in their reciprocating movement.

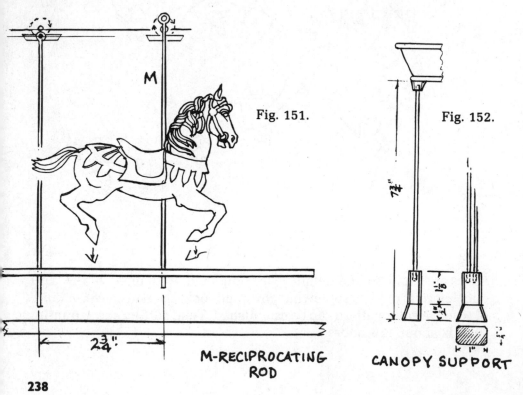

Fig. 151.

Fig. 152.

M-RECIPROCATING ROD

CANOPY SUPPORT

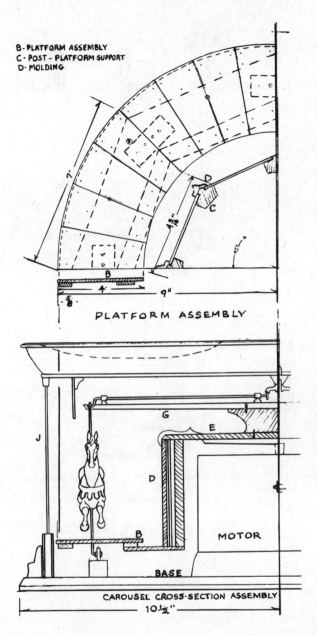

B - PLATFORM ASSEMBLY
C - POST - PLATFORM SUPPORT
D - MOLDING

PLATFORM ASSEMBLY

Fig. 153.

CAROUSEL CROSS-SECTION ASSEMBLY

239

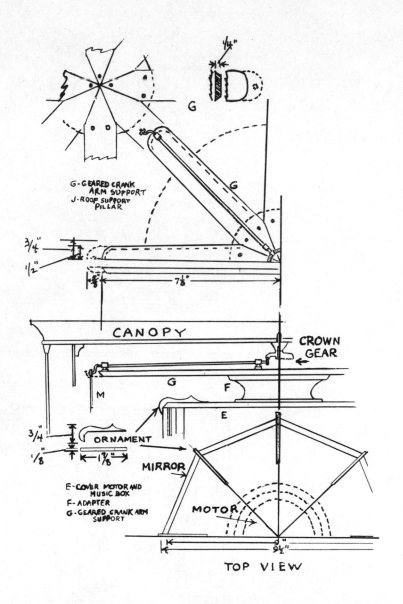

G - GEARED CRANK
ARM SUPPORT
J - ROOF SUPPORT
PILLAR

$\frac{3}{4}$"

$\frac{1}{2}$"

$\frac{5}{8}$ $7\frac{1}{8}$"

CANOPY

CROWN
GEAR

M   G   F

E

$\frac{3}{4}$"

ORNAMENT

$\frac{1}{8}$ $1\frac{3}{8}$"

MIRROR

E - COVER MOTOR AND
MUSIC BOX
F - ADAPTER
G - GEARED CRANK ARM
SUPPORT

MOTOR

$9\frac{1}{2}$"

TOP VIEW

Fig. 154.

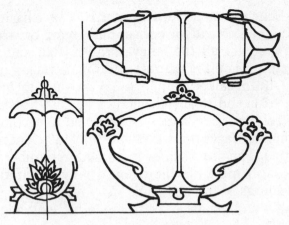

Fig. 155. Carriage.

Here are drawings (Figs. 151, 152, 153, and 154), giving further detail of the mounting arrangement of the reciprocating rod, crank and gear. A crown gear is mounted on the stationary top canopy and is fixed. As the platform and music-box assembly turn, a pinion gear on a steel-rod crank arm is rotated from the crown gear, and the crank moves the animal up and down. A roller and wavy track can also be attached to the lower end of the vertical shaft that supports the animal. The geared crank assembly can be eliminated and the carousel, with animals and sleighs in a fixed position, is still a great project to tackle.

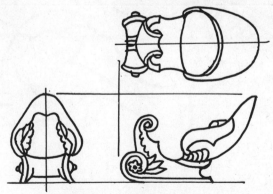

Fig. 156. Carriage.

The color scheme can be varied. I started with a basic white, with many light blue panels and an occasional edging or striping in red. Lavish use of gold for all the fancy scroll design and ornament is desirable. Trimmings on the harness and the carriages are gold highlighted. The platform can be stained in oak or walnut. Upright canopy supports. (Fig. 151) and steel rods should be gold-finished.

The carousel described here was designed to accommodate four animals and four carriages (Figs. 155, 156 and 157). This is as far as it can be simplified. The units can be increased in number as far as it is desirable, keeping in mind that they should be even in number to fit the four quarter sections of the platform.

The animals and carriages were made of lightweight pine and balsa.

The animal hair and tails can be black as well as the harness. The saddle blanket should be red, and the saddle brown, with lavish gold trim on all harness pieces. The animals can be white or light brown.

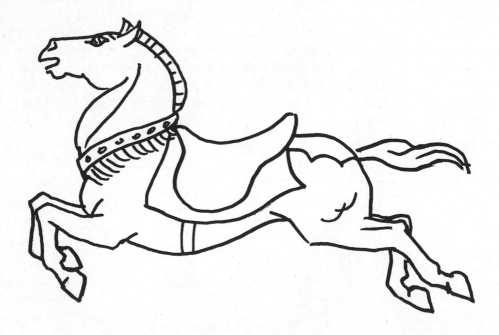

Fig. 157.

Fig. 157. (cont.)

REPLICAS

No doubt every carver has the desire to make some kind of reproduction of his work. I have been through it and have made up some porcelains and bronzes which were successful.

The first was a porcelain made from a carving shown previously. It was made from a clay moulding of a bas-relief (Fig. 158), shown earlier in wood. After testing for slight undercuts, the wood model was lubricated and moulded. I made several copies, this one in pure white porcelain and a few others in a combination of colored glaze finishes.

Fig. 158.

Fig. 159.

The second attempt was the bronze horse head, shown mounted on white marble in Fig. 159. This one was sand-moulded, but a number of later castings were made from a match-plate mould.

Among the many reproductions made from a wood model was this bronze wax-investment casting of a walnut Indian pony (Fig. 160). This is the hard way to do it because models intended for bronze

Fig. 160.

245

should be made of wax. With the grain running in line with the direction of the hind legs, they were broken in the process of mould-making. This is more serious than breaking a finger, for 75 hours were spent carving the wood.

The bronze casting was made from a rubber mould. It was cast in a Long Island foundry and, starting from a wood pattern, was quite expensive. The bronze mounted on red marble is one of my prizes. It is one of the rewards one realizes for a lot of long, hard work.

The next project will be an attempt to pour an epoxy casting, which with addition of bronze powder will make a fine little ornament, weighing about ⅙ as much as bronze.

Chariot

The tiny four-horse chariot (Figs. 161 and 162) shown earlier in Fig. 34 is detailed to scale. The chariot body is made of one piece with small insulated copper wire used as the boarding handle. The wheels may be cut from one piece, but it is more realistic to cut the hub, spokes and rims, then put it together. The rim should be made of straight-grain ash or fruitwood. The circumference of the wheel can be determined by multiplying the outside diameter by pi (3.1416). The rim strips should be boiled for quite a while, until soft enough to bend without breaking.

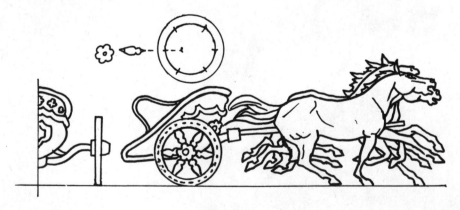

Fig. 161.

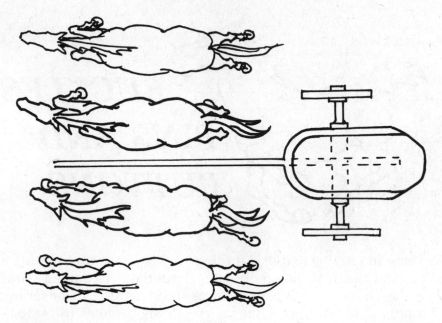

Fig. 162. Top view.

A heavier soft wire can be wrapped around the rim when assembled, twisted tight, and kept on until the glue is dry.

BUCKLES, PINS AND BUTTONS

Many interesting and useful things can be made up by using a little thought and imagination. By using the outline of a trained show horse in the various routine performances in competition, a fine series can be arranged. In this case, a fine-gaited gelding is shown (Figs. 163.–167.), all cut over the same basic pattern. They are especially attractive in walnut, cherry or some other dark wood that polishes well.

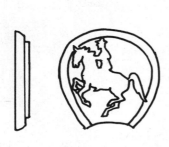

Fig. 163.

Fig. 164.

Figs. 165–167.

This series of carved horseheads for ornamental pins (Figs. 168 and 169) was cut in white pine, as I wished to make moulds and cast them with colored glazes in porcelain. The pin and clasp assemblies were taken from inexpensive jewelry and glued on the back of the pieces.

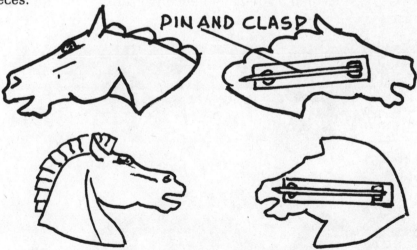

PIN AND CLASP

Figs. 168 and 169. Pins and clasps.

AFTERWORD

Now you can see why time means little to a carver. The thought occurred to me many years ago that some kind of evidence of progress could be recorded in order to show graphically what is actually cut off during each sitting (Fig. 170). I saved all the cuttings in separate piles and it was interesting to observe that, as the model was nearing completion, fewer and smaller chips were produced. In the final stages, much more deliberation is required for each chip and shaving. These separate piles accumulated in volume inversely as the total time increased.

Fig. 170.

It is not unusual to record from fifty to eighty hours on one model. There is no such thing as a time card for the true carver. His first and foremost thought concerns the degree of fidelity and quality of workmanship. When the carving is complete there can be no alteration, except in reduction if a part here and there will stand a little taken off. Unlike clay or oil painting, there can be no adding or shaping. The wood is cut so far, and work is stopped. Thus, we can assume that carving is a greater challenge for creative skill than many of the other arts.

If other wood carvers think as I do, they are their own most severe critics. In my own case, I have never completed one model that completely satisfied me. There is always some little thing that could be done better. This conclusion is carefully filed in the mind in hopes that it will influence a similar situation the next time it arises.

Other books have more elaborate information on woods and tools. My models have all been shaped with a choice of several hand knives. A motorized tool with a selection of cutters is more useful to me on bas-relief work. As stated before, the various kinds of wood each seem to have a distinctive personality. The more I work with wood, the greater my respect and affection for natural wood finishes. When my models are complete, I coat them with either linseed oil or liquid wax, depending on the degree of color I want. Oil darkens the grain, and with some woods it brings out an interesting pattern. Wax keeps the original tone in all but some soft woods. In my curly-buckeye models, wax finishing retains the ghostly grey color, and oil greatly accentuates the wavy marcel of the grain and considerable contrast of color.

My own taste forbids my painting or the addition of other materials, such as leather or metal. To me it is sacriligious to use sandpaper. I prefer knife finishing only, and have a few that have been shaved down to a relative smoothness. This is great when working with maple or cherry.

Occasionally someone asks me if I have exhibited to the public in any organized show. This is something I do not actively pursue, but I have accepted a few invitations. One of these exhibits produced several two-page rotogravure pictorial reviews in the *Pittsburgh Press*, Sunday Edition; the first on July 13, 1958 and the other on January 31,

251

1965. The exhibit that induced these stories was a hobby show in the window of the Mellon Bank in Pittsburgh, Pennsylvania. Many letters from friends resulted from this exhibit and, of course, were always warmly appreciated. Several other hobby shows and several art club shows were entered with a few ribbons received, one for best of show.

Some time ago, a winning ribbon in the handcraft section of a local church art show was received and, of course, appreciated. More recently the group was shown twice in the Butler Art Gallery in Youngstown, Ohio, the Seton Hill College Library in Greensburg, Pennsylvania and the Ligonier Library in Ligonier, Pennsylvania.

Because horses have been my specialty, I would like to suggest some things to look for when examining a carved or sculptured animal. First, look for good rhythm design and proportion of parts. Even in a standing model, the legs should not be stiff and duplicate in shape. The beast should have some indication of a natural, relaxed look with the head often slightly turned indicating that something has caught his interest.

Look for detail and expression of eyes and ears. Even his nostril should have some shape and not be just a slight gouge in the surface. Look for detail in the fetlocks, the hair on the neck and tail. The parting, or slight sway in the breeze makes these parts more interesting. Then, too, does he wear shoes if one or more feet are lifted?

If you are looking for over-simplified and impressionistic pieces, find one with some sort of good design, or my advice is to forget it.

As most of my horses are in motion, there is little symmetry in their design. I think of the axis of the shoulder joints and the hip joints as two horizontal bars supported and pivoted on a center pole—the spinal column. Then the front axis turns or drops from horizontal, then the rear axis must move in some corresponding related motion.

Any motion should have the look of effort and power exerted, even though the motion is not vigorous. Remember that the rhythm and harmony exhibited in the motion of active horses is as pleasing as good music. That is no doubt why the horse is popular, and this could be the reason that I carved so many of them.

252

CARVING WOODEN ANIMALS

E. J. Tangerman

Contents

Woodworkers' Conversion Tables

Imperial inches	Metric millimetres	Woodworkers' parlance (mm)	Metric millimetres	Imperial inches	Woodworkers' parlance (mm)
$\frac{1}{32}$	0.8	1	1	0.039	$\frac{1}{16}$
$\frac{1}{16}$	1.6	$1\frac{1}{2}$	2	0.078	$\frac{1}{16}$
$\frac{1}{8}$	3.2	3	3	0.118	$\frac{1}{8}$
$\frac{3}{16}$	4.8	5	4	0.157	$\frac{5}{32}$
$\frac{1}{4}$	6.4	$6\frac{1}{2}$	5	0.196	$\frac{3}{16}$
$\frac{5}{16}$	7.9	8	6	0.236	$\frac{1}{4}$
$\frac{3}{8}$	9.5	$9\frac{1}{2}$	7	0.275	$\frac{1}{4}$
$\frac{7}{16}$	11.1	11	8	0.314	$\frac{5}{16}$
$\frac{1}{2}$	12.7	$12\frac{1}{2}$	9	0.353	$\frac{3}{8}$
$\frac{9}{16}$	14.3	$14\frac{1}{2}$	10	0.393	$\frac{3}{8}$
$\frac{5}{8}$	15.9	16	20	0.787	$\frac{13}{16}$
$\frac{11}{16}$	17.5	$17\frac{1}{2}$	30	1.181	$1\frac{3}{16}$
$\frac{3}{4}$	19.1	19	40	1.574	$1\frac{9}{16}$
$\frac{13}{16}$	20.6	$20\frac{1}{2}$	50	1.968	$1\frac{15}{16}$
$\frac{7}{8}$	22.2	22	60	2.362	$2\frac{3}{8}$
$\frac{15}{16}$	23.8	24	70	2.755	$2\frac{3}{4}$
1	25.4	$25\frac{1}{2}$	80	3.148	$3\frac{1}{8}$
2	50.8	51	90	3.542	$3\frac{9}{16}$
3	76.2	76	100	3.936	$3\frac{15}{16}$
4	101.4	$101\frac{1}{2}$	150	5.904	$5\frac{15}{16}$
5	127.0	127	200	7.872	$7\frac{7}{8}$
6	152.4	$152\frac{1}{2}$	300	11.808	$11\frac{13}{16}$
7	177.5	$177\frac{1}{2}$	400	15.744	$15\frac{3}{4}$
8	203.2	203	500	19.680	$19\frac{11}{16}$
9	228.6	$228\frac{1}{2}$	600	23.616	$23\frac{5}{8}$
10	254.0	254	700	27.552	$27\frac{9}{16}$
11	279.5	$279\frac{1}{2}$	800	31.488	$31\frac{1}{2}$
12	304.8	305	900	35.424	$35\frac{7}{16}$
18	457.2	457	1,000	39.360	$39\frac{3}{8}$
24	609.6	$609\frac{1}{2}$			
36	914.4	$914\frac{1}{2}$			

Note: The imperial and metric sizes given for tools and joint parts, etc., cannot work out exactly, but providing you work to one or the other there is no difficulty. In the timber trade it is accepted that 1 in = 25 mm.

CHAPTER I

Answers to Your Basic Questions

What is whittling? What is woodcarving?

WHITTLE was originally an Old English word for a butcher knife, but now is largely obsolete except in Scotland and in dialect, in which it also means blanket or flannel petticoat. It has no connection with woodcarving except in the United States, where, according to Webster, the verb means "to cut or shape a piece of wood by slowly paring it away with a knife."

Actually, the definition has been more precise than that. Among whittlers it means carving with a clasp knife a *one-piece* object of wood, usually small enough to be held in the hand. However, as might be expected, modern technology has loosened the definition by providing special whittling knives with fixed or interchangeable blades, plus myriad other tools designed to do a particular job or speed the work in general. Even sandpaper might be called a multiple knife because each tiny grain actually scratches away a chip.

The same might be said about woodcarving, which originally was understood to mean the shaping of wood with traditional tools such as firmers, gouges and the adz, with riffler files and rasps thrown in. Modern technology has, however, added such tools as the bandsaw, chain saw, flexible-shaft machines, hand-held grinders, rotary and belt sanders and pneumatic or electric hammers. All sorts of accessories have been added as well, including special-position vises, multiple forms of mallet, stands and worktables of special design. Even in woodcarving, the urge to mechanize has its adherents, particularly among those caught up in the desire to make a profit, either from woodcarvings or selling the increasingly expensive equipment—or even to save time.

All this tends to obscure the fact that woodcarving, like whittling, can be and is being done with very limited numbers of tools—and no other equipment whatsoever. The carver in Bali or Easter Island, in both of which woodcarving

257

is the only industry, rarely has more than four or five tools and probably uses a shaped club for a mallet and his knees for a vise. His tools are usually home-made and cherished, not for their number or variety but for their necessity. His "shop," like the whittler's here, is portable. In fact, only in Europe and America have all the devices for saving time been introduced, and in both places we also have duplicating machines, profilers and plastic-and-sawdust moulded fakes.

What tools do you need to whittle?
(Tool illustrations on pgs. 10–11.)

YOU NEED a good knife, if you can get one. Most modern knives have stainless-steel blades, which don't rust but also don't hold an edge. Better is an old-fashioned pocketknife with carbon-steel blades (A). For conventional whittling, two blades are enough; three may be a help, but more than that tends to increase bulk and weight in the hand. I carry two pocketknives, one regular size with three blades, a pen, a spear, and a B-clip (B); the smaller, a penknife with one pen and a B-clip. Thus I have both small and large blades, wide and narrow, short- or long-pointed.

When I'm at home, I use either a fixed-blade knife, which is safer (a pocket-knife blade, carelessly handled, can close on a finger) and more comfortable to grip because of the larger handle, or two of the modern plastic handles with heavy-duty replaceable blades. One blade is a modified B-clip shape, the other a so-called hook blade designed for leather working. For most work, a blade $1\frac{1}{2}$ in (4 cm) long is plenty. Longer than that it begins to require extra gripping and may catch near the handle on parts of the piece you don't want to cut. The wider the blade, the straighter and more stable the cut, because of the added surface resting on the work. The narrower the blade, the greater the ease of carving in tight places and on concave surfaces, but greater control is needed, and there is greater likelihood of breakage.

The warning to cut away from yourself doesn't work in whittling any more than it does in peeling potatoes. The sketches (pgs. 12–13) show the many ways in which cuts can be made. You'll need them all before you're through, although some are much more important than others. Here are additional pointers:

Chips should be cut out, not wedged out—a hard lesson to learn—and a major reason why the rotary-chuck disposable-blade handles must be kept supertight. The blade may rotate in the handle or snap off. For some detail, a narrow, thin blade may be helpful; sometimes a sharp V-point is essential. Whittlers grind special knives and points for such jobs, using old straight razors, discarded hacksaw blades, even scissors or other pieces of hardened tool steel. I've made special long-handled knives to put a ship in a bottle by breaking off (with a pair of pliers) narrow sections of safety-razor blades and binding them in dowel-rod handles. An endless variety of blade shapes and lengths is possible, of course. You don't need them unless you specialize.

Beware of too-large and too-heavy handles with too-rigid, finger-shaped impressions, blades that are thin or wobble sideways and knives that do not snap open and shut securely. (The Swedes avoid this with the barrel knife, which has one blade that is opened, then thrust—and locked—through the handle. These have a sloyd blade—thick at the heel—which is stiff enough for heavy cutting, but may make trouble on delicate cuts.)

Knives must be kept sharp to reduce the cutting force required, because added force means lessened control and faster tiring, plus torn rather than cut wood fibers. Good steel, properly sharpened and honed, will hold its edge all day in whittling soft wood, but the hard wood will require a touch-up every hour or so. A portable fine-grained stone and a hone (leather glued on a stick and oiled) are essential; to do a clean cutting job in finishing you need a very sharp edge.

A knife can be dangerous, so be careful; never put anything in front of the blade that you don't intend to cut. Initially, you may want to wear a rubber or plastic finger stall on your thumb (stationery shops sell them for people who do counting and sorting) and a Band-Aid, tape, or other insulator on the middle joint of your index finger to prevent blisters. Keep your mind on what you are doing; whittling can be very relaxing, but it isn't like knitting—it isn't something to keep nervous hands busy while you watch TV or converse.

If you stick the tip of the blade into the work, be sure the pressure is in the direction of the cutting edge; a blade closing on a finger is no joke. To close the blade, hold the knife handle carefully in the fingertips and close the blade with the palm of the other hand. Don't open two blades at once. If the blade has no boss, be careful that your finger doesn't slip forward onto the sharp edge. Don't hammer the blade or use it to cut newspaper clippings or fiber tapes or fingernails—or, Lord forbid, scrape insulation from wire. Don't cut newly sanded surfaces. All these destroy the alignment of the tiny tips on the so-called feather edge of the blade, and make it dull (see Sharpening, pgs. 120–124).

259

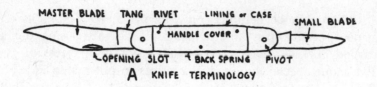

MASTER BLADE   TANG   RIVET   LINING or CASE   SMALL BLADE

HANDLE COVER

OPENING SLOT   BACK SPRING   PIVOT

A   KNIFE TERMINOLOGY

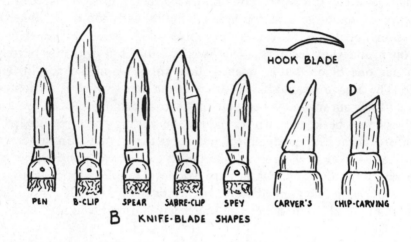

HOOK BLADE

C   D

PEN   B-CLIP   SPEAR   SABRE-CLIP   SPEY   CARVER'S   CHIP-CARVING

B   KNIFE-BLADE SHAPES

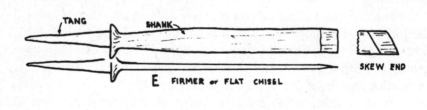

TANG   SHANK

SKEW END

E   FIRMER or FLAT CHISEL

F   SHANK SHAPES

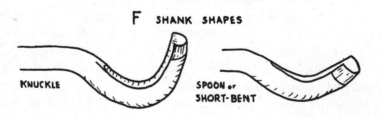

KNUCKLE   SPOON or
SHORT-BENT

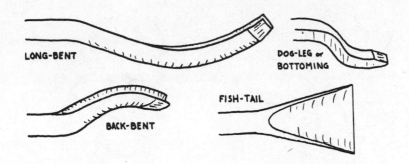

LONG-BENT

DOG-LEG or BOTTOMING

BACK-BENT

FISH-TAIL

FIRMER

FLAT·GOUGE· SCROLL or QUICK FLUTER VEINER Vor PARTING MACARONI

G TYPICAL CUTTING-EDGE SHAPES (SWEEPS)

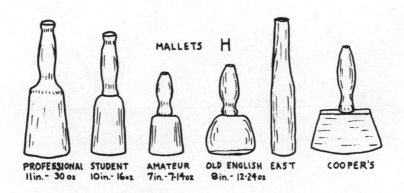

MALLETS H

PROFESSIONAL
11in.- 30oz

STUDENT
10in.- 16oz

AMATEUR
7in.- 7·14oz

OLD ENGLISH
8in.- 12·24oz

EAST

COOPER'S

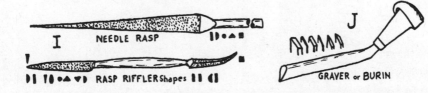

I NEEDLE RASP

RASP RIFFLER Shapes

J

GRAVER or BURIN

261

TYPICAL KNIFE CUTS

TWO HANDS

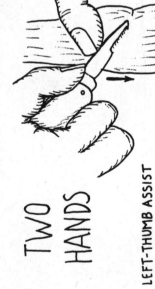

LEFT-THUMB ASSIST
Close control — more force
Short, precise cuts or shaving

LEFT-INDEX DRAW CUT
Shaving + detailing. Gives close control with more force

GUILLOTINE CUT
Adds force at blade tip.
Left index finger – or thumb push

LEFT INDEX-FINGER ASSIST
Shaving cuts. Work must be clamped or held by left hand

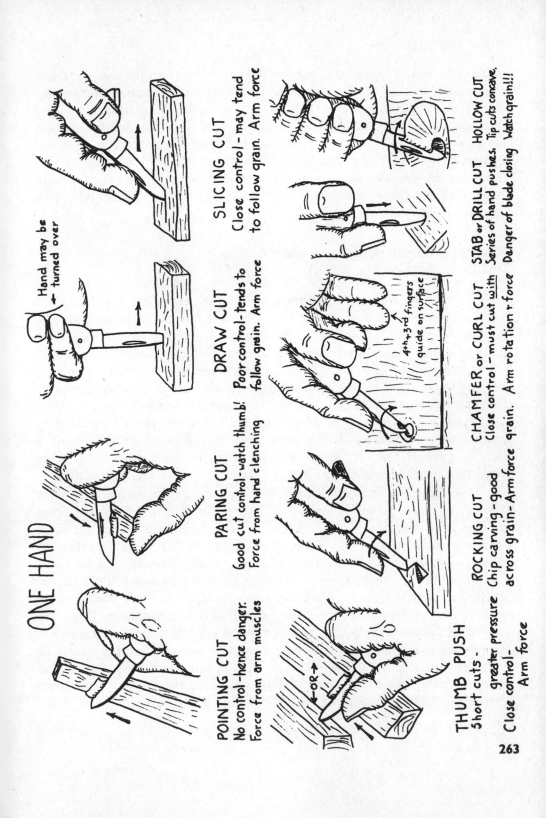

ONE HAND

Hand may be turned over

PARING CUT
Good cut control - watch thumb!
Force from hand clenching

DRAW CUT
Poor control - tends to
follow grain. Arm force

SLICING CUT
Close control - may tend
to follow grain. Arm force

POINTING CUT
No control - hence danger.
Force from arm muscles

4th & 3rd fingers
guide on surface

THUMB PUSH
Short cuts -

ROCKING CUT
Chip carving - good
across grain - Arm force
greater pressure
Close control -
Arm force

CHAMFER or CURL CUT
Close control - must cut with
grain. Arm rotation & force

STAB or DRILL CUT
Series of hand pushes.
Danger of blade closing

HOLLOW CUT
Tip cuts concave.
Watch grain!!!

Actually, even a razor edge is essentially a saw with teeth; the finer the teeth, the sharper the blade. Honing aligns the teeth; cutting an abrasive surface like those mentioned above throws the teeth out of line or breaks them off—and the blade is dull. A bit of oil occasionally on blades, pivots, and springs will help counteract rust caused by sweat, which can be highly corrosive. I know whittlers who carry their knives in oiled-leather sheaths for this reason. I also know woodcarvers who hone each tool before they use it, because exposure and time affect edge sharpness. I'm not that much of a precisionist, but *a dull tool spells trouble, and don't forget it.*

What tools do you need for woodcarving?
(Tool illustrations on pgs. 10–11.)

THE PRINCIPAL TOOL of the woodcarver is the chisel, either flat or curved. Flat chisels are lighter and often shorter than the more-familiar carpenter's chisels, and differ in that they are sharpened from both sides so they have less tendency to dig in. They are called firmers, and are available in widths from about 1/16 in (1.6 mm) to $2\frac{1}{2}$ in (6 cm) or so. The curved chisels are called gouges, and may range from U-shaped to almost flat, from 1/16 in (1.6 mm) wide at the cutting edge to about $2\frac{1}{2}$ in (6 cm). The smallest U-shaped gouge is called a veiner, and as its name implies, is used for cutting small grooves, for defining hair, and for very fine detail. A slightly larger one is called a fluter—again a descriptive name. The very large ones are primarily for cutting away waste wood and rough shaping, although they also serve in finishing large surfaces.

One tool cuts two opposed surfaces simultaneously—the parting or V-tool. It is shaped like a V, and is used in outlining, grooving and for many other purposes; it is the most difficult of chisels to sharpen and one of the most difficult to master for cross-grain cutting. Another tool, the macaroni, cuts three surfaces simultaneously; it carves a trench with flat-bottom and right-angle or outwardly sloping sides. A variant is the fluteroni, which cuts a similar trench with arcuate corners. These are rarely used and not included in most tool sets. There is also a variant of the firmer that is quite common. This is the skew chisel, in which the cutting edge is at an angle with the axis of the chisel, thus providing a point to get into corners and around surfaces. It is a versatile tool, as is the flat gouge—which may be a firmer with the cutting edge ground into an arc. The firmer tends to catch and gouge at its edges when pushed over a flat surface, and arcuate grinding of the cutting edge avoids this.

264

Wide tools, and some narrower ones, are tapered down toward the tang—which is the portion of the tool that is driven into the handle. These are called spade or fish-tail tools, and are very helpful in getting into tight places or for helping the carver to see what he is doing. The shank of a tool behind the cutting edge may also be forged into a curve so the cutting edge will be able to work in a confined place, such as a concave surface or around a curve. Depending upon the arc of shank curvature, such a tool is called long-bent or short-bent. A gouge with very short bend is also called a spoon. Normally, the arc is concave, viewed from the top, but it may be convex to handle a job such as forming the surfaces of individual grapes in a bunch or for cutting a special shape under an overhang; then it is called a back-bent tool. In present-day low-relief carving, there is little or no need for these specialized tools. Also, they are harder to use than straight ones, because of spring in the bend, and harder to sharpen.

Carving tools require the use of two hands, except tools that are very short or specialized, like Japanese tools, which have a long, thin, straight handle and a short blade. The standard tool is gripped and pushed by one hand, while the other guides the tool and controls it, keeping it from over-running or following a sudden split or breakout. This creates somewhat of a paradox, because the two hands work against each other to some degree. Note that I have not identified which hand does what, not only because the tools are interchangeable, but also because the skilled carver learns to hold the tool with either hand to suit the cut. This avoids a great deal of moving around or altering the position of the work.

In hard woods, the chisel is held in one hand, and hit with the heel of the other, or with a mallet. Thus, both hands are always in use, so the work must be held in some other way. Oriental carvers, who customarily squat cross-legged anyway, and do mostly pieces in the 1-2 ft (30-61 cm) length range, simply wedge the work into their laps. (They usually use mallets and chisels with no separate handles.) Large panels and large 3D carvings, unless they are top-heavy, usually require no holding unless very large chisels or mallets are used. The clamping method can suit the piece and be as simple as a nail or two driven through waste wood into a bench or board, or a vise. Decoy carvers, who do a great deal of turning of the piece, use a special vise with a ball-and-socket swivel that can be clamped at a variety of angles. A wide variety of clamps, in wood and metal, is available. An ancient device is the carver's screw, which is a long screw put through a hole in the bench or easel and screwed into the bottom of the work, then tightened under the bench by a wing nut. For small panels, a bench hook or bench plate is portable, convenient, and easy for you to make.

For work in harder woods, and for greater precision, it is advisable to use a carver's mallet, which is simply some form of soft-faced hammer. Then the chisel is held in one hand and the mallet in the other, so additional holding is still required. The traditional mallet is like an old-fashioned wooden potato masher, but it can have flat faces like a cooper's hammer, or simply be a club with a handle whittled at one end. Modern carvers have developed many forms of mallet. Some have plastic faces which reduce the noise, possible handle splintering and shock to the driving arm; some have lead or copper replacing the wooden head; some are even made of old washing-machine wringer rolls. This is a matter for individual selection. I have half a dozen mallets of various kinds, ranging from light to heavy, because I work principally in hard woods and use a light mallet even for most small cuts. With the mallet, I can control the force behind the cutting edge much more accurately than I can with just an arm push.

Carving tools are sized by the width of the cutting edge, ranging from 1/16 in (1.6 mm) to $\frac{3}{8}$ in (9.5 mm) in sixteenths, on up to 1 in (25 mm) in eighths, and in larger steps on up to the maximum, usually around $2\frac{1}{2}$ in (6 cm) for flat gouges. European tools are sized in millimetres: 1, 2, 3, 4, 5, 6, 7, 8, 10, 12, 16, 20, 25, 30, 35, and so on (1 mm = 0.039 in). The gouges are also usually numbered by the "London system" that measures arc or radius of the sweep; a firmer is No. 1, a skew firmer 2, a quite-flat gouge 3, and a U-shaped one 11 or 12, with the other arcs in between. For special tools, some suppliers use other numbers, their own catalog numbers, or simply show a cross-section of the arc of the sweep.

There are also many auxiliary tools, like straight and coping saws, rasps and riffler files, scrapers, hand routers and the usual carpenter's tools. (I use carpenter's chisels and gouges for roughing; they're heavier and cheaper.) Of these, the riffler files, which come in various shapes and sizes, some straight, some bent, with different surfaces at each end, are convenient for finishing in tight spots, over knots and faults, and on very small work. The adz and the axe are traditional woodcarving tools, of course, but will be discussed later as a special subject.

In some instances, you may have a choice of handle on the chisels. Usual ones are round, or octagon, tapering toward the cutting edge. Round ones are maple, ash, beech or boxwood; the octagonal ones may even be dogwood (which is preferred in Oberammergau, West Germany). Octagonal handles are less likely to turn in your hand or to roll on a bench. There are now some plastic handles as well, of course. My preference is for octagonal wood, with a brass ferrule at the tang to prevent splitting under mallet blows.

The customary way to carve is to stand up at a bench heavy enough`so it won't shift. Sculptors who work on large blocks prefer a 4-legged stand weighted at the base with a rock, so they can move around it. Some stands have Lazy Susan (rotating) tops and height adjustments. Cuckoo-clock carvers have tables with heavy, sloping tops. I often work at an outdoor trestle table or indoors on a card table, and I sit down whenever possible. The main thing is to have a stable surface which will absorb mallet blows, plus a level surface on which tools not in use may be placed. My experience is that there will be a relatively small number at any given time, so an elaborate rack of tools at the back of the bench is not necessary. It goes without saying that good lighting is a must, particularly when dark woods like walnut are being carved, and that adequate ventilation is helpful. All of these things are matters of individual preference and size and complexity of work. You don't *need* a studio unless you teach or want to create an atmosphere.

As would be expected, Americans in particular have mechanized woodcarving as far as possible. Circular and bandsaws help shape blanks, routers cut away backgrounds, coping saws, power drills and sanders are used. Carvers of totem poles and wooden Indians have adopted the chain saw—with a great gain in speed of cutting but a great potential for making the user deaf and driving the neighbors insane. Carvers of small objects and/or very hard materials use hand grinders or flexible-shaft machines with shaped cutters and claim extraordinary results with them. Some have even utilized dental drills. My experience is that they are hard to control, chew rather than cut the wood, and throw dust and chips over a considerable area, so the user needs safety glasses. I have even met a few carvers who use pneumatic or electric hammers with fitted chisels. Like the profiler and duplicator, such equipment is primarily commercial. It may save time and effort in some instances, but hand finishing is usually required anyway if the surfaces are to have any quality.

Even the authorities disagree on the proper kit for a beginner. Commercial suppliers offer kits with considerable variety, undoubtedly based on the recom-

267

mendation of some particular carver. Charles M. Sayer, who taught panel carving in particular, suggested four tools to start with: $\frac{1}{2}$-in (12.7 mm), or $\frac{3}{8}$ - to $\frac{5}{8}$-in (9.6 to 15.9 mm), No. 39 parting tool; $\frac{5}{8}$-in No. 5 straight gouge; 1-in (25 mm) No. 3, or $\frac{7}{8}$-in (22.2 mm) straight gouge, and $\frac{3}{8}$-in No. 7 straight gouge. For relief carving, he added a $\frac{3}{8}$-in, No. 3 straight gouge. H. M. Sutter, who has taught carving to a great many people during the past thirty years, starts his students with five tools, plus an all-purpose carver's knife: $\frac{3}{8}$-in No. 3 straight gouge, $\frac{5}{8}$-in No. 5 straight gouge (these two preferably fish-tail), $\frac{3}{8}$-in No. 9 straight gouge, $\frac{1}{32}$-in (0.8 mm), No. 11 veiner, and $\frac{3}{8}$-in No. 41 parting tool. Note that neither suggests fancy shapes or skew chisels—at least to start. My best advice is to start small, with the advice of a capable carver if possible, and a clear understanding of the kind of work you wish to do.

Many carvers, and some teachers, make their own tools as they find a need for them, grinding tempered steel to suit, or forging the tool and finding someone locally to do the tempering. You'll need at least a flat gouge for roughing, shaping and cleaning up; a firmer for finishing and flat surfaces; a veiner for outlining designs before they are set in, and for emphasizing lines; and a V-tool for outlining, square corners and square-bottom grooves. A gouge or two with quite different sweeps and probably a skew chisel are the first additions, followed by gouges and firmers of different widths. A good rule may be adapted from that suggested to amateur photographers when they add lenses: When you get additional tools of approximately the same shape or sweep, double or halve the previous dimension. Thus, if you have a $\frac{1}{2}$-in (12.7 mm) No. 5 gouge and want another of the same sweep, get a $\frac{1}{4}$-in (6.4 mm) or a 1-in (25.4 mm), unless you have continued need for one closer to $\frac{1}{2}$-in. The same rule might be applied to supplementing sweeps; if you have No. 3, you don't need No. 4 or 5—go to No. 6 or even No. 9.

Actual carving with chisels is to me much less complex than carving with a knife, because the individual tool is less versatile unless it is gripped in the fingertips and used like a knife. There *are* a few fundamentals. Because the tool is pushed by arm power on soft woods, it must be restrained by the opposite hand to keep it from cutting too far, a problem which is minimized when a mallet is used. (I have never been an advocate of driving a chisel with the heel of the hand; I've known several carvers who irreparably damaged their hands that way.) If you are not familiar with hammering a nail or a chisel, you must learn to watch the cutting tip, not the chisel head. The potato-masher mallet shape is a help in this because it reduces the necessity for hitting the chisel head exactly square; obviously, the angle with which the chisel is struck or pushed influences the direction of the cut.

As cutting begins, it is necessary to adjust the angle of the tool so it cuts through the wood at the desired level—too high an angle will cause it to cut deeper and deeper, too shallow an angle will cause it to run out. This is particularly important with the high-sweep or U-shaped gouges. If the cut is too deep, the edges of the gouge can get below the wood surface and cause edge tearing of fibers. When cuts are started, it is advisable to start at the edge when possible, because if you cut to an edge, the chisel may break out the fibers there rather than cutting through them. In relief cutting, it is important to outline the desired shape by "setting in"—driving the firmer or gouge into the wood to the desired depth along the line, so that cuts made to remove background wood will stop at the cut line instead of splitting or running into the design. When a chisel is driven vertically into wood, it obviously must wedge the fibers aside, so it will cause crushing and splintering of fibers along the edge of the outline. This can be avoided by cutting a groove just outside the outline with a veiner, fluter or V-tool, so the edge of the groove touches the line. Then, when the firmer or gouge is driven in along the line, the groove provides relief for the tool wedge at the surface. As a matter of fact, in shallow-relief carving, particularly in green wood, it is often possible to get the required depth of background (called "bosting") with a deep fluter alone, leaving a desirable small arc at the bottom edge of the upstanding portion.

A gouge differs from a knife in that it cuts two sides at once, so that cutting against the grain is a constant problem, not an occasional one as with the knife or firmer. In a diagonal cut, one side of the gouge will cut cleaner than the other because it is running out of the grain while the other runs in. This is the major reason for keeping the blade very sharp—to minimize the tearing in angle cuts and the breakout when one cut crosses another. Grain is always a challenge, and in woodcarving one is likely to encounter knots and other faults because the workpiece tends to be larger. It is necessary, therefore, to work with the grain as much as possible, and to proceed with extra caution when working against it. You will find that a few experiences with splitouts and the like will train you to make adjustments for grain almost automatically. You'll still be tricked from time to time by sudden grain-direction changes, hard spots, and whatever, depending upon the wood and its source. I've run

269

into bullets and nails deep inside salvaged wood, to say nothing of rotten spots or old insect bores that are not visible on the surface.

What wood is best?

THE WOOD TO CHOOSE may depend upon what is available, and what you are willing to pay for it. Many carvers salvage wood from old furniture, fallen trees, or along the shore of stream, lake or ocean. If you have a choice, what is the natural color of the bird or animal you plan to carve? What tools do you plan to use? Is the carving to be painted, textured, polished? Where will it be used or displayed?

As you can see, one question leads to another when you select a wood. If you are a beginner or a figure whittler, your best wood is probably basswood (also called bee tree, and similar to European linden). It is soft, white, easy to carve and hasn't much tendency to split. Ponderosa pine is almost as good, if you avoid the strongly colored pieces. Sugar pine, commonly called white pine, is a bit more porous, but also very good. Jelutong, a recent import from Indonesia, is like basswood. All take color well, but are too soft to wear well or carry much detail. Avoid yellow pine, which is hard and resinous.

Among other soft woods are poplar, which bruises easily and tends to grip tools, so is hard to cut; cedar, which is easy to cut but has a distinctive color; willow, which has a tendency to split; and cypress, which does not wear well. Spanish cedar, once familiar in cigar boxes, is a common carving wood in Mexico.

Many American whittlers have used local woods, particularly the fruit and nut woods. All are harder than those previously mentioned and have a tendency to check in large pieces, but they will take more detail and undercutting, give a better finish and have interesting color. Among them are pear, pecan, cherry, apple and black walnut. Of the group, walnut is probably the best American carving wood. It has a fine, tough grain, takes detail and undercuts, finishes beautifully, but frequently darkens when oiled. (It can be bleached with oxalic acid.) The mountain-grown Eastern white oaks are hard to carve, but can take detail and are inherently strong. Avoid red oak, because it has a very prominent grain and is coarse in structure. Oak has a bad name because of the cheap "fumed oak" furniture that was once all over, but it can be darkened with concentrated ammonia, or walnut-stained. Dogwood is very hard and withstands shock, but tends to check and is hard to carve.

Where they are available, butternut, red alder and myrtle are good for carving, particularly the first two. Redwood (sequoia) is durable, but some pieces have alternating hard and soft grain; this makes trouble. Sweet or red gum (also called American satinwood) is more durable and uniform than cedar, but tends to warp and twist. Beech, hickory, sycamore and magnolia are hard to cut and good only for shallow carving. Ash is stringy, but can support considerable detail. Birch is somewhat like the rock, or sugar, maple, which is hard to carve and finish, but durable. Many suppliers have soft maple, which is not a good carving wood. In the Southwest are found mesquite, ironwood, and osage orange, all very hard, inclined to split, and difficult to carve, but capable of fine finishes. Mesquite, like our fruit woods, is subject to insect attack. Holly, our whitest wood, is usually available only in small pieces. It is hard and tends to check.

Among imported woods, the most familiar is mahogany (which is not one wood but many). Quality and color (pinkish white to red brown) depend upon source and piece. Some, like the one from Honduras, is fine-grained, even though relatively soft. Cuban mahogany is dense and varies in hardness; South American varieties tend to be grainy and splinter easily; commonly available Philippine mahogany tends to be coarse in grain, but I have six samples which range from white to dark red and from coarse to dense. There are also other woods now being sold as mahogany, like luanda, and primavera, a white wood that cuts like mahogany and can be stained to look exactly like it. (Mahogany, when sanded, by the way, has a very light dust that travels all over a house!)

My favorite carving wood is Thai or Burmese teak, which is the best for exposure, does not rot, is not subject to insect attack, and does not warp or check to any degree. It is an excellent carving wood, which will support detail, but it does have a tendency to dull tools rapidly despite its inherent oil. The dulling is probably a result of silica soaked up in the marshy land where it grows. Chinese teak is red and harsh-grained, so the Chinese tended to stain or paint it black—hence the common opinion that teak is black. It is actually a light green when cut, which finishes to a medium reddish-brown, sometimes with slight graining. Another good wood is English sycamore or harewood, about as white as American holly, and available in wide boards. Lime and box, much used in Europe, are rarely available here. Both are hard woods.

Ebony, which comes from Africa, India, Ceylon, Indonesia, and South and

Central America, varies in color and marking, from a solid black (Gabon, Central Africa), to dark brown with black striping (Macassar from Indonesia, and Calamander from Ceylon). It is very hard, as is lignum vitae. In Africa and Mexico it is called guayacan and cocobola. (Avoid inhaling the dust; it causes lung inflammation.) Lacewood, briar, sandal, and satinwood are less hard and will take fine detail. All of these are more suited to carving with tools than with the knife. The same goes for rosewood, which comes from many southern countries and varies from soft brown through red and red-brown to a purple with other colors mixed in. This is a beautiful wood, but expensive, and should be reserved for pieces in which the grain and color are not competing with detail. Another fascinating wood is pink ivory from Africa, which was once reserved for Zulu kings. Anyone else found with it lost his head. It is very hard, and pinkish to red. Other woods like purpleheart, thuya, madrone, greenheart, vermilion and bubinga are also imported and offer a range of colors. All are expensive, hard to find in large and thick pieces, and hard to carve, but are, on occasion, worth it for their grain. (See the chapters on butterfly and dinosaur mobiles.)

The variety of woods available is almost endless, and my best advice is to start with the familiar and easy ones, then proceed cautiously to the exotic and expensive varieties, testing as you go. In general, the expensive woods should be selected for their color, grain, figure, or the like, not for pleasurable carving.

What size shall your carving be?

IN MOST CASES, there is no real reason why a carving must be of a particular size, unless it is part of an assembly. Size is usually dictated by other factors, like the available wood, convenience in carving, or size of tools you have. A miniature can be harder to carve than a larger piece, simply because your tools are too large, or the amount of detail you plan to include is too great for the grain or texture of the wood. Further, a miniature is hard to handle. Similarly, a piece that is overly large adds to the problems of handling and removing excess wood—you may find difficulty in holding the work, as well as in finding a place to display it when completed.

The scales of the patterns in this book vary; some original sizes are shown. This size ratio should be regarded as a general guide, not as a requirement. The patterns can be enlarged as desired by any of several methods (see appendix); only in rare instances is it practical to reduce size and retain all the detail shown. As a general rule, it is advisable to reduce, rather than increase, detail; whittlers in particular have a tendency to include so much detail that it tends to overpower the subject itself. What you are seeking is an image of a bear, not a texture that suggests a bearskin coat; or a rhinoceros, not a complex pattern of plates and wrinkles. A carving should be readily identifiable, unless you intend it for a puzzle. If a portrait of a person includes too prominent detail, we are immediately conscious of it, because we are accustomed to the soft curves in the faces of people we know.

Most of us have only a limited knowledge of animal anatomy, so we unconsciously put in too much detail "for realism." Also, we tend to think that all animals of a given species look alike. Many carvings of animals and birds are caricatures, or even crude, as a result. Some even have the joints bending in the wrong direction, or show too many toes or claws. It is better to avoid depicting claws, for example, than to depict them incorrectly. The same holds true for animal eyes and nostrils; they are differently placed and shaped than those of humans. Ear shape and position are similarly important—as important as the shape of the head itself. A sculptor uses a live model or good pictures of his subject; even a tyro must do the same if his design is to be believable.

Be sure you haven't selected a size that has details too small for your tools, or your skill, and that it does not include elements that your hand, and your eye, cannot execute. Be sure that the wood you have chosen is sufficiently dense and fine-grained for the detail you plan to include, and that the grain is not so prominent that it will overpower the detail, or indeed distort the appearance of the entire design. At least initially, don't make the piece so big that it is hard to handle or requires excessive waste removal before you can actually carve.

Particularly in three-dimensional carving, you may have to spend half your time getting unwanted wood out of the way before you can begin the interesting part of the work—actual shaping of the form. I must, however, in all fairness point out that the more nearly the design occupies the available wood, the less waste you have to remove (and in a sense the less wood you waste). Also, if you plan to sell the carving, a larger carving generally commands a higher price, even though it may require less work. People expect to pay more for something big, and less for something very small. This thinking affects inexperienced carvers, who will quote a lower price for a work of smaller size—and find to their chagrin that the time and effort involved are much the same.

CHAPTER II

Carving Animals

Suggestions for "different" subjects, poses, textures and finishes

ANIMALS, birds and fish offer a tremendous variety of designs. There are so many species, so many shapes, sizes, surface textures, poses. The possibilities for new poses, techniques, surface textures, and finishes are far greater than they are in carving figures of people. (We are one very limited species of animal ourselves, although we tend to forget it.) What's more, the typical observer has far less intimate knowledge of animal anatomy than he does of human anatomy, so he is less inclined to be critical of minor errors, or even of the exaggerations of caricature. All in all, this is a rich field for the carver.

Many carvers around the world even have specialized books on carving decoys, eagles and birds, but much of this is devoted to copying the living bird (or animal) precisely; in fact there are major awards for producing a decoy that looks as much like a stuffed bird as possible. There is, however, an entire field beyond this, that of carving birds and animals which are unmistakable but are not slavish copies of living ones. Take as a case in point the photo of four totally different treatments of the turtle. In this chapter are other examples, together with a variety of other ideas in animal and bird carving. My hope is that they will stimulate your imagination to try still others. You can go as far as you like, into great detail, or total stylization, free-form, caricature, and unusual finishes, with little fear of the nit-picking criticism that any carver of the human form is likely to get. We usually cannot distinguish individuals within an animal species, and in fact do not know anatomical details. This is borne out by general animal and bird books—in which sketches often widely disagree.

I have carved many kinds and many poses of animals in recent years, some small, some large, but most of them not the familiar domestic animals nor the familiar poses. These form a mixed grouping, which includes work done at various times, for various reaons, and in a variety of woods. Most effective in terms of observer comments has been the pair of long-tailed weasels. The stylized

Four variations of the lowly turtle, ranging from caricature to serious sculpture: the upper right figure is from the Galapagos Islands, the other three are from Mexico.

Two long-tailed weasels in mahogany. The weasel on all fours twists around the standing one. The polished finish suggests the slick coat of the animal. 4 × 10 × 10 in (9 × 25 × 25 cm).

275

Pekingese and the toucan caricature were both made from the butts of timbers discarded as scrap by a nearby piano company. The weasels were a serious effort at animal portraiture, and the musculature and poses were carefully checked with available references. The Pekingese, on the other hand, exploits the texture of the surface and the great plume of tail as well as the pug nose that characterizes the breed. Because the grain is vertical—that is, across the animal's body instead of along it—fluting with a flat gouge was relatively easy and did not generate the splinters that normally occur when mahogany is textured. Also, the tail has more strength than it would have with the grain lengthwise. The result is a piece that makes an excellent and durable doorstop, if nothing more.

The toucan is a composite or assemblage which resulted from buying a toucan upper mandible from a Cuna Indian in the San Blas islands off Panama. The body was carved in scale with the mandible, which was glued over a stub. Also, the walnut body was tinted with oils to suggest the garish colors of the bird and to carry out the tones in the actual mandible. This is a caricature, of course, as is the perplexed penguin.

PEKINGESE
Mahogany. 4×7⅜×11"
Grain vertical. Finish
is gouge fluting

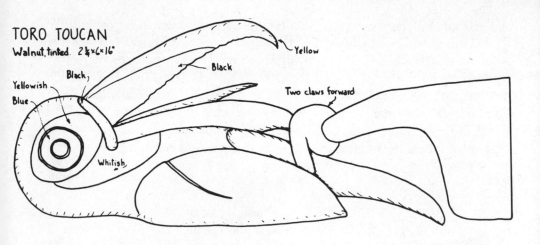

TORO TOUCAN
Walnut, tinted. 2¾×6×16"

Yellow

Black

Black

Yellowish

Blue

Two claws forward

Whitish

Mexico

TURTLE, ARMADILLO & BIRD
Originals in black horn ⓦ white trim

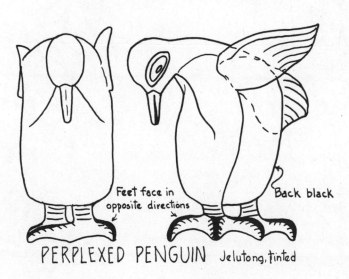

Feet face in
opposite directions

Back black

PERPLEXED PENGUIN Jelutong, tinted

The bear is a reversible piece, combining a stylized animal on one side with a caricatured troll on the other, so the exposed face can match the observer's mood. The bear design is taken from a smaller Swiss original I saw in Brienz many years ago, and I designed the troll to fit the same silhouette. (This can be done with various silhouette carvings, and converts them really into double-sided free-standing panels, thus avoiding the often dull rear view of a conventional in-the-round carving.) This piece is in butternut, a wood easy to carve, capable of taking the limited detail, and with a pleasing natural color.

BEAR & TROLL

Silhouette of bear is used for troll on reverse of a 4×6½×16" butternut block. (Some Scandinavians suggest that the troll legend is based on a bear seen dimly.)

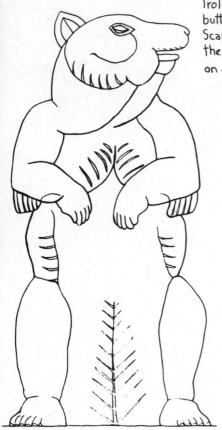

278

OWL (Granadito wood)

Earholes drilled
Eyes inlaid bone, wood centers
Beak bone
Copper leg, soldered
Wire flattened

BOAT-TAILED GRACKLE

Eyes & beak inlaid as in owl
Top views
Legs as on owl

SWAN or FLAMINGO

Details as on owl
Leg length to suit

KINGFISHER

Somewhat similar in nature but considerably smaller are the pieces whittled by others. They include four caricatured birds in granadillo wood, made in Mexico, with copper wire legs and bone eyes and beak inset. The eyes are unusual in that they are drilled rings with black wood centers, inlaid in the wood of the head. Granadillo wood (also called granadito) is a mixture of dark brown and light tan, so pleasing effects can be obtained by proper selection of the piece of wood and carving the bird in order that contrasts are obtained on wings and/or tail.

PUFFIN

Background pierced
between figures →

WOODCHUCK GROUP (for silhouettes)

Eyes are black crescents

FROG
Bass or pine with
green-gray finish
Card holder by
Fred Clark

Yellow

Orange

    The puffin poses I originally made in ivory, but they can be made in wood just as readily and lend themselves to tinting. These are fairly accurate depictions, but the bird looks much like a caricature anyway. The woodchucks were a silhouette group for the top of a breadboard, but can be done as a three-dimensional group, as a flat plaque or a silhouette carving, as you wish. The frog is a place-card holder if so desired, because his sawn mouth can hold a card or a message. Fred Clarke carved it.

280

All of these figures can be laid out on suitable blocks or boards and sawed out on the bandsaw, with details cut by coping saw. This saves enormous time in carving. The larger pieces are best done with chisels, the smaller ones with the knife. I have used a variety of finishes on my carvings in this group, each suited, in my opinion, to the particular subject. The weasels are varnished and waxed to a sheen, suggesting the smooth coat and sinuousness of the animal. The toucan is toned to contrast with the basic dark brown of the walnut. The Pekingese is textured with a gouge on all areas except the face and paw fronts. The bear is spray-varnished and antiqued with a darker stain in crevices. The frog is tinted green on top and lighter greenish-gray beneath, with oils or acrylics. The puffins are finished with oils, and the other birds left natural.

One of the most enduring of carved bird forms is the eagle, because of its association with the United States and because the bird itself is so impressive. I include three examples of eagle carvings in this group, because they are somewhat different from the norm and might not otherwise be available.

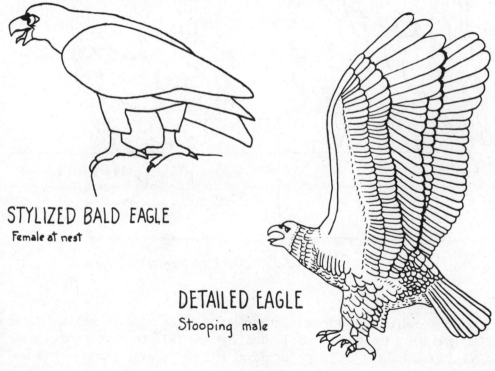

STYLIZED BALD EAGLE
Female at nest

DETAILED EAGLE
Stooping male

281

Back V

Eyes slue forward
Cross-hatch

AMERICAN (BALD) EAGLE

Feathering detailed, prominent

Legs & feet oversize,
not textured

BIG ROOSTER Mato Generalić (Yugoslavia) 1975 35"

I was also intrigued by a truly giant rooster 35 in (88 cm) high included in the Yugoslav naive art shown in the United States in 1977. In this case, the carver over-emphasized the feathering for effect, and even provided stumpy legs and

282

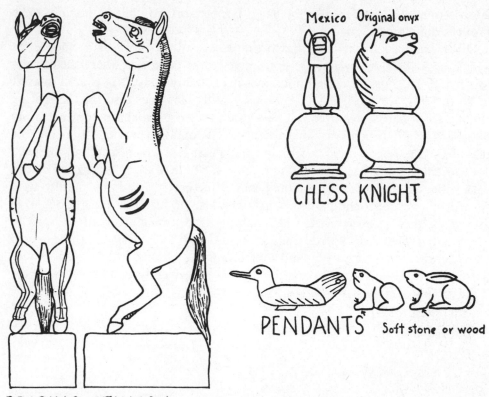

Mexico   Original onyx

CHESS KNIGHT

PENDANTS   Soft stone or wood

REARING STALLION   Bali
Original 21" high, in a white hardwood

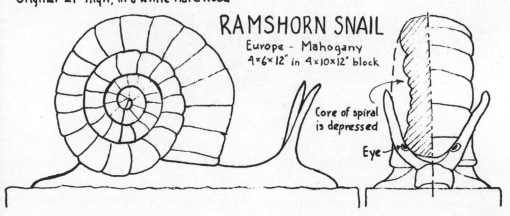

RAMSHORN SNAIL
Europe - Mahogany
4×6×12" in 4×10×12" block

Core of spiral
is depressed

Eye

feet, seemingly a characteristic of Yugoslav peasant carvings of humans. The result is quite a dramatic bird.

Other examples of stylized, and perhaps caricatured, animals include three which, as far as I am aware, are not native to the countries where the carving was made. The lion from the Philippines is probably a result of tourist interest in lions, but it was designed exceptionally well. This goes also for the rearing stallion from Bali, a distorted but very dramatic pose. In sharp contrast is my ramshorn snail, which was an experiment in making carvings that can be placed on the floor. The weasels and the Pekingese are also "floor pieces."

In recent years, it has become the fashion for both sexes to wear neck chains with pendants; the more bizarre the pendant the better. Pendants are also used for chain pulls on light fixtures, curtain pulls, or just for decoration. Two groups of these are pictured, one small stylized animals carved in horn in Mexico, the other a duck, frog and rabbit in wood. Such designs can be carved from scraps of exotic woods and are interesting alternatives to standard or heroic figures. Blanks can be carried about conveniently and carved with the knife in almost any surroundings.

Stylized lion has exaggerated musculature and mane. It is about 18 in (46 cm) long.

CHAPTER III

Animals of South America

Most are sophisticated designs and works, from one small area

FOLK CARVINGS in wood tend to result from a happy pairing of forests and skill; either alone is not enough. Thus, in all of South America, there is little folk carving except in the Andes Mountains of western Bolivia, southern Ecuador, and northern Peru (which was also southern Ecuador until Peru won it, as south Tyrol was once part of Austria). Carvings from this high terrain, regardless of country of origin, are well-formed and smoothly finished; they are not primitive but are obviously made by skilled carvers to familiar patterns attractive to tourists. Subject matter is wide-ranging, from Indian portraits through religious figures to animals, particularly the llama. Both in-the-round and relief work are done, and mahogany is the preferred material. The exact duplication of design and availability in several sizes suggests profiler roughing for quantity production, but sellers insist this is not true.

Shown here are typical animal designs. Surprisingly, there are no birds. Included are a typical pair of primitive carvings—an anteater and an armadillo—from the Amazon basin in Peru. Drawings of three ancient house posts—over 1,000 years old—from Ica and Paracas, Peru, offer very sharp contrast to the more-refined modern pieces. There is also a small panel from the southernmost city in the world, on Tierra del Fuego Island, which is a quite modern caricature of a penguin done as a pierced carving, with body areas filled with a transparent tinted plastic—quite a surprise from such a remote place, but a useful idea.

Relief carvings tend to be silhouettes and fairly large in size. The llama (pg. 37), for example, is 11 in (28 cm) tall, the llama and Indian heads (pg. 37) are 13 in (33 cm). The designs on the cap of the Indian in the Peruvian plaque are exactly the same as those on the caps of a pair of almost life-size

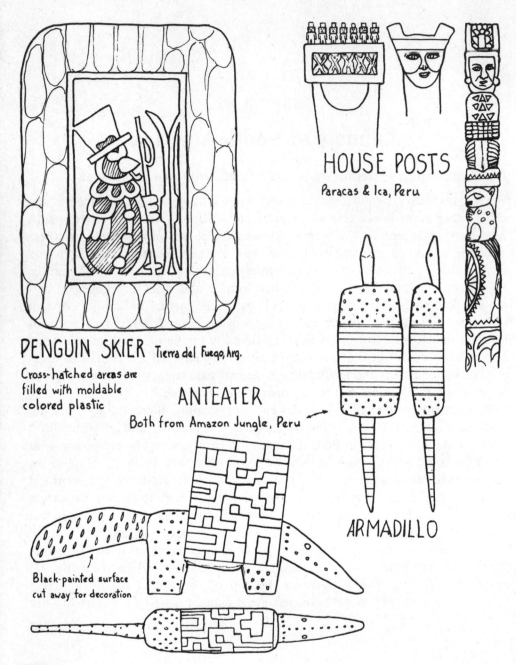

PENGUIN SKIER Tierra del Fuego, Arg.

Cross-hatched areas are
filled with moldable
colored plastic

ANTEATER

Both from Amazon Jungle, Peru

Black-painted surface
cut away for decoration

HOUSE POSTS
Paracas & Ica, Peru

ARMADILLO

286

Random
veiner cuts

LLAMA
Ecuador

INDIAN & LLAMA HEADS Peru (Plaque)

busts I bought in Bolivia, showing again that tribal boundaries often do not coincide with national ones. It is also interesting to see that one house post has an animal figure very much akin to those on Alaskan totem poles, and that the posts are silhouetted, although the half-round hole in one and the notch at the top of another are primarily sockets for ridgepoles. The intricate line pattern on the anteater's back is typical of this area, incidentally; similar designs are woven into cloth, and have been for centuries.

The llama is the traditional beast of burden, and the source of wool for cloth and meat for food. There are three species, the llama, the alpaca, and the guanaco. Another familiar figure is, of course, the bull, but the dog and cat are conspicuous by their absence. (There is an ugly rumor that they are too edible to last long among the Indians.)

Two llamas flank an alpaca. The figure at the left is from Bolivia; the other two are from Peru. Woods and facial details are the principal differences. The llama on the left is carved with the base integral, and its legs are foreshortened. Detail is avoided on all three.

The Galapagos Islands belong to Ecuador, but are now an international sanctuary, so have only two small villages of humans. However, I did find one high-quality carving of one of the turtle species for which the area is famous. The islands have never been heavily populated and the turtle was probably carved by a mainland native brought to the area as a worker in the nearby turtle hatchery.

All of these designs appear to be the products of woodcarving tools, except possibly the Amazon animals and the bull, and they show gouge marks. The Amazon animals are painted, then carved, so the natural color of the wood is recovered—a technique that I have seen previously in Fiji and among Australian Bushmen. It is, of course, now in use in the United States and elsewhere for routing name signs in laminated or "sandwich" plastics. It offers ideas for carvers as well.

Composites of wood with other materials were apparently nonexistent, except perhaps in dressed dolls. The only examples I found are shown: the use of the transparent tinted plastic filler in the penguin skier plaque and the addition of a silver chain and bell on one llama.

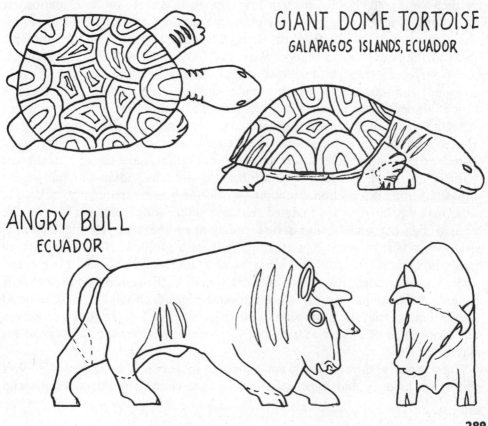

GIANT DOME TORTOISE
GALAPAGOS ISLANDS, ECUADOR

ANGRY BULL
ECUADOR

289

CHAPTER IV

Primitive Carvings of Mexico

Animals and birds are favorite subjects of folk carvers, who use what they have

CARVING is more fun, and pays better, than working in the fields, if you have the skill. That's the reason a great number of Mexican Indians have given me for their work, which they or their wives hawk in streets or hotel patios, or even along beaches. Many of these primitive carvings can be found in stores, which purchase them directly or through special buyers from the Indians. Some of the pieces are very good work and show both skill and imagination, but an increasing number show evidence of mass or hasty production.

Animal subjects are extremely popular among these carvers, and there is a great variety of techniques and designs. The figures do have an inherent strength and drama, and seem to exhibit an understanding of the animal depicted. A great many are caricatures, whittled of soft wood and painted; some are even assembled by nailing on legs, ears and tails, but others make use of the inherent shape of the wood, its figure or variations in color. One Indian who has gained somewhat of an international reputation told me that he frequently makes the same figure painted and unpainted, because unknowing customers prefer the painted figures, while connoisseurs prefer them natural. He, incidentally, produces a wide range of figures, ranging from traditional Nativity groups to highly imaginative animals. Some are hurried, some studied, some caricatures, some accurate portraits. Most are small and in-the-round, done with the knife, but occasional figures are large, and require chisels. This is unusual among commercial or professional carvers, who tend to have a specialized style and range of subject matter, but it is necessitated by the thinness of his market.

The examples shown here were collected to get a wide range of subject matter, techniques and approaches. There are some simplified designs and

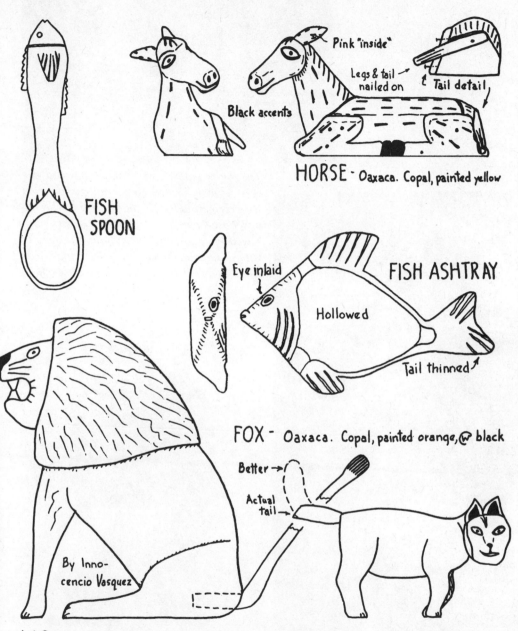

FISH
SPOON

HORSE - Oaxaca. Copal, painted yellow

Pink "inside"

Legs & tail
nailed on

Black accents

Tail detail

Eye inlaid

FISH ASHTRAY

Hollowed

Tail thinned

FOX - Oaxaca. Copal, painted orange, w black

Better →

Actual
tail →

By Inno-
cencio Vasquez

LION - Oaxaca. Copal. Painted yellow, with black lines

291

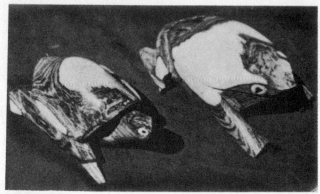

The light patches of granadillo wood are very evident on these two figures from Guerrero, which are hinged boxes. The top and base have been carved as a unit, then sawed apart, hollowed, and hinged together with a matching wood link. The hinge pin is a nail in a drilled hole and the eyes are inlaid.

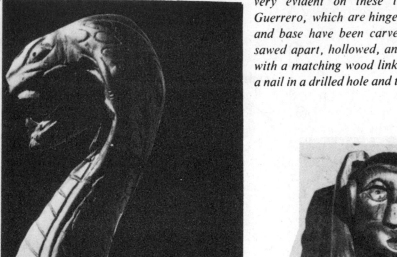

This cobra from Tehuantepec, a massive sculpture in ebony, was produced by the same carver who made the monkey. It is an extremely graceful pose and very dramatic.

many shortcuts, the result of limited skill and training as well as limited materials and tools, but in general the carvings are less inhibited than many of ours because the Indians are not trying to achieve some hazy "standard" but simply to make what they see or imagine. They're not concerned with what other carvers may think of their work, because they usually work alone.

As might be expected, work is usually identifiable by subject, finish and technique. Thus the animals carved in caricature, assembled by nailing, and painted in clear colors are likely to be from the Oaxaca area. Animals made from the highly figured granadillo wood, and somewhat more precise in proportion, are from the state of Guerrero, and are further distinguished by inlaid eyes and polished natural finish. Decorated and shaped ladles, in soft wood and unpainted, come from Uruapan. Flat trays and ashtrays in hardwood, natural in finish and with inlaid eyes, come from the vicinity of Taxco. Examples from each of these areas are included here.

A great many of these figures vary to suit the piece of wood; there are no standard patterns or shapes—just a series of ideas which are selected as available wood suggests. Many are intended primarily as toys for children—another reason for gaudy color and hasty workmanship—and the major customers are Mexicans, not foreign tourists. Tourists tend to buy either very crude pieces, or the very finished ones turned out in several factories near Mexico City—the expected cowboys, fighting bulls, and sleeping mestizos. They pay higher prices without complaint. But, occasionally, really fine pieces will be produced in an unexpected area, such as the serpent, and to a lesser extent, the monkey, which were made near Tehuantepec from local, very hard woods. (Most of Mexico's finest woods grow on the Pacific slope, particularly in the south, so are not available to Indian carvers elsewhere.) Relief or panel carving is extremely rare, probably because of limitations in wood size and shape and in tools. In addition, primitive carvers rarely think of their work in terms of panels—unless they have been influenced by religious examples seen in churches or imported from more advanced areas.

The monkey (opposite) from Tehuantepec was executed in guyacan, a dark-green striped wood, by a South Coast Indian. It is considerably more involved than the usual primitive pieces, and shows much more sense of design. It is about 12 in (30 cm) tall.

CHAPTER V

Stylized Silhouettes Create Drama

The Seri Indians of Sonora, Mexico, make ironwood carvings which are not primitive

PRIMITIVE CARVINGS tend to be crude, over-detailed, somewhat fussy; only with sophistication and training comes suave, smooth, under-detailed work. Thus it is surprising to find carvings that could readily be called modern and uncomplicated coming from a primitive people. But this is true of the work of the Seri Indians, a small tribe which 40 years ago had decreased to about 300 souls (most of them on Tiburón Island in Sonora, Mexico), existing mainly by fishing. By 1960, they had formed a fishing cooperative at Kino Bay on the mainland with other Indians and many moved back there. In 1965, Tiburón was declared a game preserve, so the tribe, gradually increasing in numbers, is now in camps north of Kino Bay.

Early in the Sixties, José Astorga, one of the tribe, made the first non-utilitarian object in ironwood for a friend from Tucson—a paperweight. Next he made a turtle, then a rather poor porpoise, then a better one. These were decorated with pearls, brads, tacks—and got worse and worse as he tried the usual barrettes, hearts, spoons, bowls. Eventually he turned back to the sea and simple fish forms—and began to become known. Others, including his daughter, Aurora, began to make the figures as well, and since then carvings have become the major source of income of the tribe.

Earlier Seri carvings, including violins, toys, yokes and such, were made of soft woods; ironwood was used only for oars and bull roarers. Desert ironwood (Olney tesota) is the second-heaviest wood found in the United States (Florida leadwood is heavier). It is a hard, dense, dark-brown to black, striated wood that is capable of taking a high polish. It grows on the desert in southwest Arizona, southeast California, and down into Baja California and Sonora. The Seri technique is to chop out a crude shape with a machete and/or a large butcher knife, then achieve the form with a large file or rasp. Hacksaws make necessary slits. The piece is sanded very smooth, then turned over to women and children to rub with rags soaked in lard, kerosene or whatever else will generate a shine. Breaks are patched with resin. Recently, more sophisticated waxes are replacing the lard and heavy oil, so the grain is more visible. The danger now is hurried and poor production to meet demand, the usual degrading process that has affected folk carving all over the world. A further danger is a shortage of ironwood. But, at the moment, they are supreme examples of what can be done with a beautiful hardwood—folk art that can stand as sculpture in its own right.

If you undertake duplicating any of these carvings, remember that a major factor in their effectiveness is the wood itself. Pine or basswood is scarcely the material. and the hard gloss of a plastic finish will not substitute for the glow obtained here by a polish that seems to be part of the wood beneath. The West Coast is particularly favored in beautiful woods, and those of the Pacific slope and coast of Mexico surpass the United States in variety, color and unique quality.

If you are restricted to familiar woods, black walnut suggests itself, and perhaps woods with a decided figure like ash or butternut, or even birdseye maple, if you dare try it. In any case, the finishing is at least as important as the carving, particularly the obtaining of smooth surfaces. Features are suggested rather than carved: the eye socket is more important than the eye, the fold of skin more important than its texture. Of the pieces I saw, I was most impressed by the mountain-sheep head, which is a difficult exercise in shaping. It is,

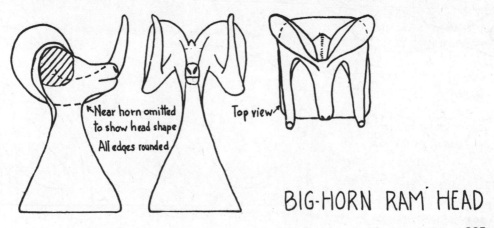

*Near horn omitted to show head shape
All edges rounded

Top view*

BIG-HORN RAM HEAD

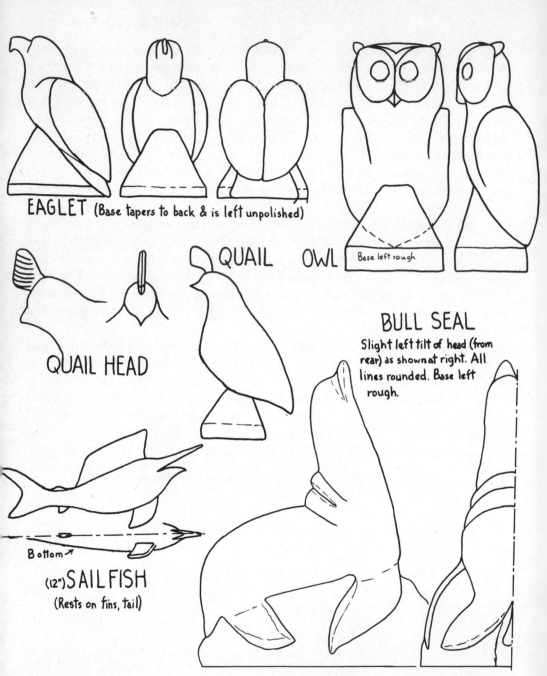

EAGLET (Base tapers to back & is left unpolished)

QUAIL   OWL

Base left rough

QUAIL HEAD

BULL SEAL

Slight left tilt of head (from rear) as shown at right. All lines rounded. Base left rough.

Bottom →

(12") SAILFISH
(Rests on fins, tail)

(*Clockwise*) *The eaglet is about 6 in (15 cm) in size. It grows out of a rough-finished base. The quail and the owl are severely stylized wood. No feathering is suggested on either. The owl is about 12 in (30 cm) tall. The seal, about 10 in (25 cm) high overall, is smooth finish over an irregular and rough base. Here the grain of the wood plays an important part in the effect, and the folds at the neck are as important as the head. The sailfish, about 18 in (46 cm) long, rests on its fins and tail. All sculptures are made of ironwood.*

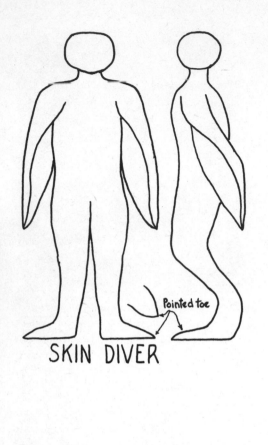

SKIN DIVER

Pointed toe

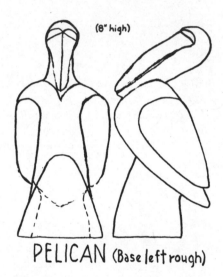

(8" high)

PELICAN (Base left rough)

incidentally, the only carving of part of an animal that I saw, and one of the few with a regular base. Also very dramatic is the seal, rising smooth from a rough base—a trick very much worth remembering.

Rather surprising to me was the absence of human figures, except for one stylized skin diver, who looks almost as much like a bird as like a human. In this figure, the line of the shoulders and arms becomes an extended fin, while the head is a simple, unadorned bump. The feet are extended, probably to suggest fins as well as to provide a stable base for the figure, but the toes are not wide across the tips, as when fins are worn, but brought to a rounded point.

CHAPTER VI

A Tale of Beavers, or . . .

How to vary a subject to suit a client's needs—rapidly

MENTION has been made of the infinite variety of designs that can be based upon a particular animal or bird. Here's a case in point. It has to do with an unlikely animal—the beaver. My experience with it derives from the fact that a particular client has sons who are members of a hockey club having the unusual name of Beaver Dam. Thus she has had need at one time or another for Christmas tree decorations, pendants and awards with some tie-in to the group. On occasion, she has given me carte blanche to provide what is necessary. Herewith are shown some of my designs, which may suggest ideas for you if you have a similar need. Many other designs are possible, of course, their form and function depending upon the animal and the need.

The beaver is not a particularly prepossessing animal, but he is appealing in that he goes his own way and lives a somewhat distinctive life. He is also rather easy to caricature because of his distinctive tail and bulky shape.

The first request I had was for awards for two volunteer hockey coaches—and they had to be produced in 24 hours! My solution was a silhouette panel of the "business end" or head of a hockey stick (sketched), about actual size—7 in (18 cm) wide. Upon it was carved a beaver and the suggestion of a dam, as well as the name of the man and the season. It was in ¾-in (19 mm) mahogany, natural finish, and was made so it could be a wall plaque, or a stand-up or lie-flat desk ornament.

The next request was for Christmas tree decorations. I made a number, including a series of miniature skates of various eras, miniature shoe skates and typical skaters; but of most interest here were a hockey goalie, a player, and two other beavers. These were 3 or 4 in (7 or 10 cm) tall, the teak beavers textured with a veiner and finished in natural color, the hockey players tinted to suggest the colors of the club.

Another request was for a pendant to be worn at the annual dinner. For this I used a scrap of holly, which is a very white wood and resembles ivory when finished. Lettering was incised, then filled with stain, much in the manner of scrimshaw, and the whole varnished over, then waxed.

A further request, a year later but also for short-term delivery, was for a somewhat more ornate award, this time for a single volunteer coach who had led the team to the championship and also conducted them on an 8-day, hockey-playing visit to Finland. The championship was to be mentioned prominently, the Finnish visit somewhat less so, because some members of the team had been unable to make the trip. My solution was a larger beaver in mahogany, mounted on brass skates of the latest hockey style, on a Mexican mahogany base. Base dimensions were 6×12 in (15×30 cm), and the beaver was about 10 in (25 cm) tall, with separate tail inserted. The beaver was carved with cap and turtleneck sweater. On one upper arm was a miniature Finnish flag. Flag and cap were lightly tinted with oils in appropriate colors. On the base was incised the single word "Champions" and the date. The base edge was carved with a random pattern suggesting the logs of a dam.

The tail and hockey stick on this beaver award plaque are inserted in holes in the body, which in turn is mounted on brass skates set into the 6 × 12-in (15 × 30-cm) base. Body is not in the round, but flattened on the sides to reduce bulk and fit available wood. Lower body is textured and tail cross-hatched. Stocking cap pompon, edge of cap and pullover sweater are tinted with oils.

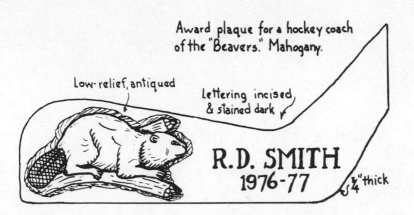

Award plaque for a hockey coach of the "Beavers." Mahogany.

Low-relief, antiqued

Lettering incised & stained dark

R.D. SMITH
1976-77

$\frac{3}{4}$" thick

$\frac{1}{4}$" wood

Beaver Dam

A HOCKEY MOTHER

PENDANT

Stick inserted

Puck inserted

Tail & skates separate

BEAVER GOALIE

Tail, skates & stick separate

Backs & legs of beavers are veiner-textured

Tail & chip added

BEAVER HOCKEY PLAYER

SHY BEAVER (Caricature)

CHAPTER VII

What a Tyro Can Achieve

Timberline Lodge, Oregon, was decorated by unskilled neophyte carvers

HALF OF OREGON'S 96,000 square miles (249,600 sq km) are publicly owned, largely by the Federal government, and half of the Federal lands are administered by the U.S. Forest Service, including the vast Mount Hood National Forest. So it was only natural that the Forest Service designed and built Timberline Lodge, the big ski resort 6,000 feet (1,829 m) up the south slope of 11,235-foot (3,425 m) Mount Hood. Further, it was built during the Great Depression, in the middle and late Thirties, as a make-work project for local people, some artists and craftsmen, but most trained on the site. The original appropriation of $250,000 ultimately grew to almost a million.

The basic idea was to spend most of the money on hand labor, using local materials and ideas. Even the woodcarving tools were made on the site. Much of the exterior of the building is made of local stone, with huge hand-hewn beams supporting the roof and interior floors. But the unique thing about the lodge is its many hand-crafted elements: 820 pieces of wood and iron work, 912 yards (834 m) of hand-loomed materials, 141 watercolors of local flowers. The unusual and powerful woodcarvings include panels in pioneer and Indian motifs, newel posts (recycled cedar utility poles) with animal-motif caps and beam-ends with animal heads. These are true folk art. All motifs are readily adaptable to smaller carvings. Such work calls for bold and deep cutting, with very limited detail.

Fawn

Bear Cub

Owl

Duck

NEWEL-POST CAPS (On sections of re-cycled cedar utility poles)

~ BEAM ENDS ~

Dowelled on

Bison

Bear

Bighorn sheep

Dowelled on!

Mountain Goat

303

CHAPTER VIII

Variations on a Theme

Even copies need not be slavish

THROUGHOUT HISTORY and in every field or profession, there have been two schools of thought, one stressing innovation, the other improvement. One worships creativity, newness, difference—in short, strives to produce or do something that has not been produced or done before. The other worships perfection, accuracy, intricacy—in short, strives to make a familiar thing better. One is concerned with ideas and dreams, while the other is concerned with reality.

There have been, and always will be, both kinds of craftsmen, both kinds of artists. Few of us are at the poles of this difference, but most of us lean strongly one way or the other. We have the whittler who strives to carve a longer or more complex chain, or the carver who tries to make a more lifelike or anatomically correct bird, or the sculptor who strives for a perfect copy of an ancient Greek figure. On the other hand, we have the whittler who creates new and sometimes amorphous forms of animals, the carver who refuses to duplicate his own or another's work even if he feels that it can be improved, and the sculptor who creates forms that are sometimes not even understandable from their titles. He is marching to Thoreau's different drummer, and the idea of sameness appalls him. Paradoxically, this difference may be the vital factor in making the individual famous as compared with commercially successful, a sculptor as compared with a craftsman. It is the innovator who wins prizes at art shows and exhibits, the craftsman who wins ribbons at fairs.

Famous artists have said repeatedly that there is no shortcut to art; it takes an enormous amount of practice, of trial and error. Only when the basics are mastered can the artist strike out on his own successfully.

There are many ways in which to be original, in which to vary even a familiar design; not all innovation must be total in concept. There may be newness in pose, in detail, in over-all silhouette, in arrangement or contrast, in texture, even in finish, for innovation is largely the meeting of a challenge adjusted to the abilities of the individual. It is a branching out, an effort to achieve something that is a definite step ahead *for the carver concerned,* an attempt to convert a mental picture into a physical one.

Most of us cannot hope to visualize the bird-and-flower compositions of the Balinese; our traditions and instincts do not seem to lead us in that direction. The cranes and snake pictured here are a simple example, in which the fragile bird legs are reinforced—quite frankly—with foliage, and the heads with crest and snake, without robbing a particle from the overall effect. The entire composition is fitted to the available wood but without being inhibited by it; there is no blocky and angular look. The composition flows upward from the base in lines that are not at all reminiscent of the original block.

For contrast, study the two Zapotec Indian (Mexico) efforts to reproduce the national symbol: an eagle on a cactus with a snake in its mouth. Neither carver was very skilled, but both achieved something which became part of a national exhibit. One worked almost entirely (except for the snake) from a single block, while the other was content to carve the bird, then mount it on a sawn assembly reminiscent of cactus. Yet both are strong and original.

The bull is in granadillo, made by a Zapotec from wood given him by a visitor from northern Mexico, and the polar bear is in sycamore chosen for the color and figure by an American carver. Each depicts its subject fairly accurately, but distinguishing characteristics of the animal and the innate coloring of the wood are emphasized. Contrast these in turn with the African animals on napkin rings, which are basically true to life, but adapted for a different purpose. These animals are miniatures, relatively speaking, and the silhouette is the important element in recognition. However, the carver avoided the ungainly effect of the over-tall giraffe by eliminating the troublesome legs.

There can be much originality in a frankly comic figure that brings a smile to the observer, as in the American goat and the Japanese owl with attached and rolling eyes. These, like the napkin rings, are made for sale, hence are simple in design, but they are different from run-of-the-mill objects. Another example of the same thing is the Noah's ark from Israel, which, like the owl, is assembled from unit carvings. This design has the advantage that the stylized ship can be assumed to have no deck, so that the body of each animal is

305

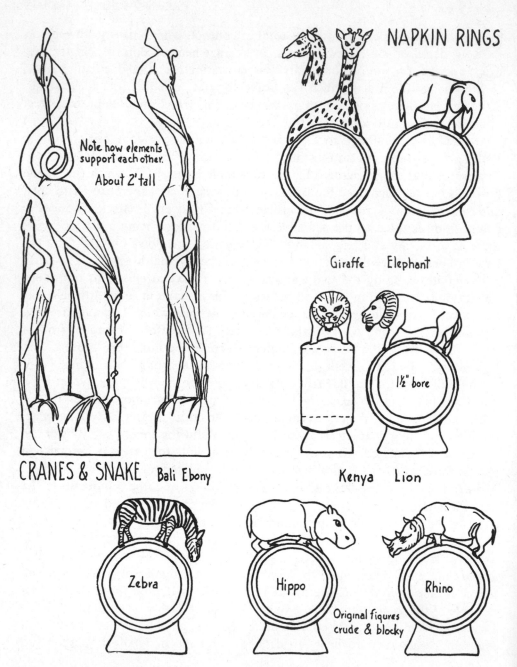

Note how elements support each other.

About 2' tall

NAPKIN RINGS

Giraffe   Elephant

1½" bore

CRANES & SNAKE   Bali Ebony

Kenya   Lion

Zebra   Hippo   Rhino

Original figures crude & blocky

306

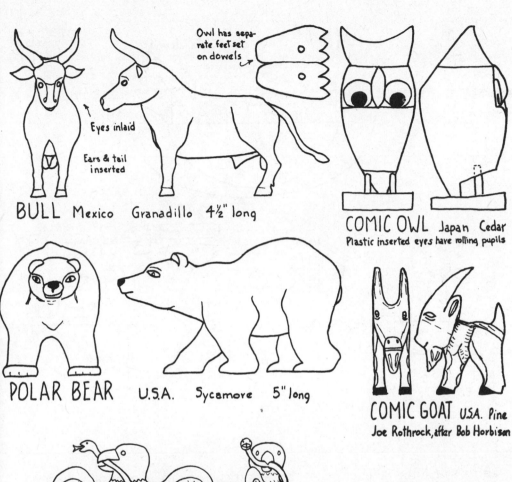

Owl has sepa-
rate feet set
on dowels →

Eyes inlaid

Ears & tail
inserted

BULL Mexico   Granadillo 4½" long

COMIC OWL Japan Cedar
Plastic inserted eyes have rolling pupils

POLAR BEAR   U.S.A.   Sycamore   5" long

COMIC GOAT U.S.A. Pine
Joe Rothrock, after Bob Horbison

MEXICAN INSIGNIA
(adapted for carving)

307

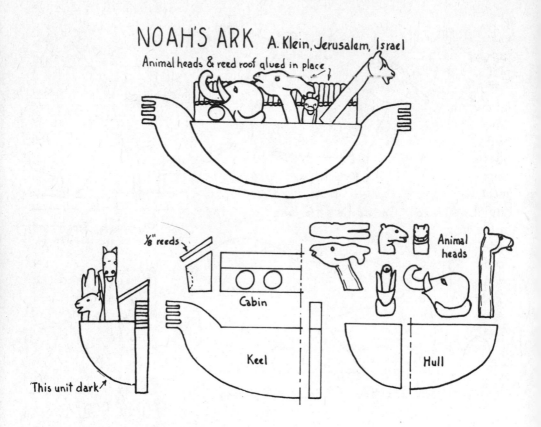

NOAH'S ARK A. Klein, Jerusalem, Israel

Animal heads & reed roof glued in place

⅛" reeds

Cabin

Keel

This unit dark

Animal heads

Hull

either within the cabin or below the bulwarks. The carvings are only the heads and necks of the animals, and they can be arranged as you wish about the composition, but the effect is unique and different. The same idea could be carried out in a fully 3-dimensional ark, with animals on both sides. The reed roof could yield to a single-piece one of textured or grooved wood, and so on, so that every ark could be an individual composition.

This suggests another idea that is relatively uncommon, that of using the same elements in a variety of arrangements, or—better still—allowing the ultimate owner to vary the composition at will, as children build with blocks. A series of building fronts against a common background, or amorphous human or animal figures that can be arranged in various ways on a base, are examples. One possibility of this sort is to provide flat elements with magnetic-tape or other "tacky" backs, and set them against a cloth-covered, sheet-iron plate or a felted board (not illustrated).

There are many ways in which some individuality may be expressed. The large-sized birds are two of my own examples. When I originally carved the "bug tree" I decided to crown it with a large cardinal. So I carved a fat, stubby bird from a wild-cherry log and put him atop an assemblage of more than 150 bugs—although the cardinal is a seed eater, not a bug eater. Some of my neighborhood "birders" were upset. After ten years, when the cardinal had succumbed to dry rot and the ministrations of friendly woodpeckers, I replaced him with a scarlet tanager, although I haven't seen one in my neighborhood in the more than 40 years I've lived here. My point is that you *can* cut loose and do as you like. You, after all, are the carver, the artist, and you have some license. Also, the bird need not be anatomically accurate unless it is being produced as a portrait. The cardinal was happily fat, the tanager has dowel-rod legs and no depiction of feathers. To anyone who criticizes, I can say that the tanager at least eats bugs, but I don't like him as well as his predecessor.

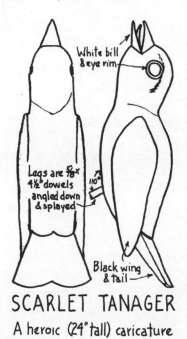

SCARLET TANAGER
A heroic (24" tall) caricature

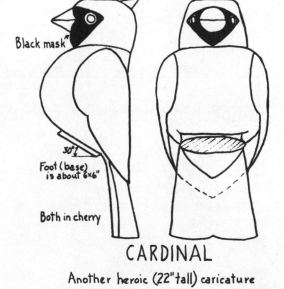

CARDINAL
Another heroic (22" tall) caricature

309

Another example of the same sort of thing is the angelfish I chose for a pendant and earring motif in the rare and beautiful pink ivory wood. Because the wood has so much color and figure, I elected to make the pieces across grain, despite the long trailing ends of the dorsal and ventral fins. As it turned out, the wood simply cannot support such long thin sections, and even a minor bump of the pendant against something hard, or something pressed against it, breaks off the fin ends. Thus I have drawn an alternate design, which ties the trailing edges into the tail. It is not as accurate anatomically, but it is much more durable. This wood, by the way, is extremely rare still.

Another example of a fish design will reinforce my point about the permissibility of varying a design as it occurs in nature. Take the loaves and fishes. Both loaf shapes and fish shapes are generally known and accepted. But the man who laid the mosaic in Tabgha, Israel, long ago distorted the fish and showed only the ends of three loaves in a basket, to depict the whole biblical miracle of the loaves and fishes. The fish are not very realistic, although still recognizable. I have adapted the group for a barette or pendant and modified it still further. This can be done, and, again, it is artistic license.

Eye is a double curl of gilt wire, formed in place

Tail curves to one face, fins to other

ANGELFISH PENDANT & EARRING   Redesign above is stronger, simpler

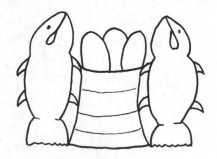

LOAVES & FISHES
Modified from the mosaic at Tabgha

As a final example, consider the doe and fawn (*ayelet* in Hebrew). I felt when I saw it in Israel that the legs were too heavy, and that they had probably been made that way because the material was stone. With the heavy legs, it is possible to saw such a figure completely from wood by sawing through at the nose, then gluing and filling the kerf later. However, the hooves were more nearly equine, as you can see from my copy of the original. So I modified the design to make the hooves more delicate, then went on to make eight further adaptations. All have a common ancestor, but they become less recognizable as they change. Three possibilities are shown here as my variations; you can certainly produce your own with a little thought. You will not have the same inhibitions or freedoms as I do, so your designs will inevitably be different. That is not necessarily bad. The point is that you can and should vary designs to suit your purposes or inclinations, and have no compunction about doing so. Sometimes, you'll improve the original idea in the process.

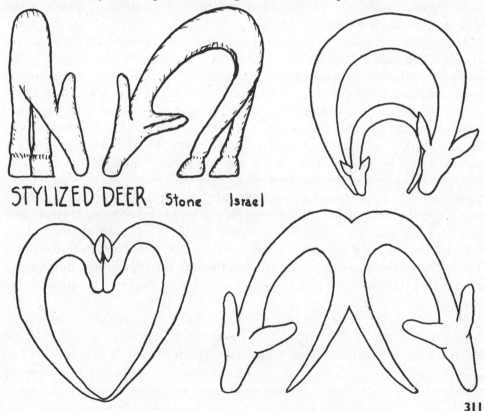

STYLIZED DEER Stone Israel

311

CHAPTER IX

Butterfly Mobiles and Ornaments

They show grain, and can be assembled of thin sections

BUTTERFLIES have long been a staple of decorative design (several are on stamps), but they are uncommon in woodcarving, probably because they are so fragile and so wasteful of wood if sculpted from a single piece. However, they do provide an unusual opportunity to display attractive wood grain or figure, exotic colors, and growth-wood and saw-cut variations because of the large and relatively flat wing areas.

Among the attractive wood-carvings you can make are single-butterfly curtain or drape decorations and three-unit mobiles. Other uses which suggest themselves are adhesive- or magnetic-backed units, pins, pendants, or desk ornaments, because these designs can be almost any size. I began with two fairly large swallowtails in purpleheart, principally because I wanted to experiment with variations in tone and wing position. My wood was 4/4-in (25 mm) finished, so I could get four wings from each blank, because wing thickness is less than $\frac{1}{8}$ in (3 mm). In this species, the wings are visibly distinct from the body, so I arranged grain to permit whittling $\frac{1}{8}$-in (3 mm) pegs at wing termini to fit into corresponding holes in the separate body. Also, this species has some white near the outer edges of the wings, so I drilled holes of suitable sizes, then shaped them with a long-pointed penknife blade. Wings were thinned along the edges to make them appear thinner and more delicate than they really are. The latter proved easier by rotary sanding than by carving because purpleheart is hard and resistant to shaving. Veins in wings were made with parallel knife cuts.

The color in the wood can be brought out by heating, and it is possible to control the depth of color in several ways. Wings placed in a small electric toaster oven will darken along edges and openings and in thinner sections first. Other zonal effects can be obtained by careful heating with a propane torch, but this is tricky because the surface burns easily. Oven heating can also be used—again carefully.

A butterfly's body is extremely complex in actuality, but it can be simplified into three major parts, the head, thorax and abdomen, the abdomen normally being about the length of the other two put together. On the head, the principal visible features are the antennae, which can be simulated with piano wire, often left with the natural curve of the coil, and with the outer end formed into a small loop. They may project from small clubs at the base, or simply from the head itself. The thorax carries all the organs of locomotion, including six legs and the four wings. It is actually segmented into three parts, but these are not visible unless the insect is dissected. The abdomen has nine segments and can be simulated as a cone, although it varies in exact shape from species to species. Also, the body itself can be small or large with relation to the wings. (If you want to be a purist, there are butterfly guides available.) But normally, bodies as drawn here are better than observers will expect. Wings can be separate pieces, or in most species can be combined because of the slight overlap. The upper wing laps over the lower midway of their length.

The principal aim is to display the varieties of wood anyway, so the wings are the crucial elements. I have tried to provide here the major variations in shape and size, and a variety of the possibilities in handling them. The monarch

The "look" of a butterfly can be changed considerably by adjusting the angle at which wings are set into the body. Note wing veining and shaped wing-edge holes. The higher the wing angle, however, the the more difficult is the balancing.

313

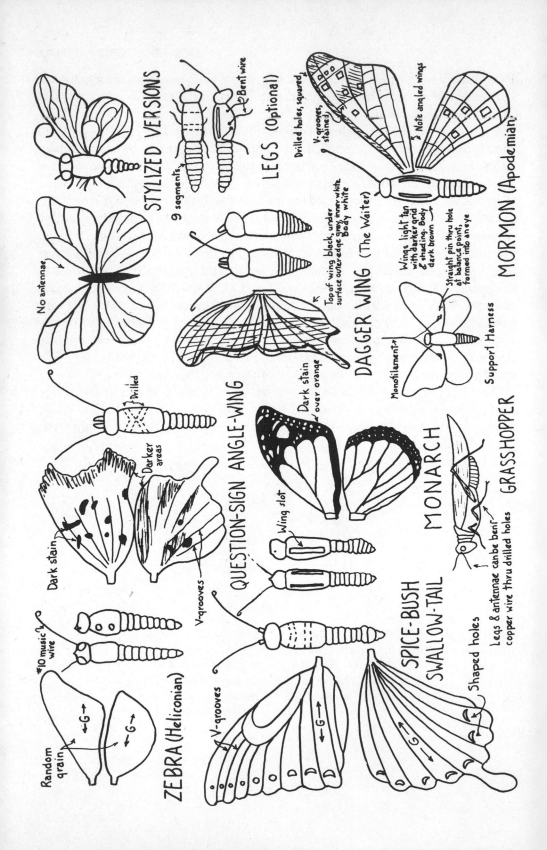

is such a distinctive and well-known butterfly that I made mine of pine and dark-stained the pattern over a lighter-colored background. In the case of multiple stains, it is advisable to give the wood a coat or two of flat (matte or satin) varnish before the stains are applied, to reduce the tendency of the stain to soak in and run. The same is true if you decide to paint butterflies in their approximate natural colors. Over varnish, color where you don't want it can be removed by wiping or scratching.

Because the wings are heavy compared with the body, you may have problems with any support for hanging. Balancing the insect fore and aft is difficult unless the wings are mounted relatively flat. The bent-pin method sketched is neat if you can find a precise center of balance and put the pins well out on the wings; otherwise it is easier to make a 4-point suspension, with a hole in each wing, so the insect can be posed at the desired angle front and back as well as side to side. Whiffletrees* for the mobile are made of #18 or #20 piano wire for the longer one, #10 for the shorter. Each whiffletree need be only long enough to clear half the width of the butterfly to be suspended at the higher level. If monofilament nylon is used for suspension, it is advisable to double-knot and glue when balance is achieved; nylon will loosen and slip if you don't.

All parts for these butterflies were made by hand, but wings can be band or jig sawed, of course, and $\frac{1}{8}$-in (3-mm) wing thickness obtained by planing or sanding. The best tool for shaping holes and veining I found to be a knife with hook blade. It is stiff enough to work any wood and is readily interchangeable with a standard blade for normal knife cutting.

If butterflies are to be used singly, you may want to add legs. These can simply be copper wire put through straight holes in the thorax. If the butterfly is to stand, glue the legs in position and splay them out to support it. If it is to hang on a curtain or drape, sharpen the two forward leg tips so they will penetrate the material, and bend them into tiny hooks. You will find that many variations are possible in wing position and angle of suspension, as well as in color, particularly if exotic woods are used. It is possible also to make butter-flies simply of two wings glued together at an angle—with no body at all. The wings can be thin slices of burl or other figured areas, and backed with a pin. However you make them, butterflies are very pleasing.

*balance beams

315

CHAPTER X

Dinosaurs Make a Mobile

Use as many units as you like, and arrange them to suit the location

MOBILES can be interesting whittling projects for a number of reasons. They are flexible in number of elements, size and composition. Elements may be alike or different, and need not all be of one wood. A mobile can offer an opportunity to work, compare and display a variety of woods. Further, the number of elements is up to you. Having made mobiles of birds and fish previously, I chose dinosaurs as my next unlikely subject, because they varied so in shape and size and because relatively little is known about them.

Wood can be selected for color and figure, because dinosaur colors are not known anyway. I also disregarded relative time and size of species, so they are not in scale and species may have lived millennia apart. Some of the figures were carved in the round, but some were flattened to catch vagrant breezes and because only thin scraps were available. I used vermilion for the stegosaurus, jelutong for the man, rosewood for the pteranodon, mansonia for the sabretooth tiger, and an unknown wood from a Vietnamese crate for the trachodon. This was to test these woods in comparison with the teak of the triceratops, the maple dowel that gives a starting shape for the egg, and purpleheart for the big diplodocus, largest of the dinosaurs. Purpleheart, by the way, is extremely hard—somewhat like ebony, but not as brittle—and has occasional checks and faults. These secrete a black dust which must be cleaned out before gluing or filling. The wood itself is an ordinary brown, but lengthy exposure to the sun turns it lavender. Heating it in the oven can turn it anything from lavender to a dark purple, with thinner sections darkening first. Mansonia, by contrast, is a tannish-brown wood that splits and splinters easily, somewhat like some mahoganies, but it finishes very well.

Figures were finished without sanding, because the small planes left by the knife will reflect light. Figures were sprayed with Krylon® matte varnish to keep them clean, but finish, at least of harder woods, can simply be wax if you prefer. To suspend them, I drilled small holes at the center of gravity and glued in eyes bent from straight pins. The proper point for suspension can easily be determined by a little trial and error with a pin. Monofilament nylon makes a good suspension thread, but must be double-knotted and glued to keep the knots tight. Initial length of the nylon should be about a foot, to allow for later adjustment.

At this point, you must decide whether you prefer a wide mobile or a long one, and cut whiffletrees to suit. I wanted one that was longer than its width, so my top whiffletree was 10 in (25 cm) long, eye to eye. Piano wire makes good whiffletrees, because it comes off the coil with a good natural curve and because it is polished; this tends to delay corrosion. It is also, of course, much stiffer than other wire of similar diameter. I used #18 wire (0.041-in [1 mm] diameter) for the long whiffletree and #10 (0.024 in [0.8mm]) for the smaller ones, but any similar sizes will do. The wire may have to be sawed, then should be filed smooth on the ends and bent with gooseneck pliers. Eyes should be small and closed tight, or you will be plagued with nylon threads slipping out during adjustment and assembly.

Begin assembly from the bottom. The general principle is to pair off two elements of approximately equal weight, one tall and one wide, and differing in color if possible. The wide one must clear the support thread for the tall one, or be hung below it. Leave the threads long and double-knot or slip-knot them at the whiffletree, because single knots will promptly loosen and come free. Considering that the whiffletrees are relatively heavy compared with the figures, they will actually make balance easier. This is important, because even the usual postal scale will not read accurately enough to get exact weights of the elements and it is preferable to have the whiffletree hang almost horizontal to keep the threads it supports at maximum distance apart. Knot a thread over the center of the whiffletree and move it until the elements below it balance, then glue it in place.

Assemble the second short whiffletree in the same way. If your mobile is to be wide, you'll tend to balance two elements against two. If it is to be long, you'll tend to balance two elements against a single one on the medium-length whiffletrees. Other whiffletree assemblies are made just as the first one was. A particularly heavy element may have to hang alone, or be balanced by a light element hung from the center of a smaller whiffletree supporting two others. I did this with the man, the pteranodon, and the diplodocus. This also serves to

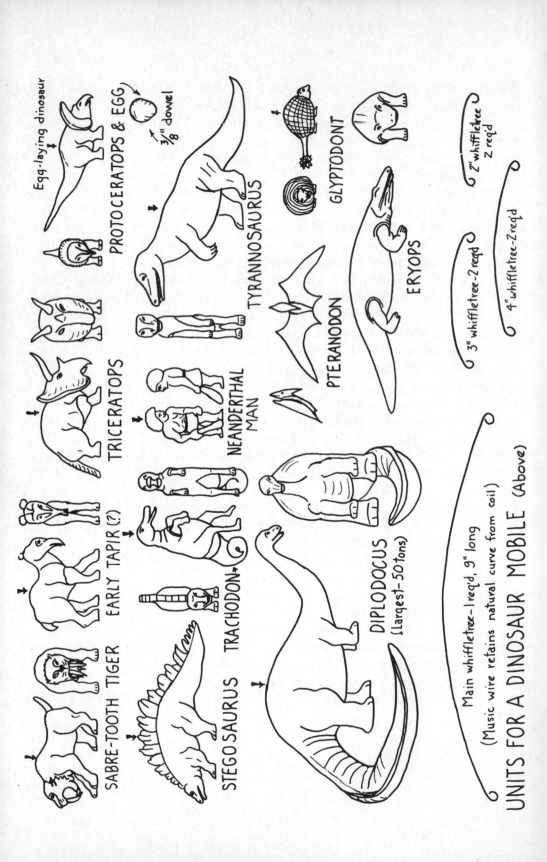

Egg-laying dinosaur

PROTOCERATOPS & EGG

3/8" dowel

TYRANNOSAURUS

GLYPTODONT

ERYOPS

PTERANODON

TRICERATOPS

NEANDERTHAL MAN

SABRE-TOOTH TIGER   EARLY TAPIR (?)   TRACHODON

STEGOSAURUS

DIPLODOCUS
(largest—50 tons)

2" whiffletree
2 reqd

3" whiffletree—2 reqd

4" whiffletree—2 reqd

Main whiffletree—1 reqd, 9" long
(Music wire retains natural curve from coil)

UNITS FOR A DINOSAUR MOBILE (Above)

UNITS FOR ADDITIONAL ARMS (Below)

These designs are adapted from sketches in "National Geographic" magazine for August, 1978, which show more details

STRUTHIOMIMUS (Running alternate)

ARCHEOPTERYX 140,000,000 yrs.
(Oldest known bird)

IGUANODON 135,000,000 yrs.

ANATOSAURUS 65,000,000 yrs.

STRUTHIOMIMUS 80,000,000 yrs.

PLATEOSAURUS 225,000,000 yrs.

TARBOSAURUS 135,000,000 yrs.

CORYTHOSAURUS 65,000,000 yrs.

Flat gouge scallops

Spurs

ANKYLOSAURUS 135,000,000 yrs.

MEGALOSAURUS 135,000,000 yrs.

fill in otherwise open areas of the mobile and make it look busier in motion.

Hang the rough-assembled mobile from a ceiling hook or a projecting arm. I use a dowel stuck under books on a bookshelf at shoulder level at convenient height, and check elements for interference, as well as the general "look" of the mobile. Usually, interference can be corrected by raising or lowering one of the two elements that collide. You may want to shorten all suspensions to make the mobile more compact. This is a matter of taste, location and strength of likely breezes—the longer the threads, the more likely they are to tangle if the wind is fresh. My mobile is about 14 in (35 cm) wide by 2 ft (61 cm) deep. You may even have to change the length of a whiffletree, particularly if you have many elements in the mobile. When everything is adjusted, glue the knots and spray the assembly with varnish to inhibit rusting of whiffletrees. Also trim off loose ends of the nylon threads.

After about a year, I felt that I wanted additional elements in my mobile. Just about that time, there was an extensive story in the *National Geographic* about recent dinosaur discoveries. So I added two more arms to the mobile (one long whiffletree) to accommodate an additional nine elements. These were in additional woods: ankylosaurus in Virginia cedar 8,000 years old, iguanodon in maple, plateosaurus in redwood, megalosaurus in shedua, archaeopteryx in pecan, anatosaurus in walnut, tarbosaurus in chinkapin, corythosaurus in basswood, and struthiomimus in Port Orford cedar. (In the original group, trachodon was in pine, tyrannosaurus in cherry and proto-ceratops in oak.) I have sketched a running struthiomimus in case you want a long and narrow element, but his legs can be a real problem to carve unless you select a hard and largely nonsplitting wood for the figure. Assembly of this group is similar to the preceding one, except that in these figures I used tiny silver eyebolts instead of bent pins. Struthiomimus, by the way, apparently lived off eggs laid by other dinosaurs, so what he is clutching is such an egg, which was simply a long oval.

Mobiles can be quite simple. To make a "hostess present" in Mexico, I found a $\frac{1}{4} \times 1 \times 15$-in ($0.63 \times 2.5 \times 38$ cm) slat of pine on the street, and whittled five birds from it, entirely freehand and of no particular species. They were suspended from white sewing thread through holes drilled with a knifeblade tip. The whiffletrees were thin copper wire from a nearby electric-motor repair shop. Birds and their suspending threads were dyed in bright colors—red, blue, green, brown and gold—in the dye vats at a weaving plant across the street.

CHAPTER XI

Simplicity Is the Mark of "Brasstown"

Animal carvings from the Campbell Folk School

FOR AT LEAST the past half-century, the John C. Campbell Folk School, Brasstown, North Carolina, has been a stronghold of American folk art. It was originally established to teach crafts to mountain people in "Southern Highlands," helping them to develop their inherent skills rather than to impose inhibiting outside ideas. Thus their carvers have utilized the native woods to make images of familiar things, usually animals and birds, that are appealing and "natural." The examples included here were selected over a decade by Val Eve, herself a carver, who worked there.

The typical piece made at the school is simple, carved almost entirely with a knife, and quite realistic. It is not ostentatious or presuming, and rarely abstract or conscious caricature. It is, rather, a straightforward expression of an object familiar in everyday life. It is likely to be sanded smooth and polished, so the emphasis is on the wood and the subject rather than the carving. Only in bird carvings does abstraction creep in, which is understandable because birds move rapidly and in flight patterns that suggest modification of precise outline and

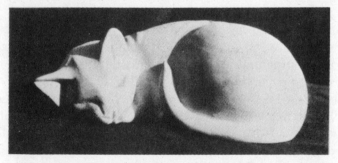

Buckeye is an excellent choice of wood for this kitten. A feline is hard to carve well because the nose is shorter than one thinks. Hind legs are very long, yet the body and tail must have sinuous lines.

321

DUSTING BIRD

BEAR Charles Church

CUB

LAMBS Hope Brown

SWAN Ethel Hoqst

DUCKLING Hope Brown

HOUNDS Jack Hall

form. This, by the way, is a common characteristic of primitive carving: it may be stylized but it is rarely abstract. Abstraction suggests the influence of outside, more sophisticated influences, usually introduced by art school-trained teachers.

Several of these Brasstown carvings are made in partially deteriorated wood, the markings of the wood and changes in color obviously being considered worth the loss in structural quality. It is possible, on occasion, to add considerable drama to a carving by incorporating such changes of texture and color into the finished design, particularly if the finish is to be natural, as in all these examples. In many instances, carvers select wood of a color to suit the design, and vice versa. Also, some carve woods wet that tend to split when dry. One carver there boiled walnut blanks for a half hour or so because he felt that this made carving easier. But beware of trying that on bigger blanks— they may split as they dry.

322

CHAPTER XII

Carving the Minotaur

Ancient Greeks believed he guarded the Maze of Minos in Crete

THE MINOTAUR is an interesting carving problem because he combines human and bull characteristics, no matter how he is made. I have carved him in low relief like a centaur, a human torso rising from a bull body, sprouting horns. The alternate is to have a bull head on a human body, perhaps with a tail added. After all, the minotaur is a creature of Greek fable anyhow, so nobody can say for sure how he should be designed.

To serve as a combined exercise in human and animal proportions, he makes an excellent companion piece for a centaur made the other way around, namely with a stallion body and human torso and head. Further, the minotaur torso can and should be compact and bunchy, while the centaur should be

Horn can be separate, of contrasting wood.

323

lighter and more lithe. I made both in mahogany, with the grain running vertically. The minotaur block was $4 \times 4 \times 9$ in ($11 \times 11 \times 23$ cm) overall, but you may prefer a slightly larger base, say 4 in (11 cm) deep by 5 in (13 cm) square.

The front and side views are sketched on the block, which is then rough-sawed on a band saw. When sawing, do the back and right side first to avoid cutting away lines. The cut-off sections can be set back in place to provide support and guidance for the other cuts, the most complex of which are those across the front of the figure. They should be done before the left side is sawed, (see photo 1). Remove the extra wood from in front of the right knee and redraw the arm and leg locations, and the roughed-out figure should look something like photo 2.

Next, begin to shape the left arm and leg, including the shoulder and tail. Be careful to leave enough wood for the flattened ears. Also, take out some of the surplus wood between the horns, but leave plenty to support these cross-grain elements, as in photo 3. Now do the same thing on the right, in effect

blocking in the body including the front (see photo 4). Shape the arms, legs, and tail, including the back raised spinal column (see photo 6). Shape the head, allowing for the flaring nostrils, ears and heavy brows (see photo 5). Shape the right foot, which is doubled under the right buttock (see photo 6). Don't forget that the toes, in this pose, are bottom up, but the big toe remains on the inside. Now finish shaping the body, then the hands, feet and tail, and finally the head and horns (see photo 7). The top of the base can be scalloped shallowly with a small gouge, and the eyes drilled for pupils or merely have a central dark spot on each eyeball. The finish should show tool marks—it helps accentuate the brute force of the animal. I used a teak oil finish and natural Kiwi® shoe polish and got just the degree of low gloss I wanted (see photo 8). Conventional wax would probably do as well.

A figure such as this should be blocky, rough-hewn, with not too much detail. He should not be sanded or polished, or he will lose force. Also, I feel that he should be in a darker wood rather than a light one, and without tinting or painting of any sort.

CHAPTER XIII

Carving the Centaur

A figure from Greek myth that offers interesting problems

CENTAURS (bull-killers) were an ancient race of men inhabiting Mount Pelion in Thessaly. They were reputedly wild and savage, and, as bull-hunting on horseback was a sport in that area, they came to be described as half-horses, half-men in later accounts, just as the Aztecs, when they first saw a Spaniard on horseback, believed horse and man to be one being. Suffice it to say that centaurs were generally considered to be evil in Greek myth, with the exception of Chiron, who was gentle and extremely wise, and had as pupils in medicine and the arts a number of the ancients, including Achilles.

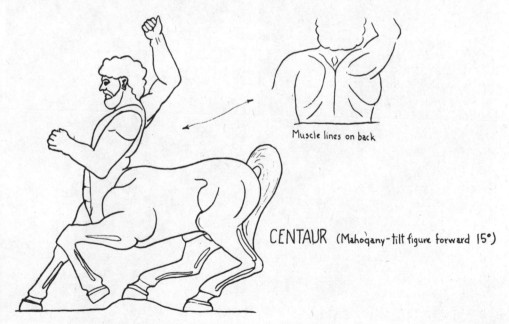

Muscle lines on back

CENTAUR (Mahogany–tilt figure forward 15°)

327

328

The usual depiction of a centaur is of the male, with a human torso running into the base of the neck of a horse. Amusingly, the human navel is shown, although the conformation would suggest that it be omitted. A little modern analysis would also suggest that the beast must have had two complete sets of internal organs and certainly must have faced some problems in deciding on a diet. Also, the centaur is often shown wielding a bow, but I have never seen a quiver or any other carrier for extra arrows. Thus I decided to show my centaur with the stabbing javelin and a couple of spares in the other hand, although his forefeet were probably his most formidable weapons. I omitted the human navel and selected a pose suggesting attack.

This figure is fairly complicated because the human and animal figures must be "faired" together to look natural. Some early painters and etchers avoided the problem by placing a wreath at the base of the horse's neck—which may also have been a device to avoid showing two sets of sex organs.

My centaur was carved in mahogany, from a block $4 \times 10 \times 10\frac{3}{4}$ in ($11 \times 25 \times 27$ cm), with the grain running vertically. The size was selected to fit the available thickness of wood. The javelins were made separately and inserted, so they could be removed for shipping. The base was slightly higher at the rear. Carving is shown step by step in the photographs.

The outline of the figure is drawn on the block, then sawed to shape (see photo 1). Note the forward tilt of the body, which adds interest and action to the pose. Because side clearances are close, waste wood is removed with a large flat gouge (see photo 2). Note the centerline drawn on the body and freeing of head and arms. Horse legs are freed from base by through-drilling and scroll-sawing, followed by chisel cuts (see photo 3). Head and extended right arm are formed first, for scale. Leg thickness and position are established, and center-line drawn. The upper torso is practically complete (see photo 4). Forelegs are shaped with chisels and knife, and back of upper torso is completed with musculature so horse portion of back can be shaped to scale. The rear legs and tail are shaped and horse torso is brought into proportion (see photos 5 and 6). Note that the tail flows back into left rear leg to reduce the danger of breakage. Musculature is refined, and javelins—$\frac{1}{8}$-inch (3 mm) dowel rods with separate whittled heads—are fitted into place. Face is refined and eye pupils drilled (see photo 7). Ground surface is gouge-scalloped to suggest rough terrain, and hindquarters are narrowed and shaped, as well as belly. Leg musculature is added (see photo 8).

CHAPTER XIV

Circus Parade and Carousel Horses

Nostalgia has led carvers into specialized areas

A NUMBER of carvers have been making models of circus wagons and carousel horses in recent years, recalling the golden age of the circuses in America from 1870 to about 1915. In 1880, there were more than 50 circuses on the road, each trying to outdo its rivals in the splendor of its parade, which was relied upon to attract crowds to the circus grounds. Larger circuses had extremely ornate and elaborate wagons, spectacles and regalia for the parade, at least one wagon reputedly costing $40,000 alone.

Biggest and most elaborate of the circus-parade models is that at Shelburne Museum in Vermont, which incorporates over 300 ft (91 m) of 1-in (2.5 cm) scale models, the equivalent of a 2-mile (3 km) parade—which no circus could ever mount alone. Models were carefully scaled from the originals or from photographs over a 25-year period, largely as the hobby of one man, with the assistance of four others at various times. It includes five bands; 53 bandwagons, tableaux and cage wagons; 400 draft, riding and driving horses; 90 ponies, mules and donkeys; 30 elephants, 33 camels, 14 zebras, 80 animals in cages, 60 lead animals, 20 clowns, 83 musicians, 170 riders, and over 130 other

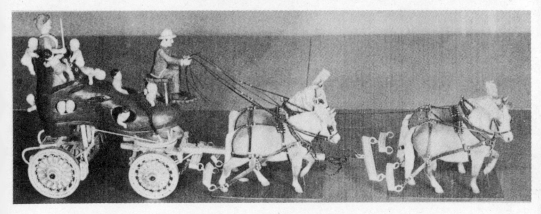

personnel. Wagons are hand-carved and painted; no two horses are alike. Pictured here are the Old-Woman-in-a-Shoe tableau wagon and the African crocodiles in tank-cage wagon, both drawn by buckskin horses, and a group of the carousel horses which are part of the same display. The parade is housed in a 500-ft (152 m) arcuate building built for it in 1965.

CHAPTER XV

Try Carving in Relief

Some of the basics—and some typical panels

WHEN YOU WANT to depict an individual animal or bird, the problem is basically quite simple—you make a three-dimensional image. But when you prefer a group, or a scene, or the third dimension must be limited either because of intended location or available wood, relief carving is the better answer. It is also a must for decoration on furniture, containers, panelling, frames, pendants, even non-flat objects such as vases, shaped pieces like wooden shoes or solid stools, and a host of other applications. Many of the carvers of ancient Europe solved their problems by carving in high relief, so that the third dimension for important figures or elements was practically normal, but this limited carving to fairly large furniture or mantels or the like, where the thickness and the weight could be accommodated. Also, problems of undercutting and support of fragile elements led to endless compromises and the necessity for many specialized tools, to say nothing of limitations in design and suitable wood. Even cleaning was complicated, and warping and cracking were common.

Carving in low relief avoids many of these problems but generates a series of others, as the ancient Egyptians discovered. Most of these have to do with the necessity of foreshortening the third dimension. In scenic carvings, there is the added complication of forcing the perspective. Early Egyptians avoided some of the difficulties by putting all heads in profile and by carving a scene in a single plane, so that their work approximated an etching or a painting with some moulding of the surfaces. It took them centuries to learn how to foreshorten the third dimension so heads could be turned without appearing to be mashed, and backgrounds could be sunken to create the effect of depth.

I mention all this because low-relief, or panel, carving is not as simple as it appears to be; in fact, many sculptors insist that it is much more difficult to

333

do well than in-the-round carving. The fact that so many neophyte carvers limit themselves to in-the-round carvings of single figures would tend to bear out this opinion. A little experience with cutting away and levelling backgrounds shows that more skill and more tools are required, as well as more patience and care.

I have, however, always enjoyed panel carving because of its versatility in design and application, as well as its challenges. There is some surprise, even some shock, when one first learns that what in life is a curve may in low relief become almost an angle, and that depth must be simulated. Much of this will become apparent through study of the examples given here.

First, a few explanations. The Italians long ago classified relief carving as high, medium and low, plus inverted relief, or intaglio. In high relief, major foreground elements are carved in the round and figures in the background are likely to be half-round, so there is little foreshortening of the third dimension.

BREAD BOARDS
Netherlands.

Veiner lines

Round off

HERALDIC LYNX

Actual size of board ⅜×4×10½"

½" gouge scallops

334

Medium relief is a compromise, with the third dimension foreshortened to perhaps half of normal or thereabouts. Low relief, or bas-relief, foreshortens the third dimension to something like 10 percent of normal; rarely is background depth over an inch even on a 12×18-in (30×46 cm) panel, and frequently it is less than that. I have carved panels as large as 30×36 in (76×91 cm) with background depth of ¼ in (6 mm) or less. Also, in low relief, surfaces may be modelled as far as possible or many may be left flat, the third dimension being suggested by the depth of the background, chamferring of edges into the background, and various kinds of grooving and texturing of the surface. This technique is particularly important when the surface is to be used as a tabletop or as a wall of something that will be handled frequently, like a jewel box.

In trench carving, a technique invented by the Egyptians, the background is *not* cut away, except immediately around the subject figures, and some of the design may actually be merely incised lines with no modelling. This technique

Simple animal forms are silhouetted atop these small bread or cheese boards from Holland. Details such as nostrils, eyes and mane separations are done with a veiner and small gouge, the bottom scallops with a gouge.

gives maximum protection to the carving by surrounding it with flat surfaces and makes possible at least the indication of a great deal more detail. Also, it is much less work, which is one reason I use it so much. As a matter of fact, most modern relief carving is low relief, even though we have power routers to remove background, probably because of available wood-plank thicknesses and cost of material. Most modern panels will be $\frac{3}{4}$ in (19 mm) to $\frac{7}{8}$ in (22 mm), or $1\frac{3}{4}$ in (43 mm) thick, corresponding to what you get when you smooth 1-in (2.5 cm) or 2-in (5 cm) lumber. Reverse inflation has even further affected the euphemistically titled 2×4, which is now nearer $1\frac{1}{2}\times3\frac{1}{2}$ in (4×8 cm). Also, much modern carving is the silhouette panel, in which outer shape conforms to the subject instead of being a rigid square, rectangle, circle or oval. Some even dare to include pierced work, so the wall or light behind shows through. Even a wall-hanging in modern homes must be thin. A number of panels and a number of in-the-round figures have one thing in common: There's no place to put them, as any carver's spouse will agree.

There are certain advantages to relief carving which are partly psychological. The drawing can be taken directly from a photograph. Blocking out and removal of backgrounds does not destroy the entire drawing, as it does in in-the-round carving. A limited area can be completed at a time, so the effect of the composition can be seen, and enjoyed, before the whole thing is finished. The completed carving can be antiqued and polished with much less fear of breakage. The carving is a scene or picture, not a group of individually carved objects pasted on a board, as so many in-the-round groups turn out to be. In this instance, perspective works for the carver instead of against him—providing he has allowed for it in the beginning. (This is an advantage in working from a photograph—the lens will have put perspective in for you.)

Only a limited number of low-relief carvings are shown here, but they cover the basics, and provide some advanced and specialized situations.

Relief carving brings with it the requirement for more tools, the chisels and gouges, their sizes and shapes dependent upon what you plan to do. The veiner and V-tool (or parting tool) are practically essential, as are $\frac{1}{8}$- (3 mm) and $\frac{1}{4}$-in (6 mm) firmers and gouges, the latter in at least two sweeps, one shallow, one deep. All of these are used constantly in carving details, regardless of carving size. I find $\frac{1}{2}$-in (13 mm) chisels in the same variety helpful as well, plus a skew chisel or a knife for corners and tricky shapes. Because I usually work harder woods, I use a light mallet almost constantly. It gives me better control of the

This figure from a kubbstol (block stool) was made by the author from an ash log. It is an example of extreme foreshortening, because background depth is only ¼ in (6 mm), while the subject is almost 10 in (25 cm) tall. It is essential to create the visual effect of depth to separate the Valykyrie and the dead warrior across her saddle from the horse. Designs of this sort require a great deal of cut and try. Staining the lines and background helps to create depth.

cut than I can get with arm power alone. This means that the work must be held in some way. Flat panels of any size will usually rest without moving much on a flat surface, particularly if there is a backstop against which they can be pressed. Smaller ones can be clamped or even nailed down—through waste wood if at all possible—or placed on a carving board like that sketched in Chapter I. This will also protect a table surface, if you work on one instead of on a bench. The work may also be held in a vise or with a carver's screw from beneath, but this makes changing of the position of the work more difficult. Very small work, such as pendants, can be placed on a sandbag.

The size and shape of the work are very important factors in tool selection, of course, but I find myself using only about a dozen tools on even the most complicated work. For low relief, the bent gouges are seldom necessary, and I carve specialized shapes (bunches of grapes, for example) with a knife or simpler chisel. I have almost a hundred tools, but it is frequently much faster to make three or four cuts with a common tool rather than hunt up, and hone, a specialized one for a single-shaped cut.

CHAPTER XVI

Machine-Roughed Carvings

Israeli and German sculptors save time with profilers and saws, even on small carvings

MANY people have taken to power equipment for roughing, and even for finishing, what were once hand carvings, often not because of economic necessity but because we have been imbued all our working lives with the importance of time. Many amateurs who try woodcarving find it to be hard and painstaking work, so use machinery, as do many professionals, who find that hand work can be a low-priced commodity. Also, when you start with milled lumber instead of a log or branch, there is less inspiration, less likelihood that the wood itself will suggest a design worthy of taking the time to "feel" it out.

Camels in olive wood are blanked on a bandsaw and largely sanded to shape, hand carving being limited largely to head, hoof and saddle details. Even the chain links are sawed from a double-drilled block, sanded and assembled by splitting and re-glueing each alternate link.

338

The process of waste removal becomes more mechanical because the design is fixed. The product is "sudden sculpture," often crude in details and finish.

In Oberammergau, West Germany, a traditional woodcarving town, carvers struggle against continually rising costs by profiling most duplicates of larger work, and abandoning familiar pieces which do not lend themselves to machine roughing or are too easily duplicated in plastics or moulded compositions. In Israel, which gains a high percentage of its income from the tourist business, central "factories" rough out small figures like the camels shown here, then hand-finish them. They are sold in shops in the souk of Jerusalem, for example, some even equipped with the stage dressing of a lathe or other machines, a few hand tools and shavings on the floor. The proprietor may—or more likely may not—be a carver. But carvings are somewhat cheaper in the factories themselves, where I got these.

The traditional wood in Israel is olive, which is slow-growing, hard, an attractive yellow and brown, and highly figured. It is fairly common because some olive groves are being replaced by housing, but it is by no means plentiful

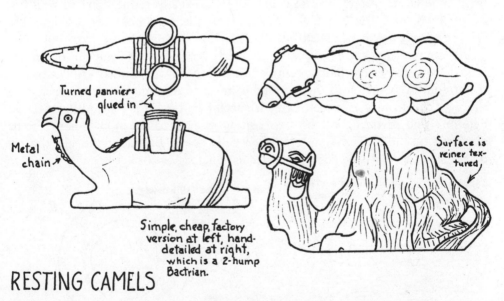

Turned panniers glued in

Metal chain

Surface is reiner textured

Simple, cheap, factory version at left, hand-detailed at right, which is a 2-hump Bactrian.

RESTING CAMELS

or self-replacing, and there is very little other wood in the area. However, among the emigrés who come to Israel are artists and craftsmen from many other countries, and these are trying to continue and develop their particular skills. Thus one finds pieces like the bear, hedgehog and fox made by a German immigrant, and the ibex in cow bone, made by a Russian emigré. (He has produced a number of other pieces in the same material, some quite complex, but his market is limited because tourists tend to buy souvenirs rather than art. Bone is not nearly as susceptible to machine production as is wood.)

The German emigré has designed his pieces so that most of the heavy work is done on a lathe. The hansa carving from Sri Lanka (formerly Ceylon), can also be turned in a lathe, including the shallow V of the outer border and moulding circles, always difficult to hand carve. Then the background can be bosted (sunken) with a small router, leaving the carving of the two-headed bird and the leaves as the hand work. It is also possible to do some portions of the feather-texturing with a stamp that makes several of the small arcs at a time. (This is not the way the original was made. It bears all the signs of being hand-textured.)

There are rationalizations for machine roughing beyond the time saving. The long legs of many animals are an onerous carving chore, so production time and the danger of breakage can both be vastly reduced by sawing out silhouette blanks. The Israeli camels are an excellent example, because not only are the silhouettes bandsawed but also the wood between the legs. Panniers, saddle components and lead chains are made separately and put on, the gross-linked wooden lead chains being ridiculously proportioned, but strongly traditional. Also, much of the forming is done on a sander or with a rasp, and the eyes are formed complete with a special cutter. Study the differences in detailing and texturing of the two resting camels to see how much can be done by machine. The simple version sells for a pittance; the elaborately detailed hand-made one costs six times as much.

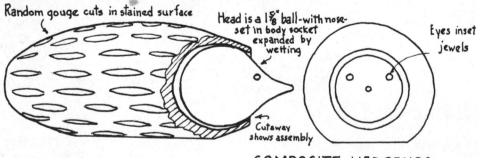

Random gouge cuts in stained surface

Head is a 1⅝" ball-with nose-set in body socket expanded by wetting

Eyes inset jewels

Cutaway shows assembly

COMPOSITE HEDGEHOG Israel

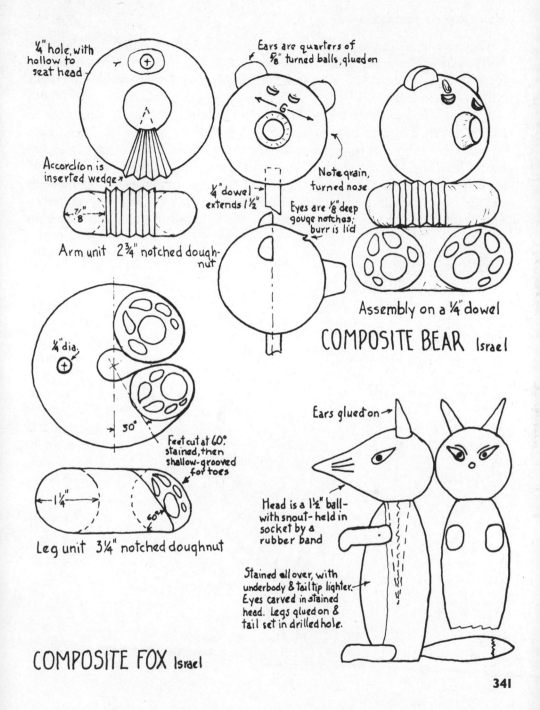

¼" hole, with hollow to seat head

Accordion is inserted wedge

⅞"

Arm unit 2¾" notched dough-nut

Ears are quarters of ⅝" turned balls, glued on

¼" dowel extends 1½"

Eyes are ⅛" deep gouge notches; burr is lid

Note grain, turned nose

Assembly on a ¼" dowel

COMPOSITE BEAR Israel

¼" dia.

30°

Feet cut at 60°, stained, then shallow-grooved for toes

1¼"

60°

Leg unit 3¼" notched doughnut

COMPOSITE FOX Israel

Ears glued on →

Head is a 1½" ball with snout - held in socket by a rubber band

Stained all over, with underbody & tail tip lighter. Eyes carved in stained head. Legs glued on & tail set in drilled hole.

341

The ibis and the duck are interesting because of another shortcut. Body shape is the same, but various species are suggested by altering neck and leg lengths and positions. This standardization makes preparation of blanks quite simple.

Because some animals are so familiar in general outline, it is possible to conventionalize or even alter or distort that outline slightly and still produce a recognizable animal. It is, perhaps, a form of caricature. This is true of the very blocky cat card-holder, which is square in cross-section and obviously sawed to shape, then sanded. Carving is minimal, because not even the features are outlined, but the silhouette, plus the slight narrowing at the nose, creates an unmistakable cat, even though its tail is the full width of the body and no

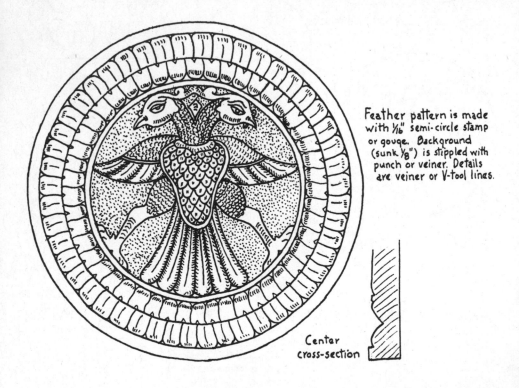

Feather pattern is made with 1/16" semi-circle stamp or gouge. Background (sunk 1/8") is stippled with punch or veiner. Details are veiner or V-tool lines.

Center cross-section

HANSA (Sacred Goose)   Sri Lanka Craftsmen
Surrounded by petals of the lotus (Pala-Petha). A traditional design, carved in a pre-turned piece of 5/8" hard, white wood.

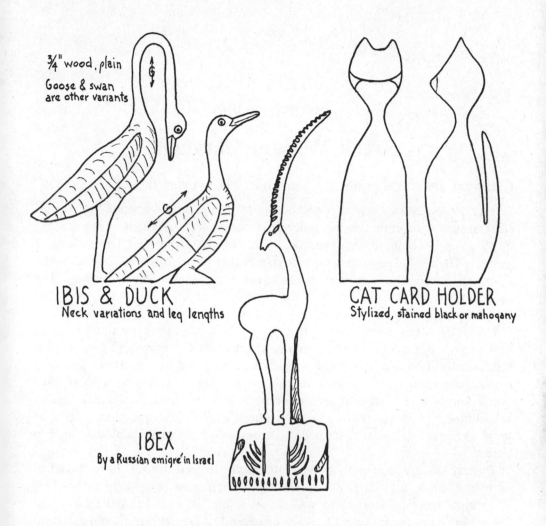

IBIS & DUCK
Neck variations and leg lengths

¾" wood, plain
Goose & swan
are other variants

IBEX
By a Russian emigré in Israel

CAT CARD HOLDER
Stylized, stained black or mahogany

modelling is done. Such a piece can be turned out by the dozen on a band saw, and be finished with a sander and staining.

The age-old skill of working ivory persists in the face of declining—almost nonexistent—stocks of the raw material. Many ivory carvers are turning to cow-leg bone as a substitute, as carvers did many years ago in Bali, where ivory is not readily available. The ibex is made in one wall of the bone and is jig-sawed to shape, with indentations of the horn and surface decoration on the base done with a flexible-shaft cutter or grinder.

343

CHAPTER XVII

Greek Peasant Carvings

Classical sculptural skills are gone, but folk art remains

WITH ITS CONSIDERABLE TRADITION in sculpture, one would assume that wood-carving would be common in modern Greece as well. Actually, even carving in stone is uncommon, and practically all of that is copied from classical models. The explanation that Greeks give is that wood is scarce, but in Israel, where the same statement is even truer, there is a great deal of carving. The practical answer is probably that the Israelis have built the craft, while the Greeks have lost it.

There are a few exceptions, but most of these appear to be not Greek as much as they are Thessalonian, because items on the mainland are peasant instruments and tools, decorated with chip carving and its variations, and they come from rural northern and mountainous areas. I described a shepherd's crook and a flute from that area in earlier books of mine. In several days of scouring Athens shops, I found one shepherd's crook and one pipe, neither as good as those I had, but described as "antiques" and thus ridiculously high in price.

Typical of the northern areas is the one-stringed *lyra* I have sketched here, well-made and carefully carved by a man now reportedly dead. This is a single piece of wood and well-finished, and is a traditional design and shape. Forming the body is the work of several days with primitive tools, and the decoration is a lengthy and painstaking process as well. The design could readily be made two-stringed to increase musical range and allow for chords, but this was never done, apparently. One-piece shepherd's pipes from the same area are usually multiple-key, having two to four flutes fanning out from the mouthpiece.

Somewhat more utilitarian, and far simpler, is the nutcracker in the shape

344

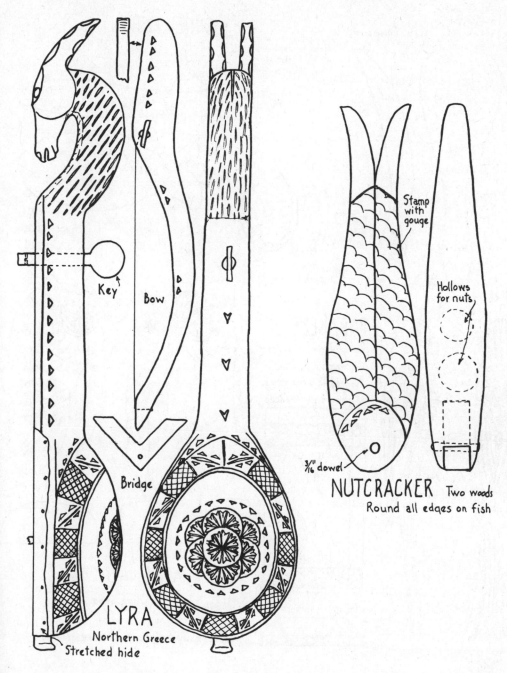

Key

Bow

Bridge

LYRA
Northern Greece
Stretched hide

Stamp
with
gouge

Hollows
for nuts

3/16" dowel

NUTCRACKER Two woods
Round all edges on fish

345

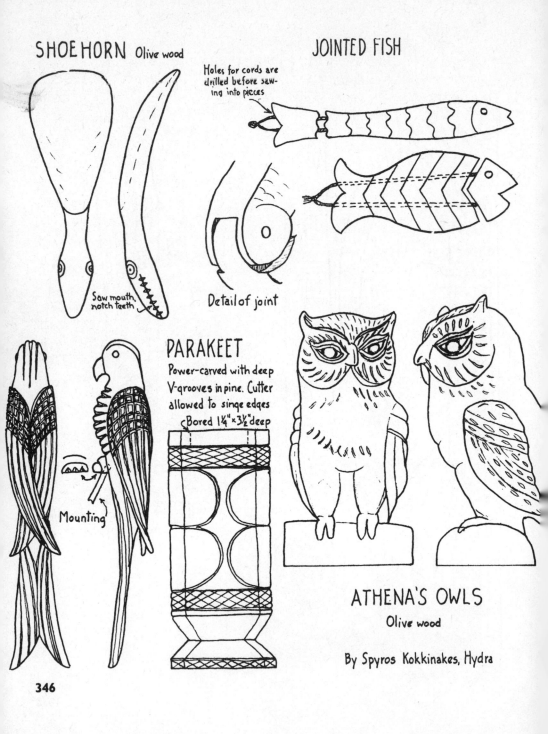

SHOE HORN Olive wood

JOINTED FISH

Holes for cords are drilled before sawing into pieces

Saw mouth, notch teeth

Detail of joint

Mounting

PARAKEET

Power-carved with deep V-grooves in pine. Cutter allowed to singe edges. Bored 1¼" × 3½" deep

ATHENA'S OWLS

Olive wood

By Spyros Kokkinakes, Hydra

346

of a fish. This is obviously sawed to shape and finished, including the joint, before the decoration is added. Because the wood is olive, the scales can be represented by simply stamping with a small gouge; the lines show quite clearly against the polished wood without actual cutting. Also, a dark stain can be applied and quickly wiped off to leave the color in the depressions. It is important to carve shallow, circular or oval "nests" for nuts between the jaws, to prevent the nut from squeezing out to the side and the meat from being crushed when the shell cracks.

There are occasional "different" carved pieces, which I found on the Greek islands in small local shops. All were of olive or other local woods. The shoehorn is a simple design, probably very old and certainly primitive. The principal problem is to use a wood that has sufficient strength in cross section to be carved thin enough for the horn. Olive wood splits and has a tendency to splinter. Maple, for example, would be better.

The jointed fish suggests a number of possibilities for other designs, although it does involve the problem of small-diameter drilling for almost its total length, and small-diameter drills are also correspondingly short. The holes can be drilled by brazing a shank on the drill bit, or by drilling to available depth, then cutting off sections until the bottoms of the holes are reached, making certain that drill "pits" are left in the stub to provide guides for the next drilling step. Assembly cords are glued into the heads. The principle can of course be applied to articulate snakes, lizards, and some birds.

The parakeet is a quite modern design, and much of the work can be done with power tools if desired. The shape is relatively simple, and the decoration entirely V-grooves, stained or singed by a rotary power cutter for an "antique" effect. A piece like this can be quite crude and still be effective.

The owl designs, made in olive wood on the island of Hydra, are unusually good, in my opinion. Owls were sacred to the goddess Athena, so owl motifs appear in a variety of Greek products, from pottery to wearing apparel, but these are free-standing figures. The carver "is quite old," so that figures like this will not be available much longer. One of the virtues of the design is that the carver avoided excruciating detail—every feather is *not* delineated; the lines suggest only general areas and directions.

CHAPTER XVIII

How Much Modelling and Texturing?

Partial answers to these basic questions, with examples

IN INDIA, and in China to a lesser degree, it was customary to cover the entire surface of a woodcarving with decoration, particularly if it was a panel in relief. In Italy, the tendency was to cover as much as 80 percent of the surface, but in other countries, this might be reduced to 30 percent or less. The Maori and the Balinese also kept surfaces busy, while, as we have seen, the Seri Indians of Tiburón carve a profile of the subject and rely on the inherent beauty of the wood and a relatively high polish to create the desired effect.

Throughout the world of carving, there have always been these variations in amount of detail in form and finish, in coloring, polishing, toning, mounting. A common present-day question is whether or not carved figures, particularly in soft woods, should be painted, and if so, to what degree. Exhibitions differentiate between painted and unpainted figures, and in decoy shows the pieces are as much paintings as they are carvings. But this was also true in Egypt and Greece, where most carvings, even in stone, were painted originally. In Indonesia, statues have been provided with seasonal or festival costumes which are changed regularly, and some of the ancients in Europe did the same thing. In many countries, careful carving of a surface was followed by lacquering in color to make the surface smooth again. Thus precedents can be found for whatever any particular carver decides to do; the weight, if anywhere, being on the side of coloring. Only in sculpture has color been banned in favor of the natural texture of the wood—and even there the surface may be textured in areas, and inconspicuous and artful tinting may be done.

Thus it is difficult to lay down rules about amount of modelling or detail, texturing and finishing. Authorities disagree at every level, as do artists and clients. It eventually becomes a matter of what the individual likes, as it always has been, plus the dictates of fashion, local or worldwide.

Actually, the density, grain, color and other characteristics of the wood; the subject and proposed treatment; the skill of the carver and the eventual disposition of the piece must all be considered from the beginning if a happy marriage of modelling, texture and finish is to be attained. If the wood has a strong figure and dense structure, it will combat any texturing or coloring, unless the coloring is opaque.

As mentioned earlier, many people once thought teak is black, because the Chinese, in particular, lacquered it to destroy the grain, and possibly to suggest ebony. Grain may also distort modelling lines and even a silhouette. I once carved an Arab stallion head in mahogany in which the grain enhanced the arch of the neck, and shortly thereafter a madonna in pine who wore a perpetual grin because of a grain line passing through the modelled mouth. (She *had* to be tinted.)

Similarly, texturing can overpower the basic design or enhance it, depending upon how it is done. The very rough coat of a bear can be simulated either with flat planes or with veiner lines, but some of the most dramatic bears I've seen are smooth and finished with a low gloss. The best decoys have exact feathering carved and painted and veined with a pyrographic needle, but most bird sculptures show no texture whatsoever and avoid the problems of eyes (glass inserts in decoys) and legs—usually metal in painted birds—by not showing either at all. The emphasis in one case is realism, in the other it is suggestion. Take your pick.

My tendency, as a mechanic and engineer, is to over-detail, to blur the profile and surface by excessive modelling and texturing. Other carvers I know are too dependent upon files, rasps and sandpaper, or upon single-coat gloss finishes reminiscent of cabinet-making. Their efforts are directed toward obtaining precision—one mark of a good piece of furniture—and art, strength and individuality may be sacrificed in the process. (I am not making a case for the slapdash wood butcher, but simply warning that exactness can be overdone.)

Sometimes, other considerations are influences. When I decided to place a heroic cardinal atop my "bug tree"—a 12-ft (4 m) surface-carved obelisk—I flew in the face of fact, for cardinals eat seeds rather than insects. Also I caricatured the cardinal, made him unduly fat although the low-relief bugs on the tree were executed in considerable detail. But I could not escape the fact that the cardinal was exposed to wind and weather, therefore had to be finished with marine varnish, which gave him a high gloss. Further, there was no

349

reason to carve feathering; it couldn't be seen from the ground anyway, and any texturing simply increased the points of entry for water and real-life bugs fond of cherry wood.

There is little point in putting a great deal of detail into a carving that will be displayed some distance from the viewer, even though detail is easier as the piece becomes larger. There is no point in carving detail and deep modelling into wood that is too soft or too inclined to split, then have to support it. If the wood is still green or its moisture content is likely to change for any reason after completion, checking will be encouraged by cut lines, and the finish will not stop it. If a piece is likely to be handled, details and weak areas are likely to be damaged; and if the wood is light-colored, they will certainly pick up soiling. On the other hand, a table top to be covered by glass can be quite intricate, because it is likely to be inspected at close range. A carving to serve as a screen is a natural subject for openwork (piercing), and the openwork may actually help reduce the tendency to warp by equalizing humidity rapidly on the two faces. The Javanese recognized these things in making moldings and other decorations for open-air shrines; they are usually pierced carvings, (as the example shows.) The openwork in the Javanese panels shown here serves yet another purpose; it gives the composition an airy quality and enables it to benefit from a suitable texture or color on the wall behind it.

Sometimes, detailed modelling is necessary to a design, as in the Celtic bird brooch, where the various levels are separated by texturing and modelling, and important elements are emphasized—in this case by textural lack. Incidentally, this particular design emphasizes another point: You don't have to stick to the letter of the original design if you are changing medium. The original was a small cast-brass brooch; mine was a 6-in (15 cm) bird carved in low relief on vermilion wood, where it was the subject of view, not primarily a decoration. So I intensified some elements. Also, vermilion takes a high polish from the cutting tool, so some texturing and modelling was necessary to make the carving stand out. I could, of course, have sanded the whole thing and blurred the lines.

Contrast the Celtic bird with the animal panels on page 102. These are obviously adapted to incising—mere carving of the outlines on a flat surface—or to shallow bosting and roughing of the background, so the elements stand out. Wavy lines under some of the animals could be incised in either case, and color could be used or the background roughened to increase the contrast.

350

BULLOCK CART Java ¾" yellowish wood

Both Balinese & Javanese carve pierced panels, but Balinese usually
choose religious or mythical subjects, Javanese choose domestic ones.

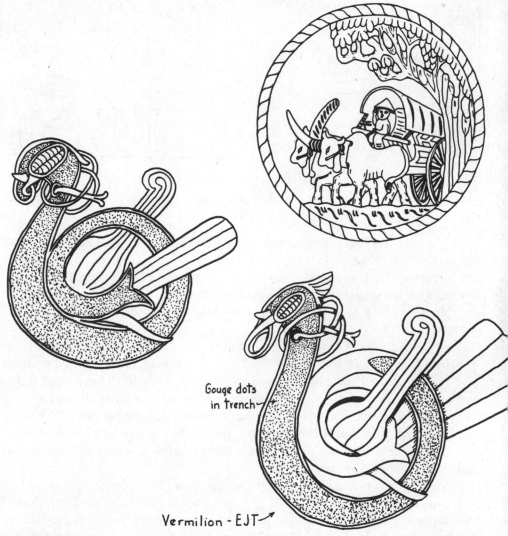

Gouge dots
in trench

Vermilion - EJT

CELTIC BIRD BROOCH ··· & modification ··· CELTIC CARDINAL

ANIMAL PANELS
Shower-curtain designs in Chiapas, Mex.

Note that the veiner, which makes these fine lines, is an essential adjunct to either knife or chisels. In fact, these designs offer so many possibilities in interpretation that I copied them from a shower curtain in Mexico—and haven't attempted to carve them as yet. The panels and the cardinal, incidentally, provide an answer to that perennial question of tyro carvers, "Where can I get new ideas?"

Another example of careful use of texturing to obtain a pleasing effect is the owl from Bali. It is, of course, a stylized owl, so its feathers are stylized outlines. The "rays" around the eyes are used to add emphasis to the eyes and bill as well as to give the "ears" shape. However, a large part of the body is unmarked except for occasional pairs of veiner lines to emphasize the curvature. The boar contrasts with it in that it is much more true to life; it has wrinkles and bends and even some white lines painted on it for wrinkles, a seemingly unnecessary addition as far as I am concerned.

Modelling is obviously necessary for the cow and dog skeletons—which aren't skeletons at all in reality. The ridges in spine and ribs and the slots in legs suggest a skeleton, which is belied by the complete head. These two, by the way, were made by Indians in the village of San Martín Tilcajete, Oaxaca, Mexico, who are primarily farmers and adobe makers. These Indians have

352

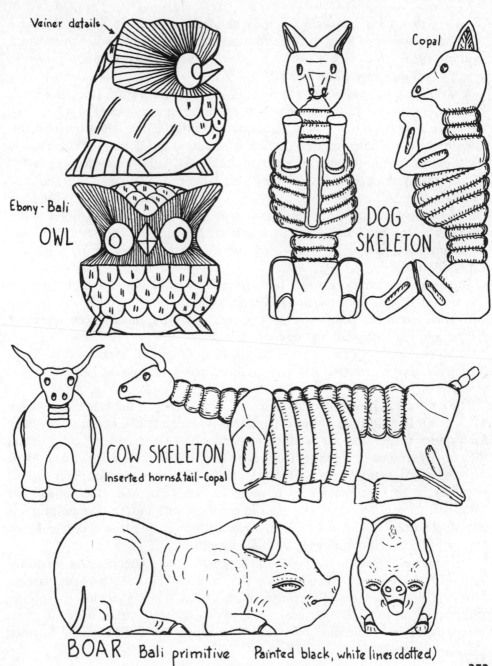

Veiner details

Copal

Ebony - Bali
OWL

DOG
SKELETON

COW SKELETON
Inserted horns & tail - Copal

BOAR Bali primitive   Painted black, white (lines & dotted)

353

become well known, however, for their carvings of similarly designed human skeletons, popular in Mexico to celebrate the Day of the Dead, November 1. Painting such figures would be rather absurd, even though they are carved in copal, a soft and very white wood.

A stylization somewhat akin to these is the armadillo, from the same town. Here the carver used knife cross-hatching to suggest the scaly coat of the animal, but again used no color. A very elaborate and imaginative sculpture from this town is the two-headed monkey, which is about 10 in (25 cm) high. I am at a total loss to explain the symbolism, and the carver had nothing to say; he felt it was strong enough to live without explanations. Strangely, he provided scales on the monkey body with random criss-cross lines, as well as on the bell of the trumpet-shaped object the monkey is holding, and drilled holes at the base of the dog head and slots in the bell of the trumpet. The result is a conversation piece, if nothing more—and one that was snapped up by a Mexico City collector.

Some carvings almost cry out for strong lines and color. Examples are the ceremonial drums from the South Pacific. The carving is simple and strong, and only resembles people by coincidence. Actually, these faces represent spirits, and are highly colored in consequence.

Another example of this is the little fish from Guerrero, Mexico. It is decorated with gouge cuts, but also has stylized color to suggest the trout that inspired it.

The ultimate in present-day stylizing and use of color is the bebek, or dragon duck, from Bali, a ritual object carved with a hidden compartment in its back for prayers to the gods. It is made in parts and carved in very great detail, then highly colored and gilded. There is no likelihood that it will not be noticed regardless of location, because the original is life-size! Designed for religious purposes, it has become a spot of color in American and other homes far from Bali, largely because it contrasts in boldness with most moderate present-day decoration. It also contrasts sharply with most modern Balinese figure carving, which relies on flowing lines for its effects.

To sum up: There are *no* rigid conventions about modelling and texturing. It appears to be more acceptable, however, to use both in moderation, particularly on small carvings. Remember always that texturing tends to subdue, rather than accentuate, a surface. Color is usually best as thin tints which are more suggestive of the color than realistic and show the wood beneath. Further,

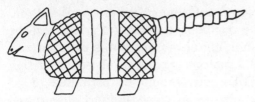

STYLIZED ARMADILLO
Oaxaca. Copal, with knife grooving

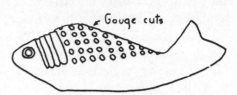

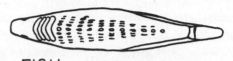
Gouge cuts

FISH - Guerrero, Mex.

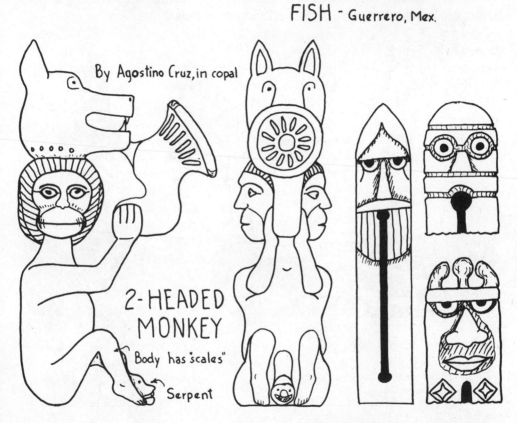

By Agostino Cruz, in copal

2-HEADED MONKEY

Body has "scales"

Serpent

CEREMONIAL DRUMS
S. Pacific (Hollowed logs)

355

color is in most cases effective primarily on soft and colorless woods with no decided grain, or where it is necessary to overcome the effect of grain, or if the fact that it is a carving rather than a molding or a cast form is unimportant. The possibilities of silhouette shape and pierced carving on flat-panel design should not be neglected. Beautiful hardwoods should be permitted to be themselves unless the carved object must serve some utilitarian purpose. Finishes usually are better if a low gloss is obtained rather than a high one, and carved surfaces should not be sanded before finishing unless the risk to carved lines is justified; it should then be done with care. Finally, and perhaps most important, all of the factors of modelling, texturing and finishing should be kept in mind when the design is selected or created.

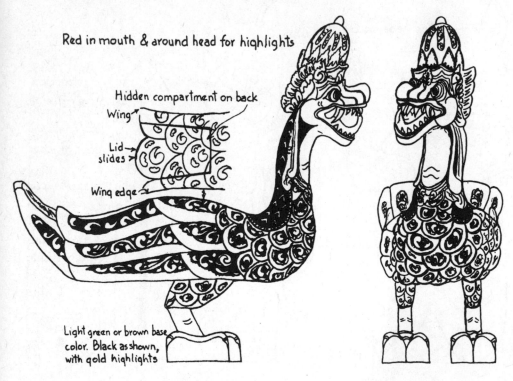

Red in mouth & around head for highlights

Hidden compartment on back

Wing

Lid slides

Wing edge

Light green or brown base color. Black as shown, with gold highlights

BEBEK (DRAGON DUCK)   Bali   Painted

CHAPTER XIX

You Can Whittle Ivory

That is, if you can find it

MAN HAS REVERED IVORY as a symbol of opulence, purity and innocence since some time in the Paleolithic Era, over 15,000 years ago. He had mastodon, mammoth, elephant, rhino, hippo and walrus tusks, and whale teeth as sources, so wherever man was, there were carved objects of ivory.

Ivory is still perhaps the finest carving material for miniatures, but it is unlikely to remain that much longer, for now all of its sources are numbered among the endangered species. Eskimos and Indians of the Northwest Coast can still get walrus ivory, northern peoples still dig up mammoth and mastodon tusks in Asia, Europe and North America, and some carvers still have private sources in Africa. But most of us must depend upon "old" ivory: pool balls, walrus tusks, big scrimshawed pieces, and the like. For others, bone and deerhorn are the alternates.

The Egyptians were carving ivory into elaborate figures, and the Chinese were making it into intricate pierced panels well over 5,000 years ago. The Phoenicians had a thriving industry; Greece, Rome, Byzantium, the Moslem countries, India, Burma, Indonesia, Japan and the Eskimos have carved ivory over succeeding millennia. Sailors of many countries perpetuated the Eskimo art of "scrimshaw"—scratching the dentine layer of walrus ivory or whale teeth and filling the scratches with India ink or colored pigment—and it is still a popular occupation. But the real art of carving ivory is relatively rare these days, except in China, India and among the Eskimos. Germany, the USSR and Japan still have pockets of ivory carvers, much of this being mastodon or mammoth ivory. In the Azores, Chile and other whaling areas, carvers have turned to whale and shark teeth; in other areas boar tusks, deer horns and bone are the materials.

My own interest in ivory has developed over a long period. I bought oc-

357

casional pieces when I could afford them as long as 40 years ago. They were mainly Chinese, but I have Russian, German, Portuguese, Indian, Japanese and Hong Kong examples. I whacked out occasional inlay and other pieces from carefully hoarded piano keys, watched scrimshaw carvers at work as far away as Hong Kong, and as near as Long Island, even tried to buy the tools from a Chinese in Hong Kong. Several years ago, a friend gave me two 10-year-old walrus tusks, so I've made over a dozen pieces of my own recently, using a pocketknife, small woodcarving chisels, coping saw and rasps. So ivory can be carved by hand, although the more prolific Germans and even Eskimos I've seen carving it in recent years were using power tools.

All ivory is essentially like your own teeth. It has an outer layer of very hard enamel, then a much thicker layer of dentine, and finally a core of much softer material that looks like slightly discolored clotted cheese pressed solid. Usual practice is to chip or grind off the enamel, both to remove surface defects and discoloration and to expose the softer and whiter dentine. This is not necessary, however—witness on pgs. 109–110 the low-relief animal poses I carved in the enamel layer. Enamel is harder to carve than dentine, but a design of any depth goes through it anyway.

Ivory has so little grain that this is unimportant. It has very little tendency to split, although old ivory does tend to separate in layers as it dries out. Thus, for example, my carvings of the polar bear and puffins are mounted on the butts of walrus tusks; partially separated portions of the dentine layer I sawed through and split off. On a conventional walrus tusk, the dentine layer will be perhaps $\frac{3}{8}$ in (9.5 mm) thick at the base and go clear through near the tip, so pieces like the Billikens can be made from it. Larger pieces, like the walrus, are carved of cross-slices, so will include some of the core material. This is slightly yellow, with a honeycomb or pebbly pattern, because that's where the blood vessels and nerves were. (The polar bear is mounted on the jaw end of such core material, which is quite dark there.)

Elephant ivory also tends to separate as it grows older, just as some woods do, particularly if the carving is kept in a thoroughly dry place. Large blocks of elephant ivory are sensitive to sudden heat changes. A high-intensity lamp too close to the block, too much concentration with a power burr or a grinder, or even sudden change from a cool storage room to a warm room may cause cracking. (Also, carving ivory with power tools may cause burning, and is likely to cause a smell like that of old bones burning.)

Red

Orange

Insert ivory legs

ARCTIC
PUFFINS – Ivory
For habitat mount

POLAR BEAR

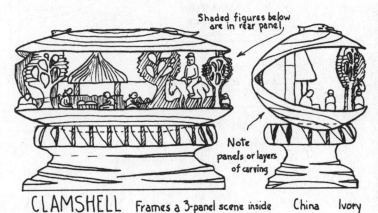

Shaded figures below
are in rear panel.

Note
panels or layers
of carving

CLAMSHELL   Frames a 3-panel scene inside   China   Ivory

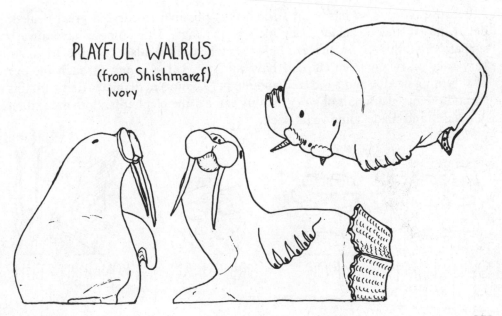

PLAYFUL WALRUS
(from Shishmaref)
Ivory

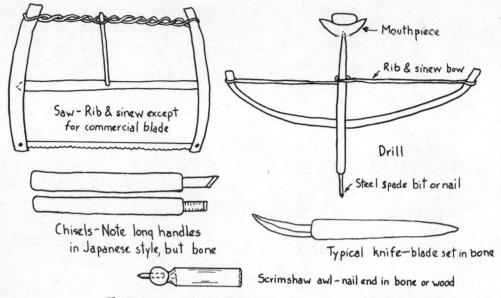

TYPICAL EARLY ESKIMO IVORY-CARVING TOOLS

Saw – Rib & sinew except for commercial blade

Mouthpiece

Rib & sinew bow

Drill

Steel spade bit or nail

Chisels – Note long handles in Japanese style, but bone

Typical knife – blade set in bone

Scrimshaw awl – nail end in bone or wood

Because ivory is so hard and strong, it is possible to carve a great deal of detail into it and to achieve lacy pierced carvings. The Chinese have always surpassed at this—note the examples sketched. It is also possible to make very small carvings from chips; I have an ivory camel going through the eye of a darning needle, and a red seed about $\frac{3}{8}$ in (9.5 mm) in diameter that contains a hundred mixed animals of ivory, mainly camels and elephants. Both are Indian in origin, and made some years back.

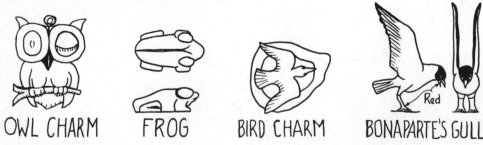

OWL CHARM   FROG   BIRD CHARM   BONAPARTE'S GULL

Red

Note: All pieces above are walrus ivory

The usual way to work ivory is to saw a blank, then to shape it as much as possible with drills, files and sanding sticks. But surface designs must be put in with an edged tool. For lines, an engraver's burin will work, as well as a V-tool or veiner if the piece can be securely held. (If the tool slips, you'll find that your hand is much softer than ivory.) A hand vise or a sandbag may be helpful, depending upon shape. But I find a pocketknife works very well, or a hook blade such as is used for leather. The included angle of the edge should be increased, however; sharpening must be frequent. Even then, chips are appallingly small.

Polishing must be done very carefully to avoid scratching and dulling the surface as well as blurring sharp edges. Ivory is such an intense white that blurred edges tend to disappear, leaving nothing visible but an amorphous blob. Very fine sandpaper or emery paper, preferably worn, can be used for rough smoothing, but for finishing, something like jeweler's rouge and a cloth is better. The final polishing, at least among the Eskimos, is with paste silver polish.

After polishing, you will probably find that your carved lines are not visible at a short distance. The Japanese and Chinese speed up the normal antiquing process (deposition of dirt in crevices) by coating the carving with strong tea or bathing it in smoke, then wiping it off. A light-colored wood stain will do the same thing, but be sure to work only small areas and wipe off the surface fast! This leaves darker tones in the crevices. It is also possible to draw in lines with India ink or to fill grooves with ink or pigment. This has a tendency, however, to give the carving a harsh look. A lighter-colored ink of the transparent kind will work better to define detail carving or important lines, but even this must be used with care. In scrimshaw, of course, which is really a form of etching, the technique was to smoke or otherwise darken the surface, then scratch the design in with a knife point, sharpened nail or awl, fill in with ink, then sand or scrape off the surface discoloration, leaving the lines filled. This is possible because ivory does not absorb the ink, as wood would, so it has no tendency to blur or spread. But beware the mistaken line! The ink will reveal *all* lines and depressions.

Eskimos carved bone and soapstone (a soft variety called greenstone), whalebone and even jade, providing their tools would cut them. They used such exotic equipment as sharkskin for sanding, and bow drills backed by jaw pressure. Typical tools are sketched.

CHAPTER XX

Bone, Stone, Shell and Nuts

Wood is not the only carving material

ONCE POSSESSED OF TOOLS, man carved anything that came to hand, from stone and shell to bone, horn, nuts and bark. Wood was plentiful and more generally useful as well as more amenable to tools, that's all. In Africa, India and parts of Europe, they carved shell, and still do. Pioneers here carved peach stones, cherry pits and other nuts, and still do. The same may be said for coconuts and gourds.

The principal problem with most of these materials is that they are harder and more brittle than wood, so tools must have a greater included angle and be sharpened more frequently. Files, rasps, abrasives, saws and drills are much more often necessary, and modern rotary tools like hand grinders and flexible-shaft tools are much faster. The bone carvings pictured here were done with a flexible-shaft tool.

Ruth T. Brunstetter of Hyde Park, New York, is a painter, art instructor and show judge noted particularly for her scenes of nature. She has illustrated several books, including a recent one of trees of North America. Recently, she became interested in animal skeletons and taught herself processes for cleaning, bleaching and preserving bones, then mounting and articulating them. She now has more than 50 skeletons, ranging from a mouse to a 10-ft (3 m) alligator and a buffalo, including most of the animals of her native state, as well as a wallaby and a barracuda. They fill her house when they aren't on exhibit, and she lectures on them in many places, including the Smithsonian.

This hobby led Mrs. Brunstetter into power carving of bones, usually buffalo, which she gets from a neighbor who has a small buffalo herd. Now her carvings are being exhibited and sold.

Eskimos carve whalebone upon occasion, and various kinds of stone,

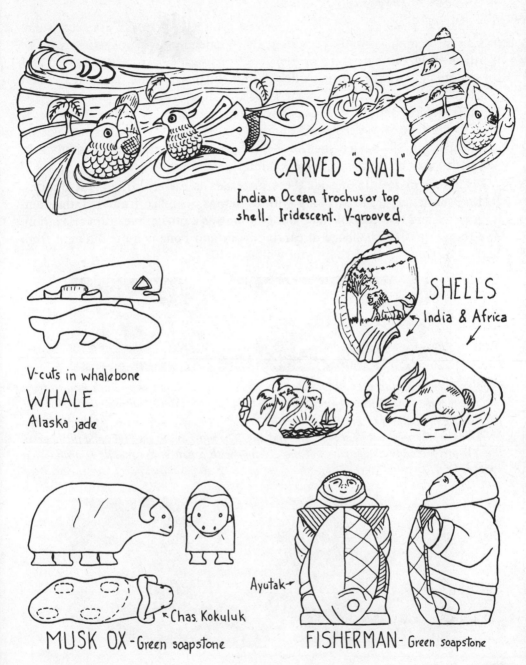

CARVED "SNAIL"

Indian Ocean trochus or top shell. Iridescent. V-grooved.

SHELLS
India & Africa

V-cuts in whalebone
WHALE
Alaska jade

Ayutak

MUSK OX - Green soapstone

Chas. Kokuluk

FISHERMAN - Green soapstone

principally greenstone, a form of soapstone (on the East Coast, gray soapstone was more common), and Alaskan jade. Whalebone and soapstone can be whittled easily, but tend to be brittle. The Northwest Coast Indians carved and formed mountain-sheep horn, as do Chilean Indians, Indonesians and Russian peasants. This material is soft, and tends to "stick" when cut. Coastal people of India, Africa, and the Americas have all carved shell, as well as using pieces of it as inlays in wood carvings; one tribe in Mexico even makes mosaics by careful placing of abalone shell in a pitch base. The composition is inlaid in wood and may be a cross, or even a miniature violin or guitar.

My intent in mentioning all these materials is merely to suggest options. Ruth Brunstetter began working with skeletons to relax from painting and housework and now has taken up bone carving as a further means of relaxation. I've found that the challenge of carving ivory and bone is quite different from that of carving wood. Perhaps you will as well.

(*Above*) *This fishpin, an example of power carving of buffalo bones, is by Ruth Brunstetter. Shaping is somewhat restricted by cutters available, but the material takes well to polishing.*

(*Below*) *Greenstone, a form of soapstone and relatively soft, is found in Alaska and has been worked there by both Eskimos and Indians. The musk ox at the right and the bear at the left are probably handmade, but the Eskimo with a fish in the middle is probably a product of a "factory" in Seattle, which imports the stone and exports "native art" for tourists in Alaska.*

CHAPTER XXI

Make Your Own D-Adzes

The favorite tool of the Northwest Coast Indians

CARVERS IN EGYPT, almost 5,000 years ago, as shown in an ancient wall decoration on the next page (courtesy The Metropolitan Museum of Art, New York) were already using the chisel, mallet and adz. The mallet was like a small bat, and the pounding surface was the butt of the handle, or the chisel was used alone if the wood was soft enough to permit it. What is most interesting, however, is the use of the adz, which is relatively unknown to most American carvers.

In various forms (see sketches), the adz was the basic woodcarving tool, not only of the Egyptians, but also of the Africans, American West Coast Indians, Eskimos, Polynesians and New Guinea carvers, among others. It is also familiar among Italians, but not among the Germans and English. Some years ago, when I attempted to buy an adz for demonstration purposes, the suppliers in New York were out of stock (although several forms of the tool were shown in their catalogs) and unworried about it, because their specialists felt that the adz was much too dangerous a tool for "amateurs."

Early adzes had heads of the hardest stone available, and it should be pointed out that they had many applications other than carving wood. They were also used for tilling the ground and for squaring timbers; the former need disappeared with the development of the plow and the latter with the ready availability of planed lumber. When bronze, and then steel, became available for blades, the adz became a much more productive tool, although it should be pointed out that even in the early days, work with the adz was often primarily the removal of charcoal—the interior shape of a canoe, for example, was roughed out by burning. Some adzes had interchangeable blades, others were double-bladed. John E. Hendricks (whose Indian name is Wahnadagee) of

Bellingham, Washington, wrote to explain to me the making and use of the
modern D-adz, one of several shapes still in use by carvers in his area.
His discussion led me to make a couple of D-adzes, which I have found to be
excellent tools, easy to control and rapid in chip removal. The American
Northwest Coast and Arctic Indians use them for carving totem poles, bowls,
spoons, ladles and the like. They also use the elbow-type (regular) adz as well,
but the D-adz has been the favorite for many years because it is easier to master
and control. Blades are made from old mill files and rasps, smaller sizes from
6-in (15 cm) files and larger ones from 10-in (25 cm) and 12-in (30 cm) files. But
let Wahnadagee tell the story:

"Handles can be plain, or quite ornamental, as show in the sketches, and
should be made of a hard, shock-resisting wood like rock maple. A channel is
cut on the striking face (the vertical bar of the D) to fit the blade, a section of
old mill file or rasp—for smaller adzes from 6-in files and larger ones from
10- or 12-in ones. The file is bolted in so it has light bearing at the bottom
towards the direction of impact. Such a tool just can't be beat for totem carving
or milling and sculpting of cedar wood in general. With a little practice, it can
do all the shaping of something even as small as a spoon up to the point of
final detail. I have one that is metal except for the grip and is a real work-horse.

While I use a hand axe for some roughing, I prefer the D-adz because you

366

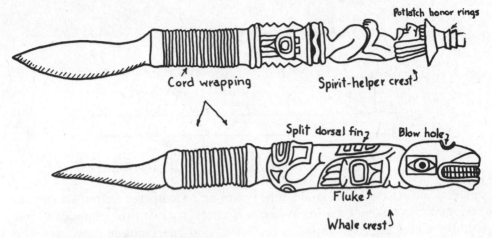

Cord wrapping Spirit-helper crest Potlatch honor rings

Split dorsal fin Blow hole

Fluke

Whale crest

N.W. INDIAN CARVING KNIVES

face the surface you're working on, rather than viewing it from one side. Also, I've always made my own tools, many of them from old saw steel. I now have many tools, but I still prefer the old ones, as well as the old ways for curing and preparing native woods such as cedar. (I make sewn-leather sheaths for all cutting edges for the sake of safety as well as for edge preservation.)

D-adzes are easy to make to suit the user. The only question that may trouble some makers is how to drill holes in a file or rasp. I have two methods: On small files, I put a plumber's-torch flame on the exact spot to be drilled, and hold it there until the spot turns bright red—about 30 seconds. Then I let it cool in air (don't quench it in water or you'll harden it again). It will then be soft enough to drill with HSS bits. If the file is smaller, or a fragment for a knife or firmer, I wrap a wet cloth around the knife end before heating. [A setup for controlling annealing is sketched—Author.]

I anneal larger files or rasps in my trash-burner stove, putting the piece to be annealed on top of the ashes and building my regular morning woodfire on top of it. I take the annealed piece out the next morning before I re-start the fire, and drill as before. This is followed by grinding off the serrations or file pattern, and cutting the blade to desired length.

The temper is tested with a file at the cutting edge; it should file about like a good axe does. One doesn't want a flint-hard edge, which is likely to shatter

367

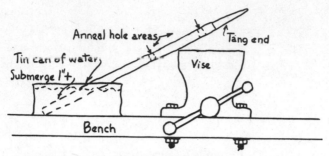

Anneal hole areas → Tang end
Tin can of water, Submerge 1"+, Vise Bench

SIMPLE FILE-ANNEALING SET-UP (Roy Hutchings)

or break off. If the blade is too soft, it can be re-tempered before sharpening. I do that, on the few occasions when it is necessary, with the plumber's torch, heating the cutting edge until it is bright red and quenching in bear's grease or old cylinder oil. (If old cylinder oil is used—which is more readily available than bear grease for most of us—be sure it is free of gasoline by pretesting a small quantity of it for flare-up.) Actually, in this case, the blade is slightly case-hardened.

Some tribes do not bolt the blade, but bind it on as on the knife pictured. This is somewhat harder to do than bolting, and in my opinion not worth the trouble. It is also possible to install a screw-clamp arrangement, but that is usually bulky and clumsy. With the bolt method, the holes in file and handle can be matched, and the only problem is some wear on bolt holes after a lot of hard use. By the way, the bolts should be of the countersunk type, so they don't project from the face of the blade.

I make blades for carving knives from worn-out carpenter's handsaws, particularly Craftsman® (Sears) or Disston® brands. To use such steel, remove the handle, then clamp the blade in a wide-jaw machinist's vise so about a ¾-in (19 mm) width of the blade is between the jaws. Start at the front or outer end of the saw. Now, beat along the blade at the top of the vise with a heavy ballpein hammer. This will start a break along the vise line. Move the saw along a vise width and reclamp, then hammer it to continue the crack. The resulting strip can be ground or broken into desired lengths and shaped by grinding. The toothed-edge strip, by the way can be made into short saws for rough-shaping soapstone (steatite), bone or other carving materials. The steel can also be formed into so-called "crooked knives" by beating a section carefully on and over an iron rod, pipe or mandrel.

368

To secure a blade into the handle, grind a slot in the handle end, then put epoxy glue (I use Elmer's®) into that slot and the slot sawed in the handle, assemble in position, and bind temporarily with cord. When the glue has set, replace the cord with a rawhide, bearhide, or fishline wrapping. Coat the wrapping with a mixture of two-thirds spar varnish and one-third turpentine or equivalent. This preservative prevents fraying or chafing. (In the old days, the preservative was a special pitch.) I prefer to sharpen such blades from one side only; this lengthens edge life and the tool cuts more like a draw-shave.

The beads and colors on knives and adzes have definite traditional meanings. Black is the decorative color for tools, which are not ceremonial. Ceremonial colors are related to the spirit language. Red denotes blood, the life giver for animals and fish. Blue denotes the Great Spirit and the Sky People, the Thunderbird's house and other spiritual things. Dark blue denotes bravery and courage; the voice of horror is in its tone. Green, yellow and brown honor our Mother the Earth; they suggest gracious giving to sustain life and the rhythm and beauty of growing things. They suggest annual renewal, the chain of life."

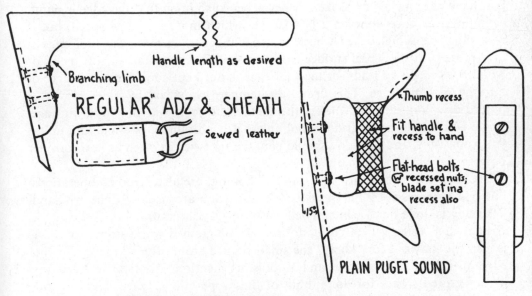

Handle length as desired

Branching limb

"REGULAR" ADZ & SHEATH

Sewed leather

Thumb recess

Fit handle & recess to hand

Flat-head bolts @ recessed nuts; blade set in a recess also

PLAIN PUGET SOUND

NORTHWEST COAST INDIAN D-ADZES

APPENDIX

Sharpening, Fitting Drawing to Wood, and Finishing

How do you sharpen tools?

THE EDGE OF A TOOL—any tool—is really like a saw under the microscope, with teeth projecting at various angles and feathery filaments projecting from them. The sharper the edge, the fewer the feathers and the smaller and better-aligned the teeth. Using the edge misaligns the teeth and blunts them, so constant, and to me boring, resharpening is necessary.

There are four steps to sharpening: grinding, whetting, honing and stropping. Grinding is the first and coarsest step and is rarely necessary, except on tools that have been nicked or broken or resharpened so often that the edge is blunt. Grinding was once done on a grindstone, which moved at slow speed, but is now done on a high-speed wheel, so the danger of burning the tool èdge is ever-present. If the wheel surface is loaded—filled with grains of soft metal or wood or even pencil lead—or the tool edge is not kept cool, there is danger of burning the thin edge. This draws the temper, evidenced by blue, brown or purple discoloration, and makes the metal soft so it will not hold an edge. Thus, you should never grind a tool unless it is absolutely essential and unless you know how, and then you should cool the tip twice as often as you consider necessary.

The next two operations, whetting and honing, are also grinding operations, but with progressively finer-grained stones. They are usually done by hand. Whetting is done on Washita, a yellowish or grayish natural stone, honing on Arkansas, a white, very hard, uniform and fine-grained white stone. Arkansas is also the material for "slips," the small shaped stones for taking the feather edge off the inside of gouges and V-tools, as mentioned later. There are now manufactured stones for doing both of these operations, often with one side for whetting, the other honing. In day-to-day carving, honing is frequent, whetting much less so unless the wood being carved is particularly hard or abrasive.

The final operation is stropping, which is what a barber does to a straight razor. It is essentially stroking the edge on leather to align the tiny teeth, and produces an ultra-sharp edge like that of a razor.

The typical tool nowadays is sold ground and whetted. It is quite sharp to the touch, but requires honing and stropping before using, if you are particular. Knives are ground so the blade itself has the proper included angle, about 15°, and require only "touch-up" for sharpening. A properly ground firmer has an included angle of about 30°, 15° each side of center, and the center line of the tip should be that of the tool also. Gouges have the same included angle, but it is all ground on the outside of the tool—the concave inner surface should be flat, and left that way.

Some carvers prefer a hollow-ground edge, one that is slightly concave, usually from the peripheral shape of the wheel which grinds them. (The hollow-ground shape is exaggerated in a straight razor.) Hollow grinding makes initial whetting and honing easier because the angle just behind the cutting edge is less than it should be, reducing drag behind the cutting edge, and is claimed to make the tool stay sharp longer. This is true in cutting soft woods, but may make the edge turn or nick on hard ones or imperfections.

I have tried to sketch the motions used in sharpening tools, both to maintain their edges and to insure uniform wear on the stone. Many stones become channelled through excessive wear in the middle, and this results in dullness in the center of a firmer cutting edge and rounding of the outer corners. (All operations on stones are done by pushing the edge toward the wheel or stone, while honing is done by passing the heel over the strop first.) The stone should be kept lubricated with thin machine oil, or even a 50-50 mixture of machine oil and kerosene, and should be wiped off and replaced when it turns gray from included metal particles. Periodically also, the stone should be washed with benzine or gasoline, or boiled in water containing a little soda. This lifts out soaked-in oil and grit. If you have manufactured stones, just heat them in an oven and wipe them off; the heating causes the oil to exude and lift the grit with it.

To sharpen a knife, I use a rotary or figure-8 motion (A), bearing down a bit harder as the edge is moving forward and lifting the handle a bit part of the

371

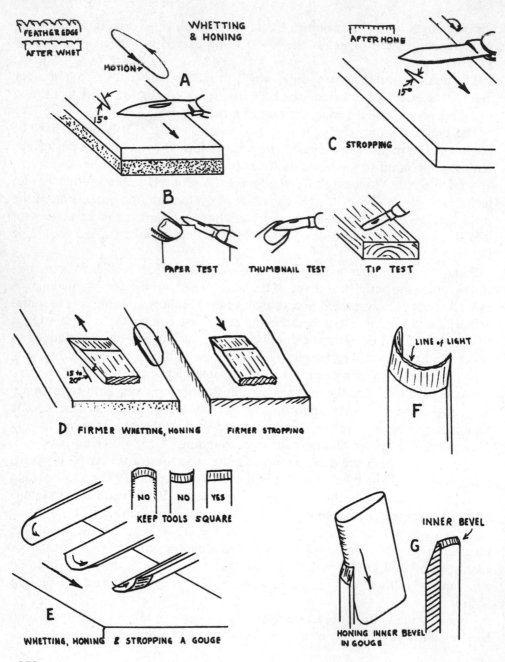

WHETTING & HONING

FEATHER EDGE

AFTER WHET

MOTION

A

15°

AFTER HONE

15°

C STROPPING

B

PAPER TEST   THUMBNAIL TEST   TIP TEST

15 to 20°

D FIRMER WHETTING, HONING   FIRMER STROPPING

LINE of LIGHT

F

NO   NO   YES

KEEP TOOLS SQUARE

E

WHETTING, HONING & STROPPING A GOUGE

INNER BEVEL

G

HONING INNER BEVEL IN GOUGE

372

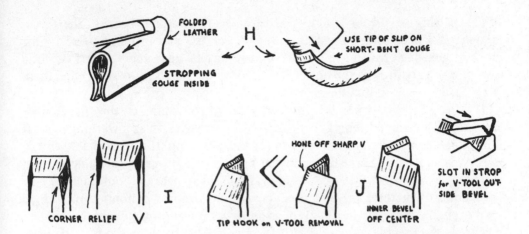

FOLDED LEATHER

H

STROPPING GOUGE INSIDE

USE TIP OF SLIP ON SHORT-BENT GOUGE

HONE OFF SHARP V

SLOT IN STROP for V-TOOL OUT SIDE BEVEL

CORNER RELIEF

I

V

TIP HOOK on V-TOOL REMOVAL

J

INNER BEVEL OFF CENTER

time to be sure I touch up the tip, which takes most wear. Unless the knife is very dull, a few swirls on whetstone and hone in turn should do it. Sharpness can be tested by trying the edge on a fingernail or on paper—it should "stick" on the former and slice the latter when drawn across (B). This operation will also detect any nicks or dull areas. Then the knife is drawn for a stroke or two over each side of the strop (C)—which is usually a piece of thin plywood with rough leather glued on one side, smooth on the other. The rough leather is impregnated with oil and crocus powder, while the smooth side has oil alone. Stropping is done with the blade heel-first; you can speed the operation by rolling the blade over the heel at the end of a stroke and reversing direction. Incidentally, it is good practice to learn to strop a tool almost absent-mindedly, so you can do it while you plan the next cut.

Carving tools are sharpened in much the same manner, particularly the firmer (D). However, the sharpening of gouges is a bit more tricky. The tool must be rotated slightly as it passes over the stone, so the entire edge is treated (E), and too much roll means rounded corners while too little means dull corners that will tear the wood rather than cutting it. Dullness in an area may be seen as a line of light (F). Also, because all sharpening is done from one side, a wire edge forms on the inside; it can be felt as a tiny burr with a fingernail. Thus the final operation in honing a gouge is to pass a slip down inside to take off the wire edge, and to do the same thing with a piece of leather in stropping. I have sketched the method (G, H). Some carvers thin the edges of chisels behind the cutting edge to relieve drag (I).

The parting or V-tool is a special problem to sharpen, because there is a tendency for a tit to form at the tip (J), or for the sides to slope back. This must be guarded against at all costs, and it may be advisable to whet or hone away just a very little of the bottom of the V at the tip so the cutting edge there is no thicker than it is at the sides.

This lengthy discussion is really only an introduction to the problem of sharpening tools and keeping them sharp, but it may serve as a warning against idle whacking or mistreatment of a tool during carving. It also explains why so many carvers hate sharpening and try to avoid it by every possible means, including disposable blades. Some of them have worked out methods of re-grinding in fixtures on belt sanders, and whetting and honing in a single operation on buffing wheels, even grinding and whetting gouges on shaped wheels as the manufacturers do. But for most of us, hand methods work best, because the frequency really isn't as great as it seems.

The carver who sharpens his own tools soon learns to treat the edges with care, both when in use and when in storage. Tools should be placed on the bench or workplace side by side, with their sharp ends toward you so you can pick out what you want rapidly and surely. They should be stored in slots so the edges don't touch, and when carried about should be in a portable carrier or in a canvas or other roll that protects the ends. Also, after arrival and before use, it is advisable at least to strop and probably to hone each tool; some professionals I know, like barbers, strop a tool just before they use it each time, and have hone and strop readily available all the time, as much in evidence as the tools they service.

How do you make the drawing fit the wood?

VERY OFTEN, the design you want to use doesn't quite fit the wood, usually because the design is too small. In these mechanized days, it is easy to make direct (same-size) copies, but the old photostat machine, which was capable of enlarging or reducing is not available except in art studios, which also often have photographic enlargers. If you can take, or have taken, a negative of the drawing, you can either have a print made of proper size, or put the negative in an enlarger and sketch the outlines to size, either on a sheet of paper or directly on the wood. For three-dimensional carvings, this is really all you need: a guide to saw away waste wood.

But let's say none of the above is available, and you have a two-view sketch that must be made double size. For a rough shape, the simplest method is to take a rubber band that is a couple of inches longer than the combined width of the wider sketch and the wood on which it is to be traced. (If you haven't one band that long, link several together.) Tie a pencil at one end of the band and make a small loop for a thumbtack at the other. Mark with ink a line one-half the distance from the tack to the pencil. Then Scotch-tape the sketch toward the left edge of a large breadboard or other flat surface that can take a thumbtack. Put the piece of wood beside it on the right. Set the thumbtack into the baseboard at the left, so the ink mark on the band is just short of the closest line on the sketch. Now stretch the band so the ink mark aligns with a point on the sketch, and move the wood blank until the pencil point is on the corresponding point on its surface. Draw on the block with the pencil and stretch the band as you draw to keep the ink line aligned with the lines of the sketch. (This is much more difficult to describe than it is to do.)

For triple size, the ink mark should be at one-third the distance from tack to pencil, and so on. For any enlargement, in fact, all you need is the ratio. Thus for $1\frac{1}{2}$ scale, divide the rubber-band length by 3 and put the ink mark at 2; for $2\frac{1}{4}$ scale, divide the band length by $4\frac{1}{2}$ and put the ink mark at 2. This method is in fact a crude pantograph, which most of us do not have.

The traditional method of enlarging is by the method of squares. Draw a grid of $\frac{1}{8}$-in (3.2 mm) squares on transparent paper, larger than the original sketch you have. Draw a similar grid on the wood blank or on a plain sheet of paper, but make the squares as much larger as you need, that is, for double size use $\frac{1}{4}$-in (6.4 mm) squares, for triple size $\frac{3}{8}$-in (9.6 mm) squares. Now lay the transparent grid over the sketch and copy the design on the block square by square. Save the grid, by the way; it can be used over and over—even on good silhouette photographs of a subject—and is particularly useful in laying out relief carvings, where precise outlines are necessary.

Another method is one I use quite frequently in laying out sketches from a photograph. Make a right-angle template of paper or plastic big enough so the arms extend to the width and height of the part of the photo you wish to copy. Set this over the photo so one arm is the base and the other just touches the leftmost element of the design, and hold it there with tape. Now prominent points can be located by measuring from the base and the side. If you lay out a similar right angle on the sketch pad, the points can be located one by one.

3 WAYS TO CHANGE SIZE

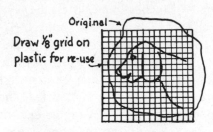

Original →
Draw ⅛" grid on
plastic for re-use

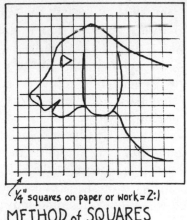

¼" squares on paper or work = 2:1

METHOD of SQUARES

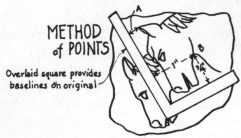

METHOD of POINTS

Overlaid square provides
baselines on original

A

B

1" ¾"

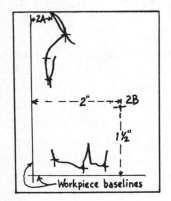

← 2A →

←— 2" —→ 2B

1½"

Workpiece baselines

RUBBER-BAND ENLARGER

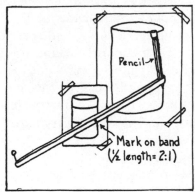

Pencil →

Mark on band
(½ length = 2:1)

Each measurement must of course be multiplied (or divided, if you are reducing) by the ratio of the size of the original to the copy, that is, twice for double size, and so on. This is slow, but very accurate, and suitable for complex designs. The sketch is of course made by drawing suitable-shape lines between the points. The number of points necessary is a function of the complexity of the design and your own skill at drawing.

How shall you finish your carvings?

FINISHING is so much a matter of the individual carving and of personal preference that it is difficult to lay down even general rules. Thus I have indicated all through this book what finish is used, as far as I can determine if I did not make the piece myself.

If a piece is made in soft wood and painted, I prefer to see the color put on thinly and wiped down somewhat, so the wood shows through in flat areas while the color accents lines and depressions. To prevent color from soaking in and over-coloring cross-grain areas, I flat-spray varnish first. Then I use oil pigments thinned with flat varnish or drier, but acrylics can be thinned and used the same way. Heavy painting creates a shiny, plastic effect and denies the hand work and the wood.

It is also possible to dye or stain soft-wood pieces; I have done both with pleasing results. I recently dyed the small birds of a mobile with cloth dyes in the absence of anything else; the colors were vivid at least. I also have a series of German sal-ammoniac-based stains called "Beiz," developed particularly for wood. These include wax, so color and polish are applied in a single operation, as with some American oil-and-wax stains. With the latter, and contrary to instructions on the can, it is usually preferable to give the piece a coat or two of flat (satin) spray varnish before staining; this prevents the stain from over-soaking in end grain and causing over-emphasis there.

For hardwood carvings, I prefer not to use fillers or much of the other paraphernalia and procedure of cabinetmaking—unless the carving is on a piece of furniture and must have a similar high gloss. There are two schools of thought on this, and all the variations between. Some sculptors like a high gloss on their work, so they sand and polish and fill and varnish or shellac, and rub down with steel wool just as furniture makers do. (There is now a plastic foam impregnated with grit, to replace steel wool.) The opposite school, of which I am a member, prefers texture, so uses sandpaper sparingly if at all, preferring to let tool marks show. Also, the wood is left without fillers or coloring, unless it be antiquing for depth, and finished with flat varnish and wax, oil and wax, or wax alone, depending upon wood and subject. We don't want a high polish, but a soft glow. There are now also several kinds of one-coat finishes, but they tend to create too high a gloss for me.

Basically, it's your choice. But test first on a scrap piece!

RELIEF
WOODCARVING

E. J. Tangerman

Fig. 1. Wide low-relief panels of local scenes face the balconies of a hotel in Puerto Moutt, Chile.

Contents

CHAPTER I

What Wood Is Best?

GENERALLY SPEAKING, THE GAMUT OF WOODS has been used in relief carving, sometimes because a wood was readily available or easily carved, sometimes because it was the right color, texture, pattern, had some significance or even rarity. Panels in churches have usually been carved in local woods such as walnut, pine, basswood, maple, butternut, cherry and apple in the United States; oak, lime, linden, apple and deal (fir or pine) in Europe; and in Egypt, sycamore and cedar. Panels carved for furniture have varied with fashion. Cherry wasn't used until 1675, mahogany didn't appear in Europe in any quantity until 1720 and teak came into use much more recently.

In the United States, the familiar woods for relief carving are black walnut, mahogany, cherry and other fruit woods; for signs or painted outdoor units, basswood and white pine are the usual choices. I have carved all of these, as well as teak, butternut, maple, pear, pecan, ash, vermilion, purpleheart, ebony and others. But for practical purposes, including available sizes and ease of working, I prefer pine, basswood, cherry, walnut and teak. Use walnut, mahogany, cherry and teak for relief work not to be painted. For exterior work, teak is superior because it does not rot or warp, and is not prone to insect attack.

Many of the exotic woods so familiar for veneering, such as avodire, satin, beef, purpleheart, greenheart, zebra and the African woods in general, are hard to carve because they split, have irregular grain or create other problems. The typical relief carving is a panel. Thus, wood should be straight-grained, so backgrounding and modelling can both be done well, without too much "figure," grain or knots, which compete with the carving, and without too much tendency to warp, splinter and split. It should also be dense enough to support detail, and preferably hard enough not to be worn away by cleaning and polishing through the years.

382

The color of a particular wood will sometimes suggest its use, such as myrtle for a mask, vermilion for a small award panel and purpleheart for an unusual subject such as a Celtic bird. But if you plan to carve in a wood with which you have no experience, try a sample before getting started on the general project. In most instances, I have indicated the woods used for the carvings pictured and described herein. Depending upon your experience with a wood, you may want to simplify the proposed design, or alter the arrangement to put a knot or flaw in an unimportant spot.

For any larger panels these days, it is usually necessary to assemble the panel from milled boards. On darker woods without conspicuous grain—walnut, mahogany, teak—the joining lines can be made to disappear almost entirely. They must, however, have smooth-planed edges for good joints, and should preferably be dowelled, glued and clamped to assure tightness. The wood should also be relatively thick; ½- and 1-in (13- and 25.4-mm) panels of pine, walnut and mahogany tend to warp and move with the weather regardless of finish. If you anticipate or encounter appreciable warpage, brace the back of the panel with screwed-on battens across-grain, or with angle irons or aluminum angles. I have used the latter in a number of instances, even to assemble a walnut mailbox of ½-in (13-mm) wood, carved on surfaces and edges. It has held for ten years, completely exposed (with marine-varnish finish). I have also seen thick relief carvings a hundred or more years old in which the center of the back was hollowed appreciably to counteract warpage, just as old-time in-the-round figures were split and hollowed out to avoid checking.

CHAPTER II

Some Suggestions on Tools

Buy them as you need them, not for stock

THE KNIFE IS THE MOST VERSATILE of woodcarving tools and works fine for carving relatively small or hand-sized pieces in-the-round; but it does have limitations in making larger pieces and cutting concave or intaglio surfaces. Some adaptations of blade shapes have been made, such as hooks and spoons, but they have only limited capacity. Though I am a life-long knife user, I must admit that there are projects for which only chisels make sense. These include almost all relief carving, unless it is silhouettes or pierced work—which is essentially flattened in-the-round carving.

This does not mean that the knife is abandoned in relief. Far from it. I find it most reliable for details and hard-to-reach places. It does mean, however, that you should have available half a dozen or so chisels and some way of holding the work securely. This is because the chisel is driven by arm rather than hand muscles, making force and length of stroke less controllable on many cuts. Also, tool selection and maintenance become more important.

Because relief carving is less portable in most instances than whittling, you don't really need a pocketknife at all; you can work quite well with a fixed-blade carver's knife in any of several shapes, as seen in figure 2. I use a fairly standard one. In either case, however, you need a good point. As to chisels, this will depend a good deal upon what you are planning to carve, whether it is small or large, simple or involved, with large surfaces or small ones. Generally speaking, small tools can be used on large carvings but large tools may not be useful on small ones. In fact, professional carvers in under-developed countries, who have only a few tools, tend to have small-bladed ones—often without handles—and only a club for a mallet. They take more cuts but reduce the risk of breakage.

384

Carver's chisels have been made and used for so long that they have their own special terminology. The flat chisel, like a carpenter's but thinner and sharpened from both sides so it doesn't dig, is called a *firmer* (see sketches). If the edge is sharpened at an angle, it is a *skew firmer*; if the corners of the edge are rounded, it is called a *bullnose* and can actually be used for many of the same operations as a flat gouge. Then there is the *V-tool* or *parting tool*, which is really two firmers joined at an angle (usually acute) along one side, for cutting a V-groove in a single pass. Variations of this tool rarely seen nowadays are the *macaroni*, which cuts a flat-bottomed trench, and the *fluteroni*, which makes a similar groove with rounded corners.

The workhorse tools of the woodcarver are the gouges—curved-edge tools that come in a bewildering array of shapes and sizes. These range from the *veiner*, with a half-circle cross section that can be as small as $\frac{1}{32}$ or $\frac{1}{16}$ in (.8 or 1.6 mm) across inside, through the *fluter*, similar but U-shaped in cross section, to large and very flat gouges up to 2½ in (6.4 cm) wide. In Europe, tools are sized by millimeters: 1, 2, 3, 4, 5, 6, 7, 8, 10, 12, 16, 20, 25, 30, etc. The arc of a gouge is called the *sweep*, commonly referred to by number according to the "London (or English) system." Thus a firmer is No. 1, a skew firmer 2, a flat gouge 3 and a semicircular one 11 or 12. (Some suppliers also assign numbers to special tools.)

Wide tools, and some narrower ones, are tapered down to the tang (which enters the handle) to reduce weight and increase versatility by giving greater clearance. These are called *spade* or *fishtail* tools. The shank may also be bent into a long arc (*long-bent*) or a short one (*short-bent*) to get the cutting edge into tight places. Some gouges are even bent backwards, known as *back-bent* tools. Small tools, such as an engraver's burin, are also made with short shanks and palm handles. They are fine for close work but cannot be used with the mallet, thus limiting their usefulness. Bent tools and palm tools are usually not required for simple relief carving; I rarely use them. The bent tools are harder to sharpen and tend to spring in use.

Carving tools may be pushed by hand in softer woods, in which case they are pushed with one hand, guided and restrained with the other. Thus the work should be held in some way, either in a vise, by a carver's screw (which goes through the workbench into the bottom of the workpiece) or, if it is a panel, by a clamp or on a benchplate (Fig. 6). I have nailed a panel to the bench through the waste wood or put it on a rubber doormat.

The regular mallet is shaped like an old-fashioned potato masher, usually in a hard and heavy wood like cocobola, and is available in various weights;

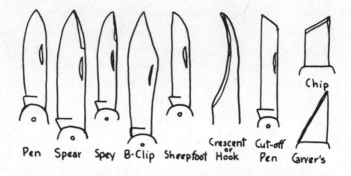

Fig. 2. Knife blades.

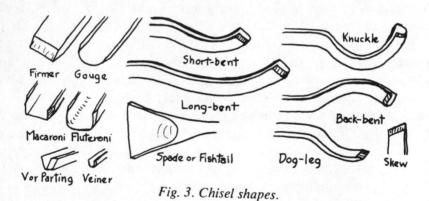

Fig. 3. Chisel shapes.

Fig. 4. Rasps and burin.

I've seen them up to 5 or 6 lb (2.3 or 2.7 kg). In these inventive days there are mallets cast of babbitt metal, turned from aluminum and made from old washing-machine wringer rolls and soft-faced hammers. In recent years, I have been using vinyl-faced ones—they're easier on my arthritis. I find that I can control the cut much better with a mallet than without.

There are also endless variations in tools, suiting the preferences of individuals or groups. H. M. Sutter, who has taught carving for over 40 years, has recently developed thin tools less likely to wedge and splinter the wood when setting-in is done (see the next chapter for Mr. Sutter's designs). Totem-pole and wooden-Indian carvers use chain saws, sometimes exclusively, while others prefer rotary grinders and flexible-shaft units equipped with cutters. I met one carver who uses a pneumatic or electric hammer, others who use belt sanders, circular saws, bandsaws or what have you. The principal intention in most of these cases is to get rid of the waste wood quickly, which is usually not a great problem in relief carving. Rotary tools can be used, but in my experience they tend to run, tear and burn the wood, and require such safety equipment as goggles and respirators. I do, however, use a router when I have large areas of background to cut down.

What tools to buy initially depends largely on what you plan to make and your personal preference. I seldom use more than ten tools, even on my most complicated carvings, but this may vary with the size of the work. I started with a kit of nine tools, about three of which I have hardly ever used. Charles M. Sayers, who taught panel carving, suggested five initial tools: ⅜- to ½-in (9.5- to 13-mm) or ⅝-in (16-mm) No. 39 parting or V-tool; ⅝-in (16-mm) No. 5 straight gouge; ⅞- or 1-in (22.4- or 25.4-mm) No. 3 straight gouge; ⅜-in (9.5-mm) No. 7 straight gouge; and a ⅜-in (9.5-mm) No. 3 straight gouge. H. M. Sutter also starts his students with five, plus an all-purpose knife: ⅜-in (9.5-mm) No. 3 straight gouge and a ⅝-in (16-mm) No. 5 straight gouge (these two preferably fishtail); ⅜-in (9.5-mm) No. 9 straight gouge; 1/16- or 1/32-in (1.6- or .8-mm) No. 11 veiner; and a 5/16- or ⅜-in (8- or 9.5-mm) parting or V-tool. My advice is to start with a similarly limited set and add tools as you need them, regardless of salesmen's suggestions. As you add tools, vary size and sweep considerably, and buy carpenter's chisels and gouges for big and rough work—they're cheaper and can take a beating. Beware, however, of patternmaker's gouges, which are sharpened inside on the concave surface.

It is easier to use chisels than knives, in my opinion, and faster on much work. When pounding, you must learn not to watch the handle but the cutting edge and to hold the mallet or chisel in either hand. Take it easy; don't try to remove all the waste wood in the first pass. In cross-grain cutting, start at an edge and work in. Don't work to the edge—you'll split out wood if you do. Keep the tools very sharp, or they'll tear wood on diagonal cuts. Soft woods require sharper tools than hard woods. Don't wedge out chips; cut them out. Don't use chisels to open paint cans or strip insulation off wires. Store them so the edges are protected—you can buy or make carrying rolls for this purpose.

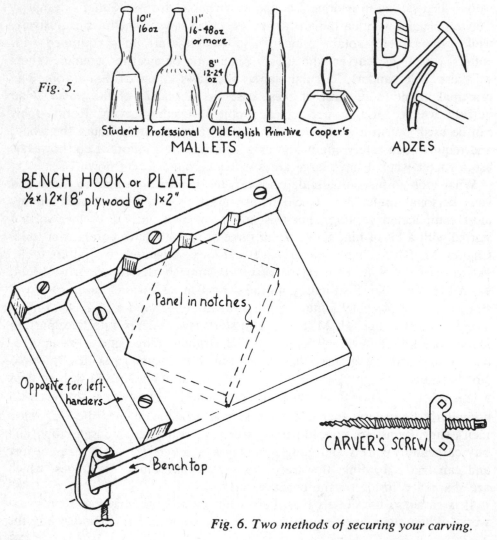

Fig. 5.

10"
16oz

11"
16-48oz
or more

8"
12-24 oz

Student Professional Old English Primitive Cooper's

MALLETS

ADZES

BENCH HOOK or PLATE
½×12×18" plywood ⓦ 1×2"

Panel in notches

Opposite for left-handers

CARVER'S SCREW

Benchtop

Fig. 6. Two methods of securing your carving.

CHAPTER III

Thin Tools Speed Setting-In

Some typical Sutter designs and ideas

H. M. SUTTER HAS MADE HIS OWN thin-bladed tools for some years because he found them better and more convenient to use on small panels. They make setting-in, particularly around curves, quicker and easier by reducing the wedging action—hence the crushing and splitting of fibres—and the number of steps. And, small tools are less clumsy for intricate work. Such tools work just as well as heavier chisels for grounding out, but are not as safe for digging or prying—which we shouldn't do anyway. Nor will they stand mallet pounding as well as the heavier chisels, though they can be used with a soft- or plastic-faced mallet. They are lighter, cheaper and less fatiguing to hold, particularly when compared to some American tools, which are much too thick in smaller sizes.

Mr. Sutter has recently found a commercial company willing to make his style of tool, so beginner sets are now available. Each consists of six tools: a firmer ¼ in (6.4 mm) wide, and gouges of ⅟₁₆-, ⅛-, ³⁄₁₆-, ¼- and ⁵⁄₁₆-in (1.6-, 3.2-, 5-, 6.4- and 8-mm) width, all No. 7 sweep. The second set has No. 7 ⅜- to ⅝-in (9.5- 16-mm) gouges and a ⅝-in (16-mm) firmer.

He rounds off the heel on each gouge and increases the length of the bevel on the firmer to make true thin blades, which allow for deeper cuts without crushing. He also reports that such tools have made a considerable difference in the quality of the work done by his students, as well as the complexity they can handle. The pine-cone design was a real challenge, even for an advanced student, but can now be done with relative ease. The same is true for the more difficult orchid design. Large curves are cut with an all-purpose knife or with larger chisels if they are available. Students have also found that this kind of tool is quite satisfactory for carving in-the-round pieces.

Several of Mr. Sutter's patterns and finished pieces are pictured here. More basic designs are shown and described in my earlier book, *Carving Flora and Fables in Wood.* My students at Brasstown, North Carolina, usually skilled as whittlers but newly introduced to chisels, have done the designs shown there and here quite successfully.

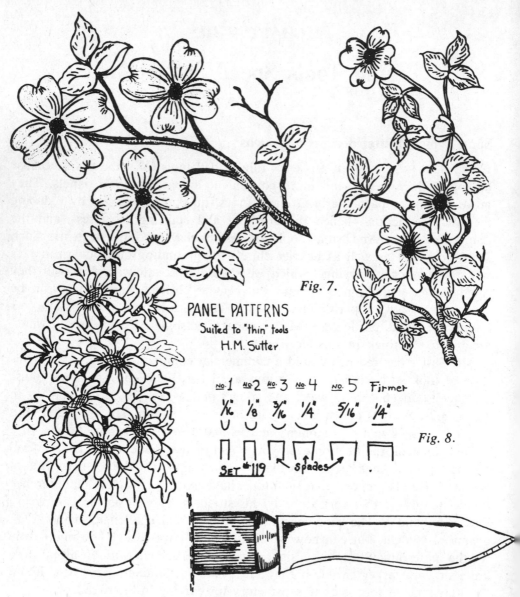

Fig. 7.

PANEL PATTERNS
Suited to "thin" tools
H.M. Sutter

No. 1   No. 2   No. 3   No. 4   No. 5   Firmer
1/16"   1/8"   3/16"   1/4"   5/16"   1/4"

Fig. 8.

SET #119   ← spades →

Fig. 9. *All-purpose knife.*

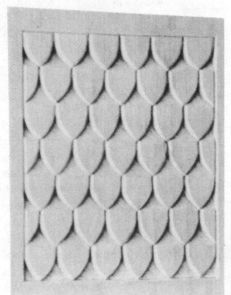

Fig. 10. Panel of overlapping simple shapes is a good exercise in setting-in and grounding. Lower portion of each leaf is sloped in to outline the next leaf shape. Conventional thick chisels would split the leaves apart in such a design.

Figs. 11–12 (above and left). This simple head can be raised above a background, trenched or silhouetted. Modelling is shallow but precise; thus, the project is more difficult than it appears to be. This is a good exercise in using the V-tool.

391

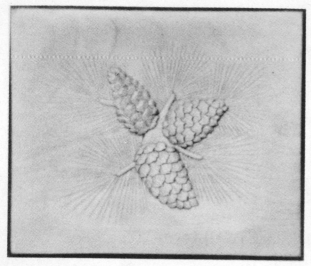

*Figs. 13–14 (left and below).
Three pine cones are another
good subject for thin-bladed
tools because of the overlapping seeds. Such designs should
be trenched, with trenching
sloping up to the surface all
around, so needles can be cut
into the surface with a V-tool.
A groove can replace a raised
rib here with no loss of realism.*

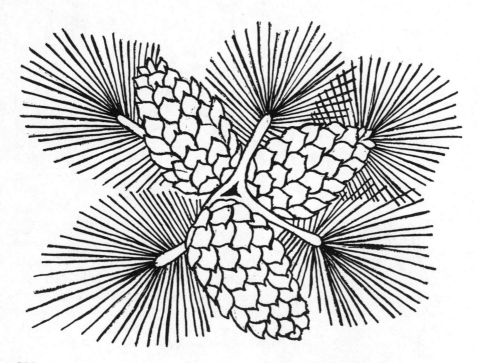

Figs. 15–16. Simple group of stylized jack-in-the-pulpits, an Art Nouveau design. Stems are V-grooves.

Fig. 17. Head of a carousel horse is difficult to carve accurately in relief because of its twist. Although the eye is correctly positioned for in-the-round carving, it appears high and too far forward here.

393

Figs. 18–19 (left and above). The rose is a complex project requiring fairly deep grounding, perhaps ½ in (13 mm) or more, to get petals well shaped. Note random-cut gouge background.

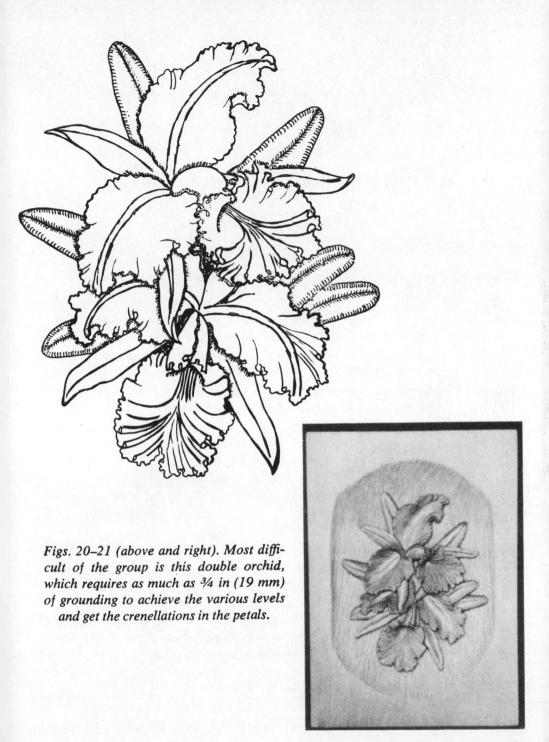

Figs. 20–21 (above and right). Most diffi-
cult of the group is this double orchid,
which requires as much as ¾ in (19 mm)
of grounding to achieve the various levels
and get the crenellations in the petals.

CHAPTER IV

An Introduction to Relief Carving

Definitions, techniques, shapes, finishes and backgrounds

CARVING IN RELIEF IS A VERSATILE approach and can offer many more possibilities than carving in-the-round, particularly when producing a legend or lettering a panel—the basics of which are covered in Chapters 16 and 17. Thus it is essential for signs, furniture, mouldings, framing and diaper patterns. It has traditionally been at least as familiar as in-the-round carving, but is less common in America where so many carvers are primarily knife whittlers. (And the knife is not the best tool for concave surfaces, part of many elements of panels.) There are also those who find relief carving to be more difficult than three-dimensional full figures, because the third dimension must be foreshortened and perspective may be involved. Further, if a regular geometric or other pattern is carved, it is easier to avoid making mistakes than it is trying to correct them. An error in an in-the-round figure, especially a caricature, is likely to go unnoticed, but an error in formal-pattern relief carving is likely to be quite visible.

Relief carving was originally just the scraping or incising of lines depicting something, probably at first on cave walls and then on wooden tools and the like. The Egyptians developed this into trench carving, which is simply digging a trench in the surface around a subject and modelling the subject itself in low relief so that no part of the design stands above the background panel level. In medieval Europe, however, and in some other areas of the world, relief carving progressed until it was sometimes extremely elaborate and might incorporate in-the-round elements or a close approximation of them.

Relief carving was thus classified by the Italians: High relief or *alto-relievo* carries projection from the background to half or more of the natural thickness of the subject. Some parts may be undercut or completely free of the

396

background. In low relief, *basso-relievo* or *bas-relief*, the projection is slight and no parts are undercut or detached. Less commonly defined are half relief (*mezzo-relievo*) and the very flat relief of medals and coins called *stiacciato*. Hollow relief, also called *cavo-relievo, intaglio-relevato*, coelanaglyphic sculpture or simply trench carving, is that in which the background is not cut away; the figure or object being carved is outlined by a deep groove but has no elements higher than the background. This technique is effective for coats of arms, monograms, initials, lettering and other carving on a flat surface, particularly if it may be damaged by bumping or abrasion. This is not to be confused with intaglio, which is most easily described as reversed relief.

Fig. 22. Detail from a massive door in the Cathedral of Seville exemplifies high-relief style of former centuries. Note that female figures and floral swags between them are practically in-the-round.

In intaglio carving, the design is hollowed out so that material pressed or poured into it comes out as an image in relief. The most familiar objects in intaglio are cookie and butter moulds. When a pattern is pressed into sand to create a mould for metal, the mould itself is an intaglio. This is not a cameo, which is normally limited to a head or bust carved in multilayered stone or shell so that the carving is in one color, the background in another. However, a head or bust carved through a surface layer of one color into a differing color beneath, so that not only color change but reversal of the depths is attained, is an intaglio and a cameo.

A figure becomes in the round only when the third dimension is correct.

397

Fig. 23. Alonso Berruguete's life-size head of John the Baptist projects from this walnut panel in the Cathedral of Toledo.

Thus, a dog or horse carved in silhouette but flattened in body thickness is still relief carving, as is pierced carving, regardless of whether it contains in-the-round elements. The same is true of high relief, which often contains foreground figures cut free of the background; they may be in the round themselves but are still part of a relief carving. I have done relief carving on trees, bowls, napkin rings and even on wooden shoes. These are, in a sense, three-dimensional, as is a mobile made up of relief silhouettes. It is possible to have two relief carvings on opposite sides of the same silhouetted piece of wood, with either the same or different subjects. It is also possible to inlay relief carvings, particularly very shallowly carved ones, with metal, stone, plastic or shell, or with other woods. Some peoples particularly skilled at relief carving, like the New Zealand Maori and American Northwest Coast Indians, inlay many of their carvings with shell as a matter of custom. So do some furniture makers, particularly in France.

Most modern relief carving is low relief and made in relatively small pieces exhibited at or near eye level. Low-relief carving, however, is particularly susceptible to light intensity and direction, so such work as a pediment high above eye level or a boat counter well below may require special correction. Also, the third dimension in any relief carving is not simply a flattened version of the actual or in-the-round dimension—it often must incorporate a difference in shape. A rounded surface may have to be carved somewhat angular to produce an edge that creates a difference in light reflection. A given line may have to be shorter or longer than a matching one on the opposite side of center, since elements that would normally be at different depths must be at about the same depth. Thus, differentials must be optical.

Effects must be created by texturing, by making a simple groove different on either side, by flattening or even gouging a surface and even by tinting and "antiquing" (my own word for darkening deeper lines and areas). Tinting or painting on relief carvings, however, is not done nearly as often as it is on the in-the-round figures, possibly because the latter are often the adult equivalent of toys while relief carvings are more nearly decoration.

It was the custom before and after Grinling Gibbons, master of the silhouetted and high-relief floral swag, to cover almost all of a surface with intricate patterns, usually incorporating vines and foliage in some fashion. One authority said that the English and Germans believed 50 percent or so of a surface should be carved, the Italians 80 percent or more and the Indians and Chinese 100 percent. Modern carvers tend to hold back, carving only portions of a surface and leaving the wood grain itself to show over extensive areas. In fact, there is much use of wood grain left utterly plain. Economy may be involved in some of this, just as it is in mounting a carved or uncarved silhouette against a contrasting background that may be glass, plastic or textile rather than wood.

Geometric patterns, bust portraits and floral groups are essentially in one plane, so perspective is not a problem; nor is composition, except in the case of the floral group. Thus, it is relatively easy to carve any of these in relief. But too many neophytes promptly decide to make a scene or multiple group. And therein often lies basic trouble, because creating an artistic composition or scene requires at least a little knowledge of art.

First are the basic rules for composition, which appear in any text on drawing or painting. They include these: Elements should not all be in the same pose, or of the same size; elements should not touch, but should either be clearly separate or overlap; a line or shape in a frontal element should not be immediately next to a similar line or shape in the background.

Eliminate extraneous details as scale is reduced. Look around you and you'll see that at a relatively short distance the nails in a fence and the veins in leaves disappear. At greater distance, the fence palings or rails begin to blur and the leaves themselves merge into a green tree silhouette. At a little distance, cats don't have whiskers, birds don't have feathers and men have no lines in their faces. If you put such details in, you create a sort of cartoon or caricature rather than a picture. It is also unnecessary to show every branch of a tree, every number on a license plate or house, every pane in a window or every shingle on a roof, particularly if it is back a bit in the composition. You don't have to fill every part of the picture with objects. In nature there is open sky, clear fields and smooth water—you'll find the hard way that adding waves, individual leaves and clouds is very difficult in woodcarving. *Suggest* a telephone or power line; don't try to carve the wires unless you need them to support a flock of birds. Leave out elements of the background that are unessential to the story you're trying to tell or to identification of the scene. Your eye does the same thing—you don't notice detail unless you study a scene very closely. A painter can grey or blur such elements, suggest them with a blob of color. But you cannot to the same degree, so it is often better to leave them out entirely. Even on a head portrait, it is not necessary to carve away the background all the way to the edge or to some rigid mechanical shape; the panel itself provides that. Framing, too, is often unnecessary, as an unframed carving can suggest that a scene goes beyond the limits of the wood.

Another vital consideration is perspective. Primitive painters and carvers are not concerned with it, but everybody else *is*, including the viewer. Under normal circumstances, it is unlikely that you will be considered a primitive; you are far more likely to be judged simply as crude, whether your friends tell you so or not. Remember: A nearby house is larger than its mate that is farther away, the rear of a house is smaller than the front and the far ends are smaller than the middle. You must learn about vanishing points and how to achieve the effect of distance on a flat surface just as a painter must. If you don't, your people and buildings will look like postage stamps poorly stuck against a background, and a continuous line of anything—road, people, train cars, flying birds—will look very wrong. Things in nature are not rigid and unchanging unless they're dead. There is always some variation between like objects, animate or inanimate. There is also perspective that effects size and shape; for example, an animal standing at an angle to you will appear to lose size at the farthest portion of its body.

Fig. 24. Small oak picture frame from Italy shows florid and deep-relief formal style of the past century. It combines several motifs and is made to appear even heavier with black stain.

Figs. 25–26 (above and right). In these panels by T. E. Haag of Tualatin, Oregon, a textured background clarifies the silky smoothness of the figure itself.

It is very easy to design a panel so that an object in the background looks too large compared to one nearer your eye, to attempt to put an essentially tall object in a wide frame or to have a free-form object in a rigid panel (or vice versa). There is such a thing as deliberate distortion for emphasis, but it is a weak defense for a beginner. You've got to learn first how to do it right, something many "modern artists" have never learned. One good way to incorporate perspective and composition into a carving is to take various photographs of the subject or scene and have a jury of friends pick the best one. Then you can project the negative and trace the parts you want or have an enlargement made to your intended size (if it is within reason) to serve as both a pattern and a guide. All in all, I find the polyglot panel (see those for a door in Chapter 15) much easier to plan and carve, because even scale is abandoned.

When laying out a panel, use pencil rather than pen unless the wood is dark and you are sure all lines will be cut away. I have had cleanup problems with soft-tip pen lines, particularly in color on light woods where the ink may penetrate and stain. On most panels, it is not necessary to sink the background very deeply. I have one in ebony in which the background is so shallow that it is really distinguished only by its surface pattern. Depth is, of course, a matter of choice. The deeper you go, the more modelling you can do (and the more like in-the-round carving it is); but you will also encounter proportionately more undercutting and lateral-view problems. It is easier, and much faster, to learn something about perspective and panel carving before you attempt a piece like *The Last Supper* for your church and find, when you've finished, that the minister or priest decides it will hang best in some dimly lit alcove.

On small panels, I often do not sink the background more than ⅛ in (3.2 mm); on larger pieces like my "bug tree," I may ground to a depth of ½ in (13 mm) or more. Several factors will determine a practical grounding depth—namely, how many elements are overlapping, how much detail is involved and how much modelling is necessary. If there are several planes of depth, it is best to ground a little deeper in most cases (at least until you learn how to make one object appear in front of another). Also, there is the matter of panel thickness; if it is relatively thin, say 1 in (2.54 cm) or less, it is inadvisable to ground deeply. If extensive modelling is to be done on a bust, for example, or on some other fairly complex figure, it may be advisable to ground as deeply as 1 in (2.54 cm). Also, when you ground, the difference in top and bottom surface areas may cause the panel to warp slightly during carving.

Cutting down the background, or grounding, is done this way: First, outline the area to be lowered with a V-tool or veiner. This cuts surface fibres and reduces the likelihood of splintering at the surface. Then drive in suitable gouges and firmers vertically along the notch to limit the cut area. I usually use small ones, such as ⅛ and ¼ in (3.2 and 6.4 mm) wide. If grounding is shallow, the setting-in or vertical cutting can be done in a single step, but usually it is best to take it in several steps to avoid crushing and breakage from the tool heel's wedging action. It is thus possible to set-in ¹⁄₁₆ to ⅛ in (1.6 to 3.2 mm) per step, depending upon wood density, hardness, tendency to split and width of sections between set-in areas (a little experimenting is advisable here). After the line is set-in, cut down the area to be grounded with a flat gouge along the cut lines, then set-in deeper—and so on. Final

403

depth can be measured with a pin gauge, a mark on a rule or scale or the like, but I find that in most cases my eye is accurate enough. This is true particularly when the background is to be textured or antiqued, in which case slight variations in depth from grounded area to grounded area are unimportant. It is also possible, if areas are relatively large and simple in outline, to rout the wood out. This assures a fairly uniform depth but may create burned lines, gouged spots and the like, as is usual with power carving.

On grounding work, I almost always use a light mallet with the chisels. It gives me better control of the tool and is less likely to cause breakouts and running of the tool into splits. Avoid wedging out chips; this causes breakouts too. Also, when grounding on two sides of a section I am extremely careful when the width of that section is ⅜ in (9.5 mm) or less on woods

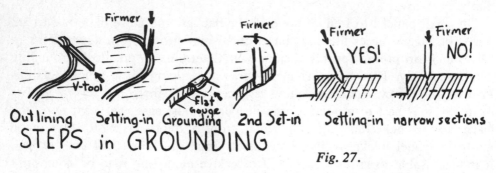

Outlining   Setting-in   Grounding   2nd Set-in   Setting-in narrow sections

STEPS in GROUNDING

Fig. 27.

such as teak and walnut. I ground out on one side as described above, but on the other I lean the tool when setting-in so that its edge cuts into the area to be grounded and away from the narrow section. The wood remaining will then be thicker at the bottom than at the top and require a follow-up operation to make the edge vertical, but this is better than glueing back a split-out section. I find, from years of performing this operation, that larger tools can do more damage than the time they save. Large gouges, for example, will tend to break out the wood inside the sweep, which is just too bad if you are outlining a convex arc. Also, the flat gouge is a much better roughing tool than the firmer, which tends to catch at the corners and gouge additional, deeper lines. (A remedy for this problem is to grind off the corners of the firmer slightly, making what is called a bullnose tool.) When the ground is fairly level, a firmer can be used for final smoothing—if you really want it smooth. In this cleanup operation, you may also find dog-leg tools very helpful for getting into tight spots. I find that in really tight corners my penknife is still my safest tool.

After you use a mallet for a while, you will develop a rhythm of, say, two or three light taps per cut. But watch out—the same strength of blow will drive the chisel in deeper with the grain than across it. You'll find it best to ground out large areas first and then go back to do the smaller and intricate areas with more care. You should also set-in across-grain first, so any tendency to split as you set-in along the grain will be halted by a previously cut line. I find that I may work progressively, doing some grounding and then some modelling and even final carving in rotation. This relieves the boredom of setting-in for days before you can get at the interesting part. I also start at the bottom of a carving in most cases. Then my hands and arms rub in some patina and, if it's a warm day, they don't erase as-yet-uncarved lines. I find, too, that I can then feel rough spots and clean them up early, thus saving final cleanup time.

Finish or texture of the background varies with subject, relative areas of background, flat surfaces in the subject, depth of grounding and the like. Large areas of background should probably be subordinated in some way, either by texturing them to break up—rather than reflect—light rays or by antiquing them slightly with stain. In the Far East, the tendency is to texture all backgrounds with small stamps; simple ones can be produced by filing lines across the flattened end of a spike. The pattern should be small, so it does not mash major fibres and cause splintering of the ground. Another device is to break up the background by shallow veiner or V-tool lines in either a regular or random pattern. An easier but less positive method is to produce a pattern of small depressions with a relatively flat spoon gouge or a dental burr or ball cutter in a rotary tool. I find darkening the background preferable because it also makes the grounding appear deeper and accents the lines of the carving. On porous woods, such a treatment should be preceded by a couple of coats of matte varnish to seal the surface and reduce contrast between end-grain and cross-grain areas. Stain should be brushed in carefully, wiped off after a short interval, and should not be a great deal darker than the surface color. On woods like apple, I use mahogany; on teak I use walnut and on walnut I use walnut stain with a little black added. (Don't use black as a background unless you intend to be startling, because black is "dead" unless it has a shine.)

When you model the surface of a design, it is actually a repetition of grounding and should be done in much the same way, with stop cuts to prevent splitting off of surface wood. The basic difference is that the modelling will probably not be more than a third as deep as the background, unless the background is very shallow. Do *not* begin by chamfering all edges the way a whittler does a dog blank. You may want to keep some edges sharp and hard so they stand out and up. Rounding an edge in relief carving tends to obliterate or subordinate it—and you want scales, feather or hairlines and the like to be visible. Small features like an eye or a brow line can on occasion be inverted as grooves instead of raised surfaces. And errors can sometimes be corrected simply by carving the erroneous area a little deeper and increasing the depth of the adjacent area until there is no sharp break. However, any really deep correction will be visible in most lighting.

Most ancient Greek statues had the eyes painted in, so the eye itself was rounded as it is in nature, and the figure appears to be blind. My remedy for this is to drill a small-diameter hole for the iris, which blocks out light and looks appropriately black. I mention this here because it is a kind of texturing you will find necessary if panels are to be convincing. A flat surface reflects light, even without sanding and reflective finishes. This is true particularly in hard woods if you cut with sharp tools rather than dull ones or rasps, rotary grinding burrs or other primarily abrasive wood removers. Thus, to reduce glare and highlights where you don't want them, you must texture the area. This can be done exactly as you would on the background—with a pattern or random cutting of shallow veiner or V-tool lines, or by stamping with very small and overall patterns. Any of these textures breaks up impinging light rays and reduces reflections.

A few more pointers: If your tool slips or something else goes wrong, repair the spot at once before you lose the chip or magnify the error. Use a good grade of glue with the cut-out chip, with another whittled to proper shape (be sure it's also proper in grain and color) or even with mixed glue and sawdust as a filler. Then work somewhere else for a while, admittedly a hard thing to do. I use Elmer's Glue-all® for most carvings but find a plastic cement better for outside work. Also, Elmer's works fine for appliquéing pieces of wood or building up a blank and, in such cases, can be cut 50-50 with water. It then penetrates deeper, dries faster and saves glue by covering more surface more easily. In any case, sand or cut away any glue spillage because it is likely to affect the finish later on.

If you want particular thickness only in some areas, buy wood in a thickness necessary for the panel and glue scraps on top in the areas that must be thicker. I've done this for a coat-of-arms on a panel, the bulge of a hull and for a special element on the front corner of a house. The same technique can be used to take care of a rotted, discolored or worm-eaten area. Just cut out the rot or knot and replace it with a selected piece of the same wood carefully fitted to the hole. It may prove better to have an irregular shape than a regular one, since masking such a line is often easier. Be sure any large filled area has the same color and grain (or figure) as the wood around it. And don't sand the area until you're done, if then—imbedded grains of sand can play havoc with the edge of a woodcarving tool.

It is also important to experiment with V-cuts or others when defining the edge of something. A V-cut that makes an accurate vee with the surface will simply be a defining line, but a V-cut with one side vertical and the other faired out onto the adjacent surface will make the edge behind the vertical wall appear to be higher than the adjacent surfaces. Cheeks can be given the appearance of being behind a nose by making the nostril lines sharply vertical and the nose outline above them more vertical than the curves of the cheeks. The same thing applies to brow and ear lines, beard lines and hairlines on faces, as well as to scenes. One panel I saw recently included three houses, each looking as if it had been pasted atop a crudely shaped mound. The problem was that the carver had a vertical V-cut along the bottom of the house so that it projected from, rather than rested on, the ground. The perspective was also wrong. These things must be learned through experimentation; you can't carve a good *Last Supper* on the first try, any more than Leonardo could paint it.

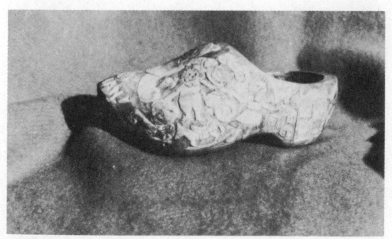

Fig. 28. Relief carving need not be on a planar surface. This is a willow-wood shoe from the Netherlands that I carved in polyglot fashion. Motifs pictured are familiar children's toys.

407

Figs. 29–30–31 (above and below). Araucano and Araucana (male and female) busts in mahogany-like rauli wood are modern high-relief silhouettes carved in Chile, where woodcarving is infrequent (possibly because of wood scarcity). Heads and chests are correct in the third dimension, while back halves of bodies are flattened. Each is about 6 in (15 cm) tall.

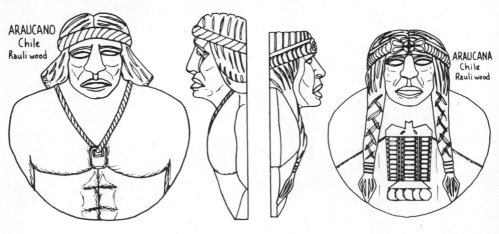

ARAUCANO
Chile
Rauli wood

ARAUCANA
Chile
Rauli wood

Fig. 32 (left). This "mask" from Easter Island is actually a flat panel for wall hanging. It illustrates the strength of stylized modern surfaces and shapes, incorporating pierced carving and simple V-groove texturing. It is about 14 in (36 cm) tall.

Fig. 33 (above). Russian bowl is lacquer-finished, then decorated in relief with gouge cuts through to the base wood.

Fig. 34 (below). Attenuated silhouette figures such as these from Israel are actually relief carvings—third dimension is negligible.

Figs. 35–36–37 (left, above and on facing page). These seem like in-the-round carving but are actually medium relief on the surface of a log. They are by Bogosav Zivkovic, and are now in a gallery in Svetozarevo, Yugoslavia.

410

Fig. 37.

Figs. 38–39 (left and below). Teak box about 4 × 6 in (10 × 15 cm) is probably from Sri Lanka; it has the familiar elephant motif on the lid and even more familiar lotus and floral designs on its sides. Backgrounds, typical of East Indian work, are stippled all over—probably with a punch—and figures are stylized to a considerable degree.

Edge of front
Edge of top panel
Elements are modelled
Hinged joint
Note that flower has 7 petals
Background stippled with punch or veiner
Lotus-petal bands on top rim

EAST INDIAN MOTIFS on a teak box

Figs. 40–41 (above and left). Two bird panels by T. E. Haag illustrate the wide range of scenic depiction possible in low relief. Figure 40 (above) shows a detailed duck against a textured background, while figure 41 (below) depicts three stylized flying swans against a patterned background. One is framed, the other has an unusual outlining with latitude and longitude lines, bowed and spaced to give the flat panel a global effect.

CHAPTER V

Belt Buckles, Plain and Fancy

Two experts share their experience with you

BELT BUCKLES ARE AN EASY, UTILITARIAN way to display both beautiful wood and good carving. Structure and design can suit your fancy, ranging from simple line patterns to elaborate modelling, appliqués or inlays of metal or stone on both exhibited front and important back ends. You can also inset small shaped pieces such as gears or animals in a plastic set into a well of wood. My childhood crony John Phillip, now of Whittier, California, and Harrison Neustadt, of Sunrise, Florida, have each made dozens of buckles for gift or sale. Mr. Neustadt has even designed jigs for bending and inserting the findings into the wood without splitting. He usually makes the buckle of wood alone, while Mr. Phillip backs the wood with a metal frame to which the findings are soldered.

The basic ingredient is an interesting piece of wood cut to a blank of the desired shape—round, oval, square, rectangular, petiolate or free form. It should be ¼ to ⅜ in (6.4 to 9.5 mm) thick and a bit wider than the standard belt widths of 1, 1½ or 2 in (2.54, 4 or 5.1 cm). If buckle length is more than about 2 in (5.1 cm), the shape should be slightly curved to fit the abdomen. If the blank is circular, it can be turned and ridged or otherwise machine-shaped before carving.

John Phillip's favorite fastening is based on a clip, or combined hook, that can be stainless steel, brass or even a coat-hanger or similar stiff iron wire. The bent form should be strong enough to resist midriff expansion after a heavy meal, so that anything attached need only support itself. The loop end (see sketches) is made to fit the desired belt width, and the hook engages in the belt holes. The belt, incidentally, is usually the kind that comes with snaps for easy buckle interchange. You can also cut an undistinguished buckle off a standard belt and rivet one of these in its place because the new assembly adds a couple of inches of length.

Least complicated is stapling the clip to the back of the blank. You can make suitable staples by bending brads into U's after sharpening both ends. The brads should not be long enough to go through the blank and in brittle or very hard wood, or in cross-grain pieces, they should be driven into pre-drilled holes. A more secure design involves routing or grooving a slot of the desired shape into the wood, then glueing the clip in securely. However, Mr. Phillip usually solders the clip onto a plate of thin stainless, brass or copper of the blank shape and contour, roughens the face of the backing and glues on the wood. The backing plate should not be more than $\frac{1}{16}$ in (1.6 mm) thick or the buckle will be overweight. You can use a very thin plate and leave it sufficiently oversize to crimp it around the wood as a jeweller sets a gem into a bezel, but this is normally unnecessary because there is little stress on the facing.

Mr. Neustadt uses no backing. His findings are just the C-shaped clip and a pin, both forced by a jig into pre-drilled holes. The findings have grooves near the ends, so glue will hold them in place.

Finish can suit your taste. I usually use a spray coat or two of matte varnish, followed by waxing. Mr. Neustadt has been using his own mixture for 20 years on all of his craftwork, including furniture, bowls and platters. It is a 50-50 mixture of polyurethane and boiled linseed oil, applied with an old sock. He says that his earliest pieces have improved with age and now have a lovely patina.

If you want to inlay metal or stone inserts in the face of the buckle, set them securely so they do not catch clothing. Mr. Phillip does it by placing the insert where he wants it, clamping it, then scratching around it with a sharp scriber. He reinforces the scribed line with a series of sharp center-punch holes, then routs the socket in his drill press with a small bit running at high speed. In this way he can shape areas that a knife would chip and break out. He drills only as deep as the insert, of course. The cavity is filled with Goodyear Pliobond® cement, enough so that the adhesive will seep out around the edges when the insert is seated. Next, he sprinkles fine-sanding dust from the wood (be sure it is the same wood) all around the edge and mixes it with the adhesive. Then he taps the insert all over with a small mallet—or hammer, if it is metal—to fill any gaps or small breakouts. He folds a small piece of waxed paper over the glued assembly to prevent sticking, on top of which is laid a block of hard wood, sawed to the same radius as the buckle top, with a gap to clear any projecting surface. He then sets three small clamps at ends and center and allows at least 48 hours drying time. When the assembly is dry, he removes block and paper, sands and fine-files the surface, then paraffin-buffs.

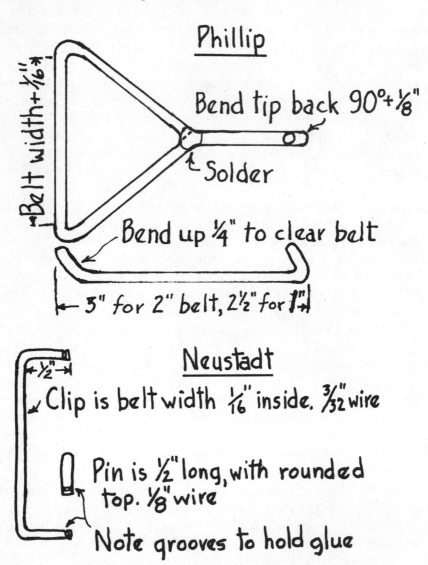

Phillip

Bend tip back 90°+ ⅛"

Solder

Bend up ¼" to clear belt

5" for 2" belt, 2½" for 1"

Belt width+ 1/16"

Neustadt

½"

Clip is belt width ⅟₁₆" inside. ³/₃₂" wire

Pin is ½" long, with rounded top. ⅛" wire

Note grooves to hold glue

Fig. 42.

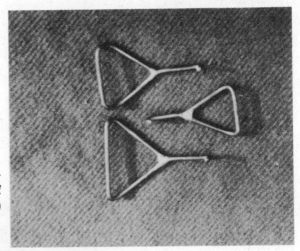

Fig. 43. John Phillip's form-ed clips to fit 1-, 1½- and 2-in (2.54-, 3.8- and 5-cm) belts. Joints are soldered.

Fig. 44. Top buckle is 1¾ × 3¾ in (4.4 × 9.6 cm), curved, of South American walnut relief-carved with a buck's head. Upper-left buckle is redwood burl 1¾ × 2½ in (4.4 × 6.4 cm), with chamfering only. One at upper right is California walnut burl, 2¼ × 3 in (5.7 × 7.6 cm), with inlaid masks of walrus ivory, hand-carved in relief. At lower left is Australian gum, turned and carved to fit a lady's 1-in (2.54-cm) belt. Lower right buckle is California walnut, 2¼ × 3 in (5.7 × 7.6 cm), with Indian sun design of darkened grooves and gold-stone insert.

417

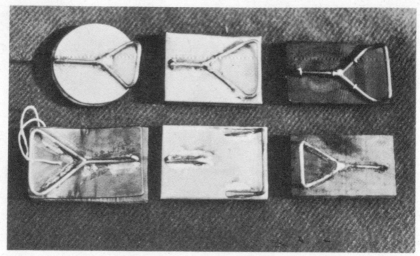

Fig. 45. Varied buckle-back arrangements by John Phillip include soldered clips on stainless (top left) and brass (lower left). At upper right is a clip secured with staples made of 1-in (2.54-cm) bent brads. At lower right, the clip has been glued into a groove. (Neither of these has a backing of metal.) At top center is a two-part clip, while at bottom center the backing of thin stainless has been crimped like a bezel around the wood front. Here, a separate pin and clip are soldered to the backing.

Fig. 46. A more elaborate clip, hinged in a soldered-on socket to give greater flexibility. The pin is soldered on separately. Face is walnut, incised with a simple initial.

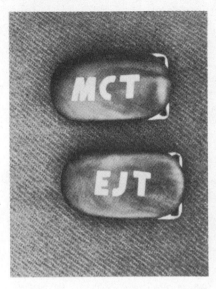

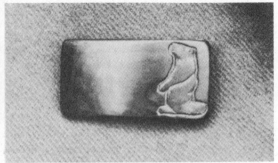

Fig. 47 (left). "His" and "Hers" matching buckles of walnut, curved, with inlaid stainless initials. By John Phillip.

Fig. 48. This walnut facing is carved with a trenched low-relief prairie dog I copied from a photograph.

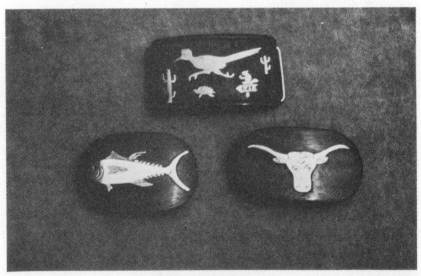

Fig. 49. More walnut buckles by John Phillip. Inserts are brass for upper one and steer head, stainless for fish.

419

CHAPTER VI

Crystal Gazer—A Composite

PERIODICALLY, I FIND IT INTERESTING to make a composite carving, combining wood with some other object or material to provide a striking contrast. Thus, I have used a gold wedding ring to make a king's crown, an actual fishing fly caught in a trout's jaw, real chain or cord and so on. The idea is merely a variation of the familiar inlaying with shell, metal or other woods for contrast. In this particular example, however, my intention was to provide some form of display mounting for a 4-in (10-cm) crystal ball I have owned for over 40 years.

The original thought was merely to carve a pedestal covered with cabalistic symbols, primarily a pillar with the ball at the top. It seemed more interesting, however, to carve a gypsy woman with the ball, so that the crystal-gazing concept would be emphasized. The objective was to feature the ball and allow it to catch the maximum amount of light. Any frontal panel seemed to enclose it too much, as did any composition in which the hands of the figure hovered over it. My ultimate choice was a side view with the ball cupped in the gypsy's hands, the entire figure of the gypsy thus becoming a silhouette and a support for the ball (Fig. 50). This effect was accentuated by the decision not to detail the figure and, further, to cover it with a scalloped texture produced with a relatively flat ¾-in (19-mm) gouge. I had a block of well seasoned maple 4¼ × 16½ × 16½ in (11 × 42 × 42 cm).

The final design was simply drawn on the block and sawed out on a bandsaw. Figures 51 to 55 explain the steps. The figure can be readily adapted to hold something else, of course. On a half-size carved later in mahogany, wood thickness permitted wider shoulders and elbows, hence more natural proportions and greater stability in the figure.

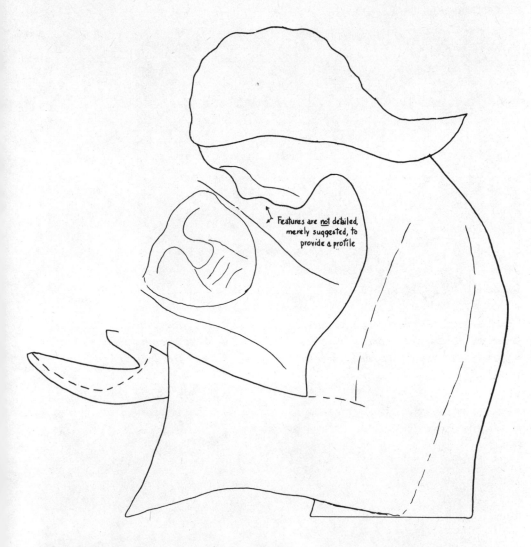

Features are <u>not</u> detailed, merely suggested, to provide a profile

Fig. 50. Crystal Gazer is maple, 4½ × 16½ × 16½ in (10 × 42 × 42 cm). It was designed to feature a 4-in (10-cm) crystal ball, and is largely a silhouette with scallop-textured surfaces.

Fig. 51. Stylized gypsy seer was carved almost entirely with ¾-in (19-mm) No. 6 gouge and finished with wax only. A later commission (foreground) included a 1¾-in (4.4-cm) Christmas-tree ball.

Fig. 52. Block is laid out with a soft-tipped pen by eye. It is then sawed out in a bandsaw. Grain is horizontal for strength in hands and ease when scalloping.

422

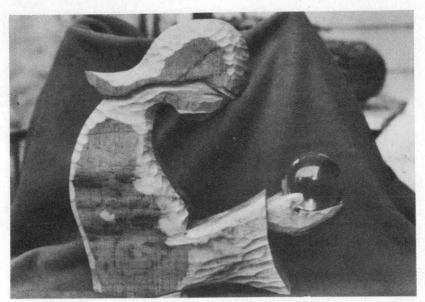

Fig. 53 (above). First cuts are made to rough-shape the figure and define hairline. Hands are hollowed and shaped early so ball can be checked in position as carving progresses. Fig. 54 (below). After rough-shaping, face is defined with simple lines that establish nose, eye and cheek, though no details are put in beyond eyebrow line. Hands are thinned and shaped, but fingers are not defined yet either.

Fig. 55. Because of horizontal grain, scalloping with the gouge is relatively easy. Scallop lines are with grain whenever possible. Nose bridge is thinned and chin rounded; hairline is sharpened with a ¼-in (6.4-mm) No. 8 or 9 gouge—also helpful in shaping the face.

Fig. 56. Doubling width of the smaller version permitted wider shoulders and elbows, thus normalizing proportions. It also resulted in greater stability, since thickness is proportional to height.

Fig. 57 (above). Half-inch (13-mm) slabs cut from sides of smaller blank permitted this exercise in head styling—something that should never be missed—as well as that pictured below. At right, head silhouette is stylized with rough-sawed surface left on bandanna for texture, while at left face has been formed and knot added to bandanna. Fig. 58 (below). Rough-shaped head at left is more defined here, with eyes, nose and mouth positioned and bandanna smooth. At right, face is fully formed, ear defined, and hair slightly textured and held by a barrette.

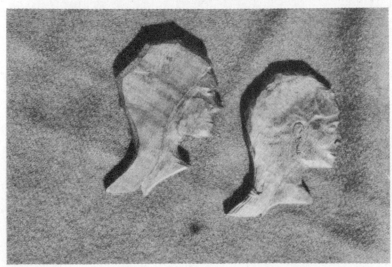

CHAPTER VII

Northwest Coast Carving Designs

The totem pole is only one example of a "different" style

SOME PEOPLES AND TRIBES are inherent craftsmen, others are not, and this seems to have little to do with their intelligence. To some degree, differences in terrain, day-to-day needs and available materials are all influences, as are creativity and sense of design. Among American Indians, the Northwest Coast tribes of Southern Alaska and British Columbia have been outstanding for their work in wood. The Eskimos of both coasts worked ivory and bone to a limited degree, as well as soft stone; but the Indian tribes of the Northwest Coast developed a much wider range of subjects and a greater sense of decoration and symbolism, of which the totem pole is a relatively recent example. Much older and less well-known are oil or grease bowls, spoons (many of mountain-sheep horn), various tools, weapons and the decorated council houses. The old arts are dying out there as elsewhere and much of what is currently available is corrupted for the tourist trade. But the work is still distinctive and interesting and includes a number of ideas readily adaptable by other carvers.

The pieces illustrated and sketched here include both traditional and more modern designs, with relatively little attention to the totem pole, which is a somewhat specialized art incorporating familial and religious elements. The word totem pole, incidentally, is a specific thing, not a general term for any vertical carved pole—particularly surface-carved ones.

Woods commonly carved in the Northwest are cedar and pine; much of the work is painted. Some pieces have inserts of abalone shell, apparently for decoration alone rather than having the significance of the somewhat

Fig. 59. Standard totem pole is a series of in-the-round animals one atop another—like this one in a Vancouver, British Columbia, park. Some, however, may be high relief with no back carving (note that this one is backed by a pine tree).

similar paua-shell inserts in Maori carving. Figures are stylized, many of them mythical or religious, and are often grouped to recall a legend or imply a force or power. Many surface-decoration patterns are incorporated, the carving done with bold strokes and relatively deep incising. Many of the old totem poles were carved with a hard stone axe (and show it), and smaller work and detail were done with the D-adze or with a triangular-bladed knife.

It is possible to miniaturize many of the designs. I have included two miniature totem poles (Figs. 62 and 63), two oil or grease bowls (Figs. 67 and 69), several charms or pendants, and a number of the Indian motifs in sketch form (Figs. 70 and 72). The shaman's mask (Fig. 61) is my own. Additional designs may be found in many books; one of the best is the analysis by Bill Holm, *Northwest Coast Indian Art*, published by the University of Washington Press. Prices in the area for elaborate pieces are extremely high— another excellent reason for making your own.

Eskimo and Indian craftsmen of today use power drills, chain saws, files and sandpaper, instead of their traditional tools, and most of their production is geared for tourists. Even so, some pieces are made on machines in cities such as Seattle, then shipped to the area; others are produced in the Philippines, Japan or wherever prices are lower. The brown bear with a salmon—a traditional Alaskan piece—is now carved by the Ainu in Japan.

The primary thing in making any of these pieces is to be bold in your cuts and sparing with the sandpaper, which blurs sharp lines. Basswood, pine and cedar are suitable woods because the pieces will probably be painted anyway. Flat designs are occasionally done in colors, and I have indicated such variations on some of the designs by shading. Miniatures, however, can simply be flat carvings with the background sunk rather deeply in proportion —this makes the carving stand out in bold relief. Some of the designs are quite complex, and are modern variations of old designs that, through the years, have become increasingly abstract and symbolic.

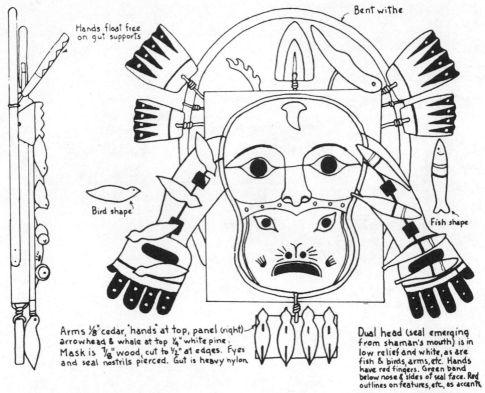

Bent withe

Hands float free
on gut supports

Bird shape

Fish shape

Arms ⅛" cedar, hands at top, panel (right)
arrowhead & whale at top ¼" white pine.
Mask is ⅞" wood, cut to ½" at edges. Eyes
and seal nostrils pierced. Gut is heavy nylon.

Dual head (seal emerging
from shaman's mouth) is in
low relief and white, as are
fish & birds, arms, etc. Hands
have red fingers. Green band
below nose & sides of seal face. Red
outlines on features, etc, as accents.

SHAMAN'S DANCE MASK (Alaska)
Late 19th Century. Painted: green, red & white

Figs. 60–61 (above and left). I made this tinted miniature of a shaman's dance mask from the late 19th century. The original was so elaborate that it was probably carried rather than worn. It depicted animals and was used to assure success in the hunt.

429

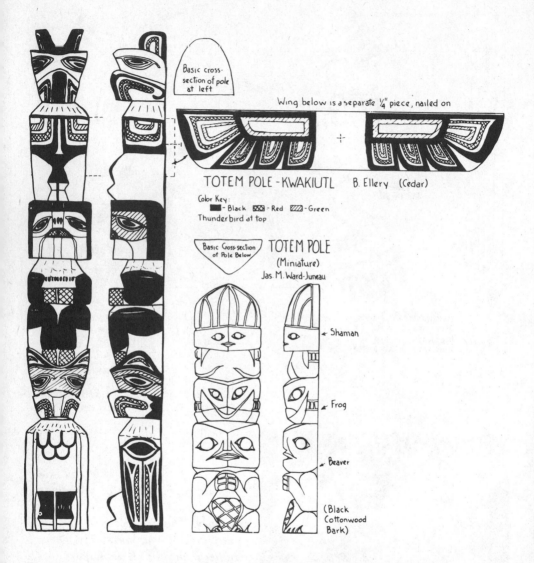

Basic cross-section of pole at left

Wing below is a separate ¼" piece, nailed on

TOTEM POLE - KWAKIUTL   B. Ellery (Cedar)

Color Key:
■ - Black   ▨ - Red   ▥ - Green
Thunderbird at top

Basic Cross-section of Pole Below

TOTEM POLE
(Miniature)
Jas. M. Ward-Juneau

← Shaman

← Frog

← Beaver

(Black Cottonwood Bark)

Fig. 62. Patterns for miniature totem poles pictured at top of facing page.

Fig. 63. Miniature totem poles such as these are primarily tourist items, though they may be faithful copies. The one at left is about 12 in (30 cm) tall and painted, and shows two birds sandwiching a human figure. Totem pole at right is about 6 in (15 cm) tall and unpainted, and is a shaman atop a frog atop a beaver; it is particularly interesting because it is carved in black cottonwood bark rather than the usual cedar.

Figs. 64–65 (above and left). A traditional Northwest Indian carving is this black bear with a salmon. They are now imported from Japan and made there by the Ainu for less than they could be in Alaska. Design can be either in-the-round or relief.

431

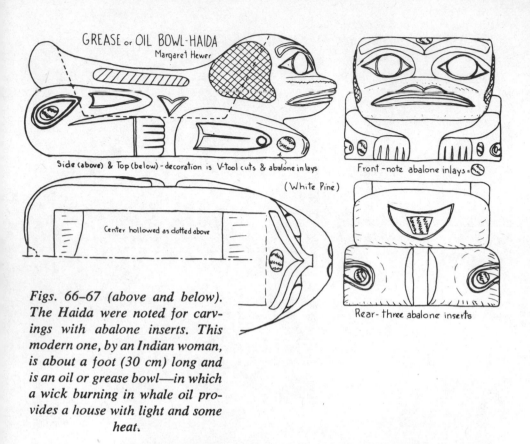

GREASE or OIL BOWL-HAIDA
Margaret Hewer

Side (above) & Top (below) - decoration is V-tool cuts & abalone inlays

(White Pine)

Center hollowed as dotted above

Front - note abalone inlays =

Rear - three abalone inserts

Figs. 66–67 (above and below). The Haida were noted for carvings with abalone inserts. This modern one, by an Indian woman, is about a foot (30 cm) long and is an oil or grease bowl—in which a wick burning in whale oil provides a house with light and some heat.

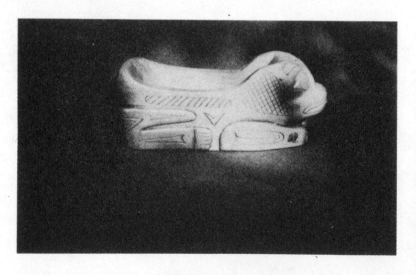

OIL BOWL-TLINGIT

Cross-section
from below head
(cedar)

(Miniature)
J.O.Rowan-Kekh

Center hollow

Figs. 68–69 (above and below). This miniature of a Tlingit oil bowl was made by J. O. Rowan of Ketchikan, Alaska. It is a sea otter on its back, with paint spots replacing the shell inserts used on full-sized carvings. Stylizing makes it practically a shaped panel.

WASGO or MONSTER

Can be panel or in-the-round figure

Fig. 70.

DOG

Indian motifs and charms.

Fig. 72.

DOLPHIN or KILLER WHALE

Fig. 71.

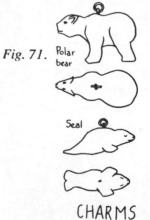

Polar bear

Seal

CHARMS

Eskimo or Indian
(Black Cottonwood Bark)
Shown actual size

CHAPTER VIII

Carving a Cameo

IF YOU HAVE A PIECE OF WOOD WITH STRONG CONTRAST between strata, or between heart wood and growth wood, it is possible to get a special effect— that of a cameo such as is carved in multilayered shell—by having the figure in one color of wood against the background of the other. Woods like walnut and apple can provide such a contrast, and a number of foreign woods can provide very strong contrasts, if that is desired.

The subject can be a mammal or a bird, or even a scene. An interesting added effect is obtained if the carving is made in a section of log, with or without the bark. As an example, I used a green section of apple, complete with bark, selected from a pile I was splitting for firewood. The blank was roughly triangular in cross-section, about 4 in (10 cm) deep by 6 in (15 cm) wide by 18 in (46 cm) long.

My design was a Nereid (water fairy) that followed the curvature of the log, with hands and feet disappearing into the ends of the block, and the background cut away to expose the growth wood. Because of the particular twisted pose, the figure is practically in the round. Carving followed the conventional cycle of setting-in, grounding out, then modelling, all of the heavy work being done with relatively flat gouges and firmers in the ¼- to ½-in (6.4- to 13-mm) range, with details carved by knife. There was no detailing of the face or hair, and the sides were left somewhat rough.

Carving wood while it is green is easier than carving it when it is dry, but here it was necessary to give the finished carving several coats of matte varnish, particularly on the ends, to avoid or reduce checking during drying. It may also be necessary to touch up the back of the figure with stain to accentuate the contrast and emphasize the shape without extensive under-cutting.

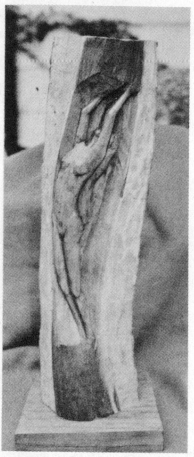

Figs. 73–74. Nereid (water fairy) follows the curvature of the log. Effect is similar to that of appliquéing a figure on a contrasting background, except that the carving is integral and less contrived in appearance.

NUDE
Apple 16" on 24" pc.
Medium to high
relief

436

CHAPTER IX

Variations on a Bird Theme

How the carver makes a design his own

YEARS AGO, I WAS FASCINATED BY THE STUDY of gravestone rubbings that showed how a skilled itinerant stone carver had gone from town to town westward from New England. His designs and techniques were readily recognizable from those of both his contemporaries and his imitators. The same thing is true of familiar woodcarving designs; they may be "standard" but, unless they are turned out on a duplicator, there will be slight but identifiable variations piece to piece. This is true whether it is all the work of one carver or that of several in turn. I have seen copies of my designs that are better than my originals because the carver has more skill or took more pains. I have also seen copies that are so painstaking that they have somehow lost verve and fire. I have made copies of Oberammergau splinter angels and similar work, and mine were not as strong as the originals because the German carver made strong cuts with single strokes while I whittled little chips to make sure I copied precisely. Making a given design over and over again should obviously lead to improvement, but sometimes it leads only to change because the individual is not capable of further improvement or becomes bored with the repetition.

To illustrate facets of this question, I have selected two groups of designs (Figs. 75 and 76), one with Indian variations on a bird profile, the other showing variations in the design of an American eagle for the top or splat of a wooden clock-case.

The bird designs are symbolic, and don't to my knowledge attempt to depict any particular species. They are shown in a 1916 book, *Evolution of the Bird in Decorative Art*, by Kenneth M. Chapman; all are suitable for incising, inlaying, or similar applications. They show how far stylizing can stray from the near-exact reproduction of the decoy-carver.

437

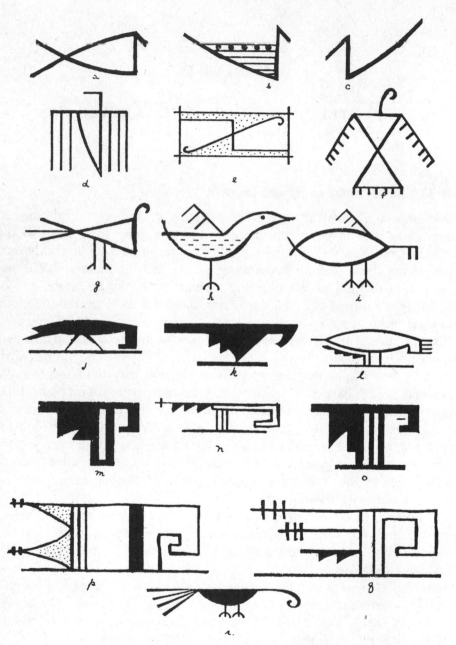

Fig. 75. Symbolic bird variations—American Indian.

1 Chauncey Ives 30-hr long case. Rare

2 G & E Bartholomew 30-hr long-pendulum

3 Riley Whiting #2 (Note differences)

4 Marsh-Gilbert 8-day.

5 Ely Terry & Son 8-day.   S.B. Terry

6 Rare

7 Silas Hoadley 30-hr. Note shield

8 Universal Eagle- many 30-hr clocks

9 Hopkins & Alfred   Rare

10 Putnam Bailey - One of a kind ?

Fig. 76. Variety of American eagles.

The second group of sketches depicts research by Sheldon Hoch of White Plains, New York. He has carved mahogany copies of these eagles from his own or others' photographs of the originals. These were shown in the *Bulletin* of the National Association of Watch & Clock Collectors (Feb., '81, pp. 20–9) in which Mr. Hoch explained his project of "Hunting for Birds and Beasts in Connecticut Shelf Clocks." They are all from the American Empire period, running through Andrew Jackson's presidency (1829–37). Most clocks of that period had wooden Terry-type movements and hand-carved cases with splats depicting eagles, acanthus leaves, pineapples, paws and varied birds and beasts. Such clocks were turned out by the hundreds by a number of makers using duplicating machinery for the works, and sold for about $8. You can imagine how much the carver got for a splat; it behooved him to cut corners and work fast. None ever took time to sign his name.

First designs of this period were apparently baskets of fruit and horns of plenty (cornucopias), which were on short-case clocks. Eagles came later, usually on long-case clocks, and were more prevalent on eight-day wood-movement and 30-hour long-pendulum clocks. Each maker had his own design, almost a trademark, probably made by one or two carvers. One or two makers had more than one design, and some occasionally had unique ones. As wood-movement clocks lost out to brass-movement ones, makers like E. Terry, Jr. and Boardman & Wells went to increasingly unique, often one-of-a-kind casings with splats to match, featuring coats of arms, stylized birds and beasts or what-have-you (sometimes to order).

There are relatively few left-facing eagles. (I seem to recall that left-facing was thought to be unpatriotic by some purists.) Right-facing ones are essentially alike, suggesting a common ancestor or source design. In fact, some of the carving conventions, for feathers to name one, are repeated. Some designs have crests, others do not.

Captions with sketches identify makers. Note that both Terry designs (5 and 6) use the scroll, and that Silas Hoadley reinforced the patriotic motif with a shield (7); this design also had "The Union Be Preserved" carved on the case. Only two birds have feet (9 and 10), and were carved by the same Connecticut man for a New York company.

CHAPTER X

The Maori—Masters of Low Relief

Some of the motifs developed in a special style

IN CONTRAST TO MANY PEOPLES WHO DEVELOPED the carving of three-dimensional figures, the Maori became particularly adept at relief carving and developed a distinctive and elaborate style. Like all Polynesians, they were highly design-minded and deeply religious, and their work reflects that as well as their isolation in far-off New Zealand. In contrast to many peoples in remote locations, their work actually improved for a time after the white man came, because he provided them with steel tools to replace their greenstone ones, developing a greater crispness and cleanness.

The Maori are thought to have come from Tahiti in three great migrations, the first in the 10th century and the last about 1350. The white man came in the 16th century, when their work was at its peak. By the 18th century, the Maori had become Christian, had abandoned their own gods and with them the depictions that had made their work so strong. Thereafter, the carvings became more rococo and less original, and by the 19th century, carving had already disappeared in some areas.

There is little question that some of the Maori legends about the development of carving contain elements of truth. One is that Rauru, son of Toi-kai-rakau—meaning "carver of wood" or, literally, "eater of wood"—came with his father in about 1150 and settled in Whakatane, where he developed the distinctive Maori style as opposed to his father's Tahitian or Marquesan style. This was taken up by other carvers, who had plenty to do because the climate caused rapid deterioration of most carving, and also because the house and possessions of a dead man were considered taboo, so left to rot. Much of the carving was panel work, considered sacred, and used on houses and canoes.

The carver had priestly rank and was considered gifted by the gods. He washed his hands before and after carving, begged the pardon of the trees he cut, believed his work area was contaminated by the presence of women, fire or cooked food and never blew chips away because he considered that sacrilegious!

Maori carving is different in that it features spirals, particularly 2-, 3- and even 4-way ones, usually enhanced by paua-shell inlay. Panels are often pierced and double-sided, as on a canoe prow or the outer end of a barge board (a decorative facing from ridgepole down below the eaves). In-the-round figures were limited to such uses as peak ornaments on roof fronts (the roof beams were considered ribs of the head at the peak) and on the bases of house support posts and pillars. Much of the carving was designed around the human figure, although the figure tended to be a stump type with folded and undersized legs, a rounded belly and three-fingered hands. Fish, birds, lizards, dogs and rats, plus a few legendary concoctions, were auxiliary motifs (no larger animals existed there at that time). Exposed tongues, along with spirals in the carvings at body joints and on cheeks and foreheads signifying tattoos, reflect Maori ideals and customs. To the Maori, a grimacing, tattooed male face with protruding tongue, dilated eyes and defiant hands was the essence of strength and virility.

The most highly carved building was the *pataka*, an elevated storehouse set on posts, often with bargeboards and threshold across the front incorporating pierced and shell-inlaid carving as well as carved pillars. The council houses (*whare whakairo*), which doubled as sacred buildings and residences for distinguished visitors, also contained much interior carving of posts and beams. Painting was common, the favorite wood totora—which in recent years has become so scarce that old canoes have been cut up to provide carving wood. Some of the characteristics discussed here are shown in the sketches, which also suggest the extreme elaborateness and detail of the stylized designs. There was almost no realistic carving or attempts at portraiture, though ancestor worship was tremendous.

Fig. 77. Panel in pine by Austin Brasell shows motifs that are usually background or secondary to a principal figure depicting an ancestor. White spots are paua shell; size is ¾ × 15¾ × 15¾ in (1.9 × 40 × 40 cm).

Fig. 78 (below). Typical Maori motifs.

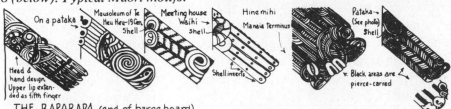

THE RAPARAPA (end of barge board)

On a pataka
Head & hand design
Upper lip extended as fifth finger

Mausoleum of Te Heu Heu-19 Cen. Shell

Meeting house Waihi - shell

Hine mihi - Manaia terminus

Pataka→ (See photo) Shell

Shell inserts

← Black areas are pierce-carved

PILLAR-7'tall N.Y.Wld's Fair.'39

PILLAR-Bird Also N.Y.'39

MASKS (Wm. Redman)
From museums
Note reduced detail on fish-hook at top.
Black is shell

Shell

Ridged

POURANGAHUA-Detail
Flying from Hawaiki on the magic bird (manaia?)
Note knuckled fingers, toes
(Source of outer-space tales)

PANEL (Redman)
Rotorua style-see knuckles. Good god defeats bad (bottom)

ARAWA MASK
Brow & mouth decoration is interwoven incised lines. Eyelids are latticework. Tongue is a decorated loop. No shell in eyes.

NOTCH PATTERNS (Wakati)
Chip-carved triangles
Diamond (from triangles)
Overlapping chevrons
Dragon-tooth (bottom)

ROTORUA MASK
Diamond-pattern eye & mouth decoration (like chip carving). Over lapped wedges in brow plus lines. Split tongue.

Core+5   S   X

Single 2-way 3-way 4-way
SPIRALS

TATTOOED HEAD
(3D Carved)

LIZARD - an unusual form (stands vertical)

PIERCED SPIRAL

MANAIA in oval-note bird mouth

443

CHAPTER XI

Try Far Eastern Panels

Sri Lanka, India, Nepal, Tibet
and Kashmir have carved for centuries

INDIA, SRI LANKA, KASHMIR, NEPAL AND TIBET all have a tradition of wood-carving that spans centuries. What survives from the old days is very competent and ornate, and is usually religious in tone. The modern work is turned out largely in "factories" for the tourist trade, and the carvers are *not* hobbyists nor artists but craftsmen earning a living. In most instances, there is one artist-designer and several carvers, often in shops with practically none of the amenities such as power saws, grinders or even electric power and light. The factory is primarily a place to work and a sales outlet. Tools, too, are limited in number; many are homemade strictly for the particular work a carver does. There may be an antique vise or two, and nothing but the floor for a bench, but there are also helpers to do preparation, sanding, finishing, polishing and other onerous chores.

In contrast to the United States, where a high percentage of carving is in-the-round and small enough to be held in the hand for whittling, many of the carvings made in this area are in relief. This ranges from very shallow, as in the case of the queen in ebony (Figs. 86 and 87), to quite-high-relief copies of old work (particularly in India, where some copies are claimed to be antique fragments). What's more, the variety is marked; carvings may be framed or unframed, geometric shapes, free-forms or silhouettes, non-planar or pierced work, in a bewildering variety of woods. Carving is of good quality, as are designs, and although it may also have pieces from other factories for sale, a particular factory is likely to be specialized. Thus, in Sri Lanka, panels are carved in the Kandy area, ebony 3-D figures in Galle, masks of *nux vomica* in one particular south-coast

444

Fig. 79. A carver works on a mask of nux vomica (a wood like balsa, with poisonous berries used in medicines) in a factory in Sri Lanka, while his partner tests the edge on his chisel. Carvers are pieceworkers, with nothing beyond a circular saw, flat table and bench and a tool or two apiece.

village, and so on. I could have traded a pocketknife in any factory for a really good carving; one carving school up a dirt road outside Sigiryia, Sri Lanka, had a cheap set of six American tools kept carefully in its original cardboard box. This school had no power, so used gas-pressure lamps at night for its 15 or so apprentices, who were schoolboys aged 12 to 20, who went to school in the morning and then came to apprentice in afternoons and evenings for eight long years. They should be good!

There are many varieties of wood in these countries, and factory managers are quite conversant with them; one Nepalese manager had an exhibit of woods for potential quantity buyers of carvings. Each was labelled with its correct Latin name. Ebony still seems to be available, although expensive— relatively. Most carvings are made in hard woods, so the mallet—often just a carved club—is as common as chisels. Sandalwood carvings are expensive and limited to India. One figure, the Zogini, is in a wood listed as adinacopifolia, and is carved in one piece despite elaborate projections. Pieces tend

445

to be finished in low matte or satin, and high gloss is reserved for furniture—something Western carvers have not yet learned.

The variety in shape, technique and treatment is quite wide in these examples, which is relatively rare in areas where carving was developed later than it was here. It is interesting to me that Kashmir and Tibet both tend to carve a variety of walnut, while Nepal, India and Sri Lanka have much more variety in woods. Yet Tibet and Nepal are alike in that the population is heavily Oriental; indeed, there are 10,000 Tibetan refugees in Nepal, itself a small country. Sri Lanka, with 10 percent of the population Tamil—or recent Indian—plus tens of thousands of southern Indians as "temporary laborers" in the tea country, proclaims that it is Sinhalese (although its population is apparently Indian in origin as well). Sri Lanka is very Buddhist, India is not and so on. This affects the kinds of carvings that predominate in each country, as the pictured examples show. And it also suggests, once again, the tremendous variety available.

Fig. 80. This Nepalese scene is in sisso, an antiqued light wood, and depicts village and city with adjacent countryside. Dominant is a stupa (temple) with "paper" prayer streamers from its peak, surrounded by typical multi-storey brick and stucco buildings. Stylized rural area in foreground and at left includes rice paddies. Size is ⅞ × 6½ × 11 in (2.2 × 17 × 28 cm).

446

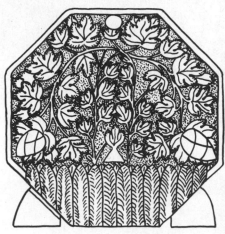

Figs. 81–82–83 (above, right and below). From far-off Tibet comes this octagonal triple folding tray in walnut. The 7-in (18-cm) sides fold down (below) to reveal carved-tray inner surfaces, plus a tilting tray in the middle. Motifs are floral.

*Fig. 84. All carvings are not tradi-
tional. Here are modern treatments of a praying girl in ebony
½ × 4½ × 15 in (1.3 × 10 × 38
cm) each. They were carved in Sri
Lanka, and have a minimum of
modelling and decoration—quite
unusual there.*

*Fig. 85. Krishna and Raddha
(Hindu god and consort) are
depicted here in fret-sawed bam-
boo. Parts are carefully cut and
glued to a backing, and some are
even broken at proper points to
flatten the natural curve of the
stem and heighten the three-
dimensional effect. Figures are
about 12 in (30 cm) tall; from
Sri Lanka.*

Figs. 86–87 (above and right). Contrast in subject and wood is shown in these two panels. Above is a low-relief ancient queen in ebony 2¾ × 4 in (7 × 10 cm); below, a cheepu or demon head and hands in a relatively soft wood, stained black—a 7-in (18-cm) pierced carving.

Fig. 88. A panel like this delights Sri Lankans—and me. It is 6½ × 12 in (17 × 30 cm) and combines a bullock and an elephant, face to face to a greater degree than expected because they share a face and an eye.

449

Figs. 89–90–91. The lotus has deep
religious significance to Hindus and
Buddhists alike, and is a frequent design
motif. Here are an 8-in (20-cm) disk
and a 5¼ × 8-in (13 × 20-cm) panel
(below) from Sri Lanka that feature this
design.

Fig. 92 (right). Moonstone is familiar as the base step to Buddhist temples, and depicts the seven steps to Nirvana. In stone, it is usually a half-circle. This one, in wood, is a complete circle 14 in (36 cm) in diameter, but shows only five steps—it lacks a ring of sacred geese and another floral ring. Carving is excellent and crisp, particularly on the animals.

Fig. 93. Head-size mask of nux vomica is by Ariyapala, the best of Sri Lankan mask carvers, and is the most elaborate. Called Maha Kola Sanni, it incorporates 18 smaller masks, each a specific for curing a particular ailment in ritual healing dances. Masks cure boils, arthritis, fever and even nervousness.

451

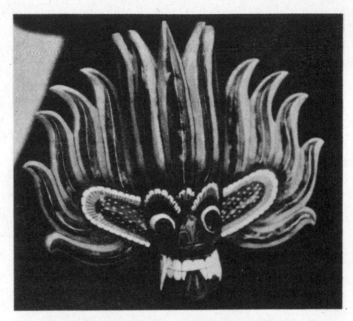

Fig. 94. Another head-size mask, depicting the fire demon featured in Kandy dances. A mask such as this takes about a week to complete, including carving and elaborate enamelling. Side projections are removable and plugged into the semi-cylinder face.

Fig. 95. Indians are masters of horn carving. Here are four examples—lion, goose, horse and pigeon—all basically relief because third dimension is flattened.

452

Figs. 96–97. Another delight to Sri Lankans is this variation of the Chinese puzzle box, with elephant and lotus-blossom border on its cover. It looks like a 6 × 9-in (15 × 23-cm) light-colored book, but then back-bone is pushed down and back, allowing central panel to slide to the side, revealing the ¾-in (19-mm) "secret compartment."

BOX COVER

"Secret" panel in mahogany book-shaped puzzle. Sri Lanka

Fig. 98. Unusual panel in a walnut-like wood in-cludes growth wood and depicts three demons. It is a sort of caricature, un-usual in Sri Lanka, and is 4 × 8 in (10 × 20 cm).

453

CHAPTER XII

Memories of Lebanon

Various scenes are combined in a cherry panel

GEBEL, OR JBEIL, IS IN LEBANON; it was Byblos (from which we get the word *bible*), oldest town in the world, and has been inhabited for at least 7,000 years. This cherry panel, ¾ × 7½ × 22½ in (1.9 × 19 × 57 cm), a retirement present for a Marine officer who served in Beirut some years ago, illustrates a number of basic principles of relief carving.

Fig. 99.

- The scene incorporates elements from many sources, including postals, transparencies and travel folders. The terracing at right is a composite of four sources, while the village at left is five. Some elements are introduced from elsewhere, such as Sparrow Castle, at upper right, and Pigeon Rocks, at bottom center.

454

- Point of view is offshore and above, so roofs can be seen on nearby buildings, giving them a third dimension. Distant structures such as the castles loom over the scene, suggesting the rise of ground. Bottoms of walls of foreground buildings and pillars are sloped backward to meet the ground. Perspective is adjusted to suit location from a higher elevation since most available photos were taken from ground level and incorporate little distance.

- The knot and knothole in the board were incorporated in the scene—one as a ruin, the other as a mountain. The knot and the graining dictated selection of this particular board for the scene.

- Relief is shallow in this case, not much over ⅛ in (3.2 mm) in the foreground; thus, depth is enhanced by antiquing. Relief depth is greater in the foreground to suggest the haziness and blurring that occurs with distance.

- Number of elements is not too great, and detail surrounding each is reduced so that each stands out. This is decided partially by size and wood. There are few indications of brush and trees and there are no people. These clutter up the picture and are very difficult to carve realistically to scale. Texturing suggests terrain characteristics, and does not compete with elements.

CHAPTER XIII

I Sing Behind What Plough?

The saga of a symbolic panel

THIS PANEL EXEMPLIFIES SOME OF THE PROBLEMS you may face if you attempt a commemorative relief. It is in walnut, $1\frac{1}{2} \times 24 \times 36$ in (3.8 × 61 × 91 cm). The John C. Campbell Folk School, Brasstown, North Carolina, has used this symbol for most of its 55 years, but solely as a silhouette with the caption, "I sing behind the plough." The story is that the silhouette was drawn from a photo that is no longer available, and the slogan was taken from a Danish folk song by Mads Hansen, written in 1866.

I offered to make a relief panel from the silhouette as my contribution to the 1981 "Work Week" at the school, thus adding an additional hurdle—the necessity of working against a deadline. The only drawing approximating the desired size had been used for a banner, which was far away in Raleigh. There was a metal cutout on the school sign, so this was copied on a 1-in (2.54-cm) sheet of plastic foam, cleaned up, and reversed by photocopying portions and assembling them. Then began the laborious job of drawing in detail, which started with the discovery that the rear horse had only three legs and that there was no plough. This was confirmed next day when a 50-year-old Danish woodcarving of a man ploughing was produced, and when Murray Martin, a retired woodcarving instructor at Brasstown, came up with a $2\frac{1}{2}$-in (6.4-cm) brooch depicting the same scene—one of three cast in Denmark perhaps 50 years ago. It also bore more of the legend: "I am a common farmer, I sing behind the plough, I am happy and free." The brooch was too small to show all necessary detail, but permitted roughing-in of the figure details and started me guessing as to the rest. Some research in old books helped on harness detail, which was further improved by the recollections of two visitors who had ploughed with two-horse teams in their youth in nearby Georgia and Mississippi. Meanwhile, I had begun trenching for the silhouette, which took a day or two. I arbitrarily decided on a depth of ½ in (13 mm) and maintained uniformity with a brad driven into a stick to make a gauge.

The area around Brasstown is mountainous, and the top of the 3-piece panel assembled by the Cabinet Shop contained a white top of growth wood; so I bandsawed away the "sky" to leave some light-topped hills, as if a lowering sun were hitting them. Lettering 2 in (5.1 cm) tall was laid out to form a base cup for the carving, and to center the important third of the quotation on the bottom—this necessitated adding the word "for" to the third line. That seemed a minor change, because a translation of the original Danish by J. C. Auberg is quite different from the previously quoted lines.

Modelling the figures took four days and four long evenings. I decided to cut away the background to trenching depth at the top, leaving the full depth at the base and half-sides in which to incise the lettering with a V-tool. Background above the lettering was textured with a flat gouge and some texturing was done on the bodies of the horses to avoid shine from flat surfaces. The finished carving was given one coat of Deft® to seal it, then an old can of fruitwood color stain was discovered and used for antiquing. This took another day and a half, leaving a half-day to drill and file hangers, find wire and test the carving in its location over a fireplace.

Fig. 100. Commemorative relief panel in walnut, based—in part—on an old silhouette.

CHAPTER XIV

The Kubbestol—A One-Piece Tradition

Scandinavian block stool is a carver's challenge

THE KUBBESTOL IS A VERY OLD FORM OF BLOCK—or solid—stool, made in Scandinavia from a hollowed tree trunk. Early ones were low-backed, with little or no decoration, but those made in Minnesota resemble a chair, with both the back and solid skirt decorated with relief carving.

This stool was made from a section of the trunk of an ash—carved green. A 3-ft (0.9-m) length, 16 in (41 cm) in diameter, was cut halfway through in the middle, and one half was then split away. I used a chain saw to cut a series of radial segments in the remaining half, and split them out to leave a 2-in (5-cm) ring of living wood for the back. Then the chain saw, with a 14-in (36-cm) arm, was used to plunge-cut a central plug out of the solid base, about 1½ saw-widths on a side. This is much harder than it sounds, because the saw tends to run instead of cutting, and it overloads as well. We drove out the heart plug with a sledge, and I immediately stripped the bark and rounded up the hole with a 2½-in (6.4-cm) flat spade gouge, since ash will check overnight and removal of the heart wood inhibits that action (at least to a degree).

The original log weighed about 175 lb (79 kg). With the core removed, it was reduced to about 80 lb (36 kg). Next day, minor checks showed around both ends of the solid skirt section, but these did not progress; in fact, they eventually closed as more of the interior wood was removed. I did not 'attempt to round up the skirt because I wanted to maintain diameter and strength as well as provide some interest in the shape. Wood was removed with a 1-in (2.54-cm) carpenter's gouge and a 2½-in (6.4-cm) flat gouge in a continuous process around the interior. When the walls and back were approximately 1½ in (3.8 cm) thick, the bottom end was cut true and smoothed. The top was rough-shaped to design, then thinning was continued. At this point, the stool was 33½ in (85 cm) high and roughly 14 in (36 cm) in diameter, with a seat height of 15½ in (39 cm). When wall thickness was down to 1 in (2.54 cm), it weighed 30 lb (14 kg) and had no visible checks.

Figs. 101–102. The Scandinavian Kubbestol, or block stool, has been made for centuries. This one is more elaborate than usual, with most surfaces carved. It is ash, about 14 × 33 in (36 × 84 cm), and weighs 24 lb (11 kg). Seat is red Naugahyde® atop plywood. Back view (right) points up benefits of antiquing with dark stain, painted on interstices and lines and then rubbed away. This provides surface contrast and emphasizes the patterns, along with the shape of the log itself and darker streaks in the grain.

From various references, I gathered designs for Odin (or Wotan), Thor and Freyr (sons of Odin), Freya (sister of Freyr) and Frigga (Odin's wife). To finish, I needed a Valkyrie, a female warrior who brought the bravest of the fallen heroes to Valhalla. The gods were spaced around the skirt, with Thor positioned front and center. This was because my design had the god placed on a natural bulge of the wood, and his two goats, Tanngnjost and Tanngrisir, in a hollow where I'd left a little inner bark—which would give them a variation in tone and texture.

Odin was the most powerful of the Norse gods. He invented poetry, liked history and sacrificed one eye for wisdom. His pet ravens, Hugin and Munin (or Thought and Memory), flew daily to the four corners of the universe to bring him its secrets. He was also the god of the dead to whom the Valkyries brought the souls of slain heroes to live again in his banquet hall. Odin also invented writing and the runes, peculiar letter forms that are thought to be derived from the practice of divining by throwing sticks—they are patterns of short straight lines such as thrown sticks might make.

I incised the name of each god and added a line of runes in the band at the front of the seat. The line is simply a phonetic translation of a toast I made up: "May you sit in the laps of the gods." For the outside designs, I arbitrarily decided to sink the background ¼ in (6.4 mm), so it was a natural for a power router—which took only three hours for the entire job. However, setting-in the recessed areas of the irregular face and cleaning up the background around each figure took a couple of days. I found that a deep gouge (fluter), with about a ³⁄₁₆-in (5-mm) curve at the bottom and high parallel sides, could be driven along the lines to avoid the usual veiner outlining and wearisome setting-in. It leaves a small radius at the base which is desirable in many instances and is not visible after antiquing, anyway. For this, I use a very light mallet so that the tools never overcut or overstress the wood surface. Also, I use smaller and smaller firmers and gouges as the work progresses—even down to ⅛- and ¼-in (3.2- and 6.4-mm) widths.

Ash will support considerable detail if tools are kept sharp and you take it easy. The wood has a tendency to leave small, fuzzy splinters on occasion, and these must be removed almost individually. (I know a sign carver who uses a blowtorch for this purpose, thus saving a considerable amount of time.) Also, on my blank there was a strip of dead wood and one area that had been attacked by insects. This area required more careful cutting than the rest and the holes had to be filled with glue and sawdust. I usually pour the glue into the hole, then pile sawdust on top and knead it down. That's much easier than working with a gluey mixture. After a few minutes, the surplus sawdust can be blown off.

My sketches included a considerable amount of detail, probably more than you will want to put in. I eliminated a few fine points here and there as I carved because they were not essential and were beyond the capacity of the wood grain or surface to take.

For the surface carving, I used $\frac{1}{16}$-, $\frac{1}{8}$-and $\frac{1}{4}$-in (1.6-, 3.2- and 6.4-mm) firmers, and similar small gouges of various radii, alternating with a sharp-pointed knife. Details of faces and hands, the lining of beards, and the heads of the animals were knife jobs for me, as was the rounding of axle spokes, horns and such, but I used the veiner and V-tool as much as possible because they are much faster. Even so, each god-design took the better part of a day. Just for kicks, I used an ornamental brass upholstery tack for the central boss of the Viking's shield, and put black gimp tacks as center bosses in two Viking shields on the ship. The ship, by the way, was positioned so that the handhole came in the center of the sail. For all this work, it is easier and faster to transfer the tool from hand to hand than to move the piece. It takes some practice, but it can be done. Doing the designs on the inside of the back was something else again, because of the extreme curvature. Most of the design could be outlined with a $\frac{1}{8}$-in (3.2-mm) round gouge and close details outlined with a veiner, but I found that a short-bent gouge was essential in some areas. The short-bent gouge was too long to use with the mallet for short distances, particularly near the top where the back "ears" come so far forward. The tool could be used alone, however, by pushing and rotating it—somewhat akin to what an engraver does with a burin. Setting-in the background was comparatively easy because cuts could be made with a flat gouge along the grain for most of it, and the rest removed with small flat gouges (although near the seat area it may be necessary to have the arm holding the chisel come up through the skirt).

The conventional Kubbestol, by the way, has a flat wooden seat cut to the inner contour of the skirt top and tapered slightly so that it can be wedged and nailed in place. I elected, instead, to have a thin plywood seat, recessed about $\frac{1}{2}$ in (13 mm) so that a foam-padded cushion could be set in. The plywood could have been held by cleats, but I wanted to thin the top of the skirt anyway, so I decided to cut a $\frac{1}{2}$-in (13-mm) step $\frac{3}{4}$ in (19 mm) deep all around. I made this step only approximately level, because I wanted air spaces around the edge of the plywood to avoid a differential-humidity problem inside the skirt when the chair was set on a rug—which would effectively seal the bottom. An alternate design would have been simply to drill a few small holes in the plywood seat, but that would have been hard on the cushion.

The cushion, by the way, was made of three ½-in (13-mm) layers of discarded foam plastic from an ironing board, covered with a dark-red vinyl. My wife decided that it should be a welted rather than a boxed edge, so the welting would just cover the inside edge of the skirt. The cushion was made to a cardboard pattern, painstakingly cut to fit.

Light sanding with a worn-out piece of fine sandpaper removed most of the burrs and slivers on the piece; a pocketknife took care of the difficult ones. The ground was not smoothed but was left with flat-gouge lines showing, while the surfaces of the designs and the borders were smoothed. Further, as each design was completed, it was sprayed with satin varnish to protect it against grime. All surfaces were finally sprayed with a second coat. Then a teak oil stain was applied and immediately rubbed off flat surfaces, to leave the darker color in carved lines and adjacent to the pieces, thus creating an antiqued effect. This required some touch-up here and there with a small brush, as well as some scraping where too much stain was absorbed, but the spray varnish makes such touch-ups relatively easy.

The inside of the skirt was also varnished to equalize surfaces, as was the underside of the seat, which, by the way, was oak-faced plywood (which approximates the ash in color and figure when varnished). Before inside varnishing, some additional slivers were removed from behind the figures to cut weight and equalize wood thickness to some degree, so final weight is about 23 lb (10 kg) without the cushion, and wood thickness is about ¾ in (19 mm). As a final finish, an additional spray coat of satin varnish covered the stain, followed in turn by two coats of wax and a final top coat of neutral Kiwi® shoe polish buffed with a soft-bristle shoebrush, which gives a slightly higher gloss than the wax. The result is a chair with a warm tan-to-brown color range and a surface which exudes soft reflections and shows the carving quite clearly.

Fig. 103. This 80-lb (36-kg) rough shows chain-saw marks, has 2-in (5-cm) walls and required one day to produce. Core hole was plunge-cut with a chain saw, then interior and exterior surfaces were shaped with 1- and 2½-in (2.54- and 6.4-cm) gouges.

Fig. 104. Progressive shaping and thinning brought walls down to 1½ in (3.8 cm). Some inner bark was left in hollows of the naturally contoured skirt, in the event that the darker tone would help design.

463

Fig. 105. Six designs were spaced around the skirt, scroll-banded at the top and plain-banded at bottom. Similar scroll-banding at back enclosed two Vikings that flank a scene symbolizing the origin of man, with a Viking ship across the waist. Here the background has been routed ¼ in (6.4 mm) deep.

Fig. 106. After mechanical routing, design outlines were detailed and areas bosted where the router could not reach. Also, a ¼-in (6.4-mm) ledge was cut inside top of skirt down ¾ in (19 mm), to support a ¼-in (6.4-mm) contoured plywood seat and leave a ½-in (13-mm) rim to enclose the padded cushion. Weight is now 30 lb (14 kg).

Figs. 107–108 (below and right). Back was carved first. It was necessary to plug and tone an area just over the head of Aske, the first man (Embla was the first woman).

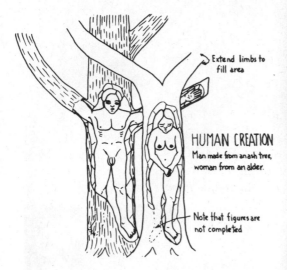

Extend limbs to fill area

HUMAN CREATION

Man made from an ash tree, woman from an alder.

Note that figures are not completed

Fig. 109 (right). Drape lines of Frigga's skirt are established with small gouge cuts and then faired in. Wool on distaff is suggested by veiner lines. Frigga was Odin's wife and queen of Asgard, patroness of ships, and brought lovers together after death. With her is Fulla, keeper of her jewels.

Fig. 110 (above). Freya was the most propitious of the goddesses, who loved music, flowers, fairies and elves, so human lovers invoked her. She is usually shown driving a chariot drawn by cats and is sometimes confused with Frigga or even Saga, goddess of poetry. Freya was Odin's daughter and Freyr's sister.

Figs. 111–112 (left and above). Thor, the Thunderer, and Freyr, Odin's sons. Thor's chariot is drawn by Tanngnjost and Tanngrisir, his goats; note that bark is left on them for texture and tint. Freyr, or Frey (above), god of the sun, is usually shown riding high over the mountains on a boar —thus, his image is placed high on the skirt, with mountain range in miniature along base line.

Fig. 113 (right). Symbol on inside back of Kubbestol is the Norse sign for eternal life, said to have been the favorite design of Helen Keller because she could trace it with her fingertips. Gods on the stool are identified by runic characters, a very old alphabet said to be derived from the thrown sticks used in divining. Germany and Scandinavia used it as early as the fourth century.

Fig. 114. Odin (Wotan, Woden) was the principal Norse god, but not the first, nor, indeed, the Supreme Being. He ruled the universe and gathered fallen heroes for an ultimate battle with the giants. His wolves are Geri and Freki, and his ravens, Hugin and Munin (Thought and Memory). This is the largest and most detailed motif and is placed at the center rear of the skirt, where a broad arcuate surface was available.

467

VALKYRIE ("Chooser of the Slain")
Note: Norse warriors wore chain-mail shirts

Fig. 115.

Figs. 115–116. The Valkyries (Choosers of the Slain) were messengers for Odin and brought the bravest of fallen heroes to Valhalla, Odin's banquet hall in Asgard, after their veil of death was removed in the forest of Glasir. A Valkyrie wore a chain mail shirt and a winged helmet that enabled her and her horse to fly. She was armed with a spear, and her armor shed a strange flickering light—the Aurora Borealis.

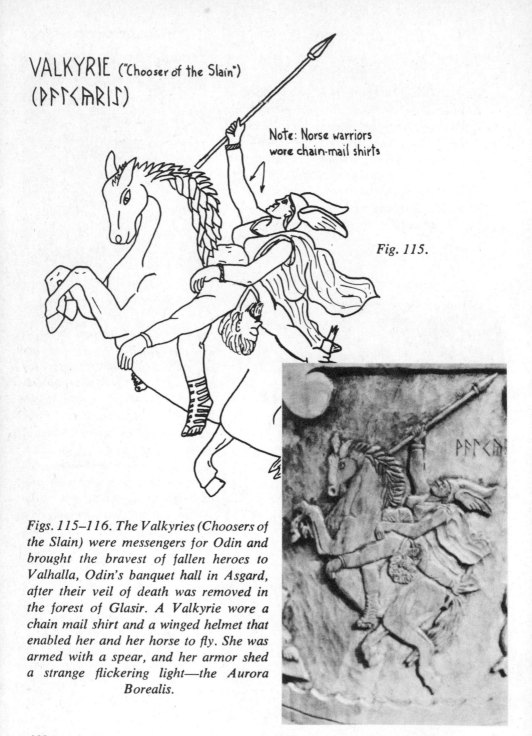

Figs. 117–118 (above and below). The Viking ship was low in the waist and high at prow and stern, both often decorated. Though shallow-keeled, it was fairly seaworthy and was apparently the last survivor of Roman and Greek designs in northern Europe. Crews ranged from 30 to 60, a third at the oars—which were used much more than the awkward square sail—the other two-thirds ready to fight, with their shields draped along the bulwarks. It was steered by an oar at stern right.

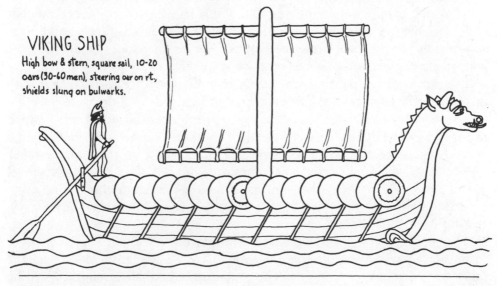

VIKING SHIP
High bow & stern, square sail, 10-20 oars (30-60 men), steering oar on rt., shields slung on bulwarks.

469

CHAPTER XV

Ecology II—A 6-Panel Door

478 flora and fauna carved in teak polyglot panels

EVER SINCE I BEGAN TO CARVE THE "BUG TREE" back in the mid-sixties, I have been fascinated by polyglot grouping of low-relief subjects without any elaborate background or tracery to connect them. There are infinite possibilities, and I have only begun to explore them in more than a score of panels. Not all of these polyglot carvings were on flat panels; I have carved on a half-dozen wooden shoes, a walrus tusk or two and many other surfaces. The subjects have included flora and fauna, vegetables and fruits, musical instruments, toys, fabulous figures—anything in which there are a number of readily recognizable shape variations. I have even mixed flowers and birds successfully. One carver wrote me that she carves only shoes of all vintages, and so she carved various shoes on a wooden shoe.

This series of six panels is my best example. They are in teak, and vary in size as well as thickness. The eight panels I carved for a door eleven years ago were in an essentially rotary design, around a central doorknob—which most of us don't have. This is a vertical grouping on a more conventional door. I had a piece of 4/4 teak, a piece 1¼ in (3.2 cm) thick and another 1⅜ in (3.5 cm), which could be combined into a 1¼ in (3.2-cm) whole, so these pieces were the basic elements. It took some scrambling to find more teak, but I got a ¾ × 9⅜-in (1.9 × 24-cm) plank 13½ ft (4.1 m) long— at a bit over $100! About half of it made the four smaller panels. The group had to be relatively narrow, because the front door on which the panels were to be placed was to be covered year-round by a glass storm door, and the knob was of course on one side. The grouping is flexible, so panels could be

Fig. 119. Six teak panels are combined on a plain pine door to display 478 species of local fauna and flora in mid-New York State. Panels vary in thickness as well as size.

set any distance apart, from zero to perhaps 3 in (7.6 cm). I figured on 4½-in (11-cm) clearance on sides and top, 6 in (15 cm) at bottom to clear an inadvertent kick. Because the house is in the country, I chose flowers, trees (leaves), birds, bugs, local animals and fresh-water fish as my subjects.

Sizes of elements and subjects can suit your own purposes and design; they are, however, dependent to some degree upon your ability to draw. It is easier to trace them directly from references such as field handbooks, though these tend to standardize the size and pose because of the standard illustration size. Better and more versatile are the lengthier texts, including books for children, which will show larger and more varied poses than the usual handbook top views of insects and side views of animals and fish. I trace from the original when the size is suitable, using a scratch awl (to avoid marking up the book) and carbon paper directly on the wood, then strengthening the outline with a soft-point pen.

I find it best *not* to design the entire panel in advance. I trace or copy the designs as they seem to fit, and stay roughly one row ahead of my carving. That keeps me from forgetting details of the designs and then inadvertently cutting off a leg. Further, it reduces the likelihood of missing lines in copying, and the possibility that the design will be partially erased by the friction of my hands and arms over it. I also find on teak that the oil in the wood has a tendency to fade drawn lines over a period of time.

In the sizes with which I work, I am not concerned about relative scale of various elements. An eagle may be 5 in (13 cm) long, a wren or humming-bird 2 in (5.1 cm), and they may be side by side. Any attempt to maintain scale would result in highly disproportionate units. Besides, when you're copying directly from texts, scale is not constant either.

In these sizes, the tools must be small. I have perhaps ten chisels ready, but some are almost never used. The ½-in (13-mm) firmer, for example, is useless except for smoothing a surface. Tools used constantly are the V-tool, $\frac{1}{16}$-in (1.6-mm) and ⅛-in (3.2-mm) flat gouges and a hook knife. Less frequent is the need for the veiner, ¼-in (6.4-mm) firmer, ¼-in (6.4-mm) gouges of several sweeps, a ⅛-in (3.2-mm) fluter and a regular pocketknife. Many of the areas are so small that miniature tools would be a help. Always remember the sizes of your smallest tools and the character of the wood when you design; if you don't, you'll have excessive splitting and breakage.

Polyglot panels are a particularly good exercise in using the V-tool because there are endless leaf veins, fish fins, bird and insect wings to be lined—a job usually too fine for the average veiner. You may also want to do some texturing, such as cross-hatching, and there is inevitably the need for separating planes. By tilting the V-tool to one side, you can cut a vertical wall on one side and a longer slope on the other, making the side with the long slope appear below the one with the vertical wall. The tool is also handy for cleaning out around a design after grounding-out, notching vertical walls to suggest a ragged edge and a variety of other purposes. But you must keep it sharp.

When notching or grooving fine lines, I hold the V-tool by the blade as I would a pencil, making the cut with the fingers alone. The length and direction of the stroke are thus controlled more precisely. Precision and control can be further enhanced by gripping the panel with the other hand so the middle fingers of the tool hand press against the thumb or index finger of the holding hand to act as a stop. (I intentionally avoided using the designations "left" and "right" because you should learn to make such cuts with either hand, thus saving board rotation.) To carve panels like these, I either lay them flat on a bench or prop them against the bench with the lower end on my knees, sitting down whenever possible. This makes panel position much more flexible, and the panel is usually big enough to stay in place without clamping. When at an angle, the panel will also rid itself of most of the chips as you work.

The hook or pull knife is also particularly useful on work like this because the heel of the blade will not nick adjacent surfaces, the point is narrow and the concavity makes it stay in the cut rather than jump out on occasion (although it does tend to jump free at an edge).

It is possible to shortcut the usual lengthy procedure of outlining and grounding-out, because most elements are round-edged somewhat anyway. I do not outline with the V-tool before setting-in. My designs tend to be small, so a 1/8-in (3.2-mm) firmer will handle most of the setting-in except for sharp curves. I set-in less than 1/8 in (3.2 mm) on the first pass, depending on the wood. (Teak tends to crush and splinter if the tool is driven in deep enough to cause serious sidewise wedging.) I remove the waste, then set-in again. Also, all setting-in is done with a light mallet. I find I develop a pattern of blows (two or three taps with the grain, three or four across it), which makes the work go fast.

In panels like these, it is unnecessary to get the entire background bosted to the same depth or even maintain a precise plane surface. This is because the background areas are quite small and are eventually stained dark anyway, so a little unevenness will help avoid the light reflection given by a flat surface. It is also unnecessary to texture these backgrounds, thus saving time.

On large panels, I bost the background down a bit over ⅛ in (3.2 mm). This is deep enough with background staining and makes undercutting unnecessary. If the area is small or complex, I set-in in three steps to reduce crushing of delicate elements. Obviously, you can't set-in the two sides of a thin element such as an insect leg or antenna in the conventional way. If the section is very narrow, particularly across-grain, I set-in with a knife and may ground-out with it as well. On teak, any section less than about ¼ in (6.4 mm)—particularly across-grain—must be treated with great care. Setting-in can be done with the chisel on almost all sections if you slope the tool edge away from the vertical on the second side and set-in in three or four passes. This leaves a sloping side that can then be cut vertical safely because the obstructing wood outside is gone.

My custom is to set-in larger areas first as far as possible and skip over the interior bosting between two adjacent slender sections. Then I go back, pray, and do the small areas. You may find it advisable to leave extremely slender sections a bit over-width initially, slimming them down with the hook knife as you complete carving. It may also be possible to put a mark on the major setting-in tool tips to indicate the desired setting-in depth, but then you'll have to renew the line every time you sharpen the tool.

Try to keep in mind the cutting problems as you lay out the panel. Leave yourself enough space to clear your smallest tools. Adjoining subjects should be as different in shape and size as possible. A panel of fish, for example, tends to be monotonous because so many of the subjects will be generally similar in shape and positioned horizontally; break it up with angled poses, leaping fish or even a crab or turtle. Also, a panel containing birds, which have a recognizably similar conformation, must also attain interest by the use of variety in pose. Further, all birds have bills that usually end in a point, so if the bill is across-grain, it is edgy to carve. (Of course, if you get the bills with the grain, the legs will be across it—so you can't win!)

You can avoid some of the grief with legs by having flying or sitting birds, or by arranging poses so that the legs of one bird are apparently behind the body or wing of another. With insects, observing grain for six legs and two antennae is impossible particularly because they stick out at odd angles and tend to curve. Some support can be gained by intersecting them, overlapping them or having long antennae or legs run across an adjacent body or wing—thus vastly reducing the cutting depth necessary. In most cases, antennae and legs, especially on insects, are so small that only undetailed general shape is necessary, without such projection as fuzz, kinky joints and such. Besides, such details will not be seen on a large panel.

You may have a problem grouping elements and deciding which details to include. Should this leg extend over that animal's back? What do you do about the long antennae of some insects, the long tail of a bird of paradise? The coward's way out is not to include difficult subjects. Mine is to draw the subjects where I think they belong, showing overlaps. Then I decide each situation as I reach it, often placing a leg over an adjacent wing to reduce the depth of cut.

When laying out a polyglot panel, it is very important to make a record of each subject as it is drawn in. I simply draw approximate blob shapes on a pad in approximate position, and write across the blob the name of the subject, the reference (A, B, C, etc.) and the page number. Then when I do detail carving, I can find it again quickly. This also serves as the base for the ultimate identification key and helps avoid including different poses of the same subject drawn from different references. The key, by the way, can be tied in with an approximate tracing of the finished panel, with numbers written on an enlargement of the photograph of it or on a tracing made over the photo.

Border width can be what you wish; I find that about ⅝ in (16 mm) looks good and allows room to drill for the fastening screws. These, by the way, are No. 8 1½-in (3.8-cm) brass flathead screws, set in recessed holes and capped by plugs of the same wood glued in to match the grain, then sanded smooth and finished. Screw holes are oversize to allow slight shifting if either door or panel is affected by humidity.

Panels can be almost any shape or size, and can be made up of individual subjects alone. What you use depends upon purpose and time. Out of curiosity, I kept records on this door panel by panel. Total carving time was about 375 hours, of which 25 were general preparation of boards, obtaining materials, planning of the door design and drilling screw holes and installation. The flower panel, for example, required 113½ hours and contains 162 designs, while the animal panel (smallest of the group) took 33½ hours and included 41 subjects. All were done roughly in order of increasing difficulty. Layout time, in two cases, was 17 percent of the total for the panel while carving time was a bit under an hour per subject, ranging from 1.06 to 1.6 units per hour. (I carve relatively quickly, so your time may not be as good— as it is with m.p.g. estimates for present-day cars.) It is also interesting to note that these six panels include 478 separate designs, as compared with

459 in the eight panels of the larger door I did eleven years earlier. This indicates that I had a more compact layout in this case, probably because I used more designs directly from references without enlargement.

As you may know, in the elaborate panelling and pierced-work carving in medieval churches, the monks and their lay assistants occasionally worked in designs that are secular and sometimes even bawdy. This was also true of the single designs for misericords—the little projections under fold-up church seats upon which weary buttocks could be rested during lengthy periods when church attendees were ostensibly standing—several of which are illustrated in my book, *Carving Religious Motifs in Wood*. This was probably to relieve the tedium of carving endless vines and religious symbols. Something similar occurred in these panels. Thus, you will find a tree frog basking on a basswood leaf in the tree panel, a sea horse, a crustacean and a sea snake (saurian) among the fish, as well as The Little Mermaid—definitely a mammal. Among the animals are domestic beasts, and among the insects are two spiders and a mite, all arachnids, a worm or two, a fish (being juice-sucked by an insect) and even the White Rock girl; she is watching a frog catch a dismayed damselfly. Among the flowers are a snail, an inchworm, a snake and a female gnome collecting Dutchman's-breeches. Not exactly formal, but why not? They give an added fillip to the careful searcher. A doodlebug catching an ant, a tarantula hawk stinging a tarantula, an insect attacking a fish, the White Rock girl watching the frog—these are all little scenes incorporated in the panel. They relieve the monotony and expand your experience.

Fig. 120. Flower panel is 1-in (2.54-cm) teak, tree panel comprises two glued pieces 1¼ in (3.2 cm) thick, and fish panel is ¾ × 9⅜ in (1.9 × 24 cm) wide. Flower panel is the largest of all six.

Fig. 121. All three of these panels are ¾-in (19-mm) teak 9⅜ in (24 cm) wide. Insect panel is most complex of the group because of antennae and legs.

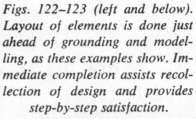

*Figs. 122–123 (left and below).
Layout of elements is done just
ahead of grounding and modelling, as these examples show. Immediate completion assists recol-
lection of design and provides
step-by-step satisfaction.*

*Fig. 124. This panel was a
design test for my first ecol-
ogy door in 1970.*

CHAPTER XVI

How to Carve Lettering

Design is as complex as execution

LETTERING ON A CARVING may have one or more purposes. It can be just a signature and/or date, a title, a dedication, or the major subject of the carving itself. If you carve a likeness, you will almost certainly want to add a title. The Arabic alphabet is cursive (script) and flowing, thus lends itself to endless variations and is easy to incorporate in a design, but our Roman alphabet is rigid and much more difficult to use. Once it consisted only of capitals, and before that simply incised strokes, but the addition of lower-case letters for ease of reading, and of the running-hand, cursive or script forms for easier handwriting, tremendously complicated the job of the carver. Today we have vertical letters and sloping letters (italics), and many alphabets have weighted lines and curves and lines to end each basic stroke. These letter terminals are called *serifs* and are a major problem in relief carving, particularly across grain. Also, letterers add flourishes called *swashes* to the tails of letters—as some penmen do—or make elaborate tails and loops called *uncials*.

All this does not mean that any lettering you do must be elaborate—or boring. You can vary the designs to suit your purpose, as long as the letters are recognizable and legible, and you can finish them in many ways. The effect of raised lettering can be achieved by stamping or otherwise texturing the background around it; letters can be outlined (if they are large enough), inlaid or even carved with channels or grooves in the wider verticals of capital letters. But the easiest form is V-groove incising, particularly if the wood and the tool sharpness permit use of the veiner or V-tool, or you are working in end grain. You *can* go all out and do raised lettering as a con-tinuous cursive strip, as if a ribbon had been laid on the surface to form the letters. If you undertake that, be prepared for trouble, and except no sympathy from me. It is my firm belief that much lettering on carvings, particularly titles, is unnecessary and looks crude, even if the carving itself is well done. If you must have elegant lettering, have it engraved or etched on a brass or silver appliqued plate.

Even the simplest lettering is difficult to carve. The difficulties include line width, spacing and depth, and increase with smaller size and more complex letter forms, such as serifs and swashes, as well as if the letters must project rather than be incised, because the eye picks up very small variations in the curve, spacing or width of a line. Further, calligraphy—the design and execution of ornamental lettering—is rising in public favor, so many people are more conscious of letter forms.

It is a paradox that the typewriter and most other forms of commercial type place each letter in a block of uniform width and height, while the calligrapher and the handsetter consider a great many spacing variations essential. Small wonder that carvers go to templates and routers to produce passable lettering!

There are an endless number of rules that the sign painter and the hand typesetter, as well as the calligrapher, follow. Some of the simpler ones are: The letters i and l require only ½ space, while the letters m and w require 1½; a punctuation mark requires ½, with a single space between words and at least a double space between sentences. Letters that are very boxy, like capital H, need ½ space between, but rounded ones like O, P and Q can be crowded closer to adjacent letters. Letters like o and c actually look smaller in a line of type than do many others, so they can be made slightly taller. A letter like t, particularly a capital T, can be crowded slightly closer to adjacent letters like o or a because of the projecting crossbar on top. This is also true of the letter f on its right side. Interline spacing can vary widely, from one-half the total line width to more than twice the line width, but line spacing should be widened as line length or letter weight increases, for ease of reading.

There are many other rules, some of which will vary with the particular alphabet being used. For example, in the large plaque pictured (Fig. 125), the t, l, and f are special forms requiring a full space in width. My best suggestion for the beginner at carving letters is to use a simple sans serif alphabet. Gothic, script, italic and archaic alphabets are much harder to carve well.

There are occasions when all these suggestions must be abandoned, as in designing and carving the legend of the bird (Fig. 135). This is the old Celtic story, so it seemed appropriate to design it with an alphabet from *The Book of Kells*, and to use a decorative band from that book as well.

My first idea was a simple carving of the bird suspended from a thorn, the whole composition "white on white" except for a vermilion drop of blood.

Fig. 125 (above). Gothic letters in relief, Spanish, 14th or 15th century. Fig. 126 (below). Gothic letters from the tomb of Richard II, and others, about 1400.

Fig. 127 (above). Incised letters from the Forum at Rome. Fig. 128 (below). Elizabethan lettering from an incised inscription at North Walsham, Norfolk, England.

**ABCDEFGHIKLMNP
QRSTWY! 1234567890
abcdefghjkmprstuvwxyz**

Fig. 129 (above). Engraver's Old English.

**ABCDEFGHIJKLM
NOPQRSTUVWXYZ**

Fig. 130. Modern initials.

**ABCDEFGHIJKLMNOPQRSTU
VWXYZ&   1234567890$
abcdefghijklmnopqrstuvwxyz**

*Fig. 131. Caslon Old-Style alphabet, the basis for numerous modern
type faces.*

***ABCDEFGHIJKLMNOP
QRSTUVWXYZ&
abcdefghijklmnopqrstuv
wxyz   1234567890$***

Fig. 132. Ultra-Bodoni Italic; note slant and extra-fat letters.

**ABCDEFGHIJKLMNOPQRSTUV
WXYZ&   1234567890$
abcdefghijklmnopqrstuvwxyz**

*Fig. 133. Sans Serif, which must be carefully spaced between letters
for ease in reading.*

Then I realized that the carving might well be meaningless to most people, and the legend itself should be included. This suggested that the plaque take the form of an illuminated manuscript, with the bird as the ornamental initial. It seemed advisable to include some other decoration for the "page" as well, so the idea of including a side band combined with the thorn branch was born. Fortunately, the ancient Celts were fond of designs of vines growing from pots, so the branch could simply be an extension. It could also incorporate some of the complex patterns the Celts used in the bird itself, so I braided the extended tail.

My original plan was to carry the thorn branch out to form an ornamental T and to begin the legend with the words, "There was once a bird . . ." This would have necessitated a tag line at the end "—Celtic legend," which can be hard to handle, and the words did not fit well in the line width. So I converted the opening to the present one and avoided both problems. The word "Celtic" gives a better start than the rather flat "There," and the thorn branch could make a C as readily as a T. Also, the word "bards" is a bit more graphic than the word "legends," which would have crowded the line anyway.

The second line presented a similar problem: If the bird were considered impersonal, I might have used "that" instead of "who." And so it went through the quotation. My point is that unless a quotation must be exact, it is possible to rewrite it slightly as you go to avoid splitting a word or over-spacing words; hyphens and gaps don't look well in a line. I was, of course, trying to make all the lines the same overall length. Typographers and cryptographers avoid this problem by having one edge or the other of the column "ragged"—that is, they allow the lines to come as nearly as possible to the desired width, but to vary slightly on one side, usually the right. (This would have been perfectly possible in this case, because the alignment needed only to be with the band at the left.

Another alternative, for short quotations or lettering, is to center each line, thus leaving both edges ragged. A third alternative is to increase the width of each letter, or the spaces between letters and words, to make the line come out even (note the difference, for example, in the spaces between words on the bird panel from line to line). A fourth alternative is to reduce letter size slightly after the first few lines, this is common in newspapers and similar printing, but less common among typographers (note that my fifth and subsequent lines are slightly smaller).

In addition, there is the problem of the space between design and lettering. On the sixth line I elected to split the difference between the lengths of preceding and following lines; it could have been the width of the line above (leaving an unsightly space below the bird), or as long as the succeeding line (crowding the design too much). These are, of course, very much matters of personal opinion and taste.

There is also the matter of lettering size and spacing. In this case, I used a ⅜-in (9.5-mm) letter height for capitals, which gave the lower-case letters a basic height of ¼ in (6.3 mm), plus "upstanders" and "downstanders," as they are called. The spacing between lines is also ¼ in (6.3 mm), which is enough as long as an upstander on one letter doesn't exactly meet the downstander of another. I was lucky.

The old Celtic alphabet had no k, and its capital G looked something like a reversed capital F. You will note that the little wedge-line atop the t and g is higher than the line of letters, and that the f is slightly higher and adds a downstander (which our alphabets, except the script, have lost). Also, the s has a larger loop on top than on the bottom. All of these things further complicate the lettering design and execution. I replaced the capital G with a more modern form, added the k and changed the ampersand to a later design in the interest of readability, but I left the i as it originally was, without the dot above, because the dot is a nuisance anyway.

I have gone into considerable detail here on design, because books on lettering design are not readily available, at least in my experience. There are, however, books showing alphabets, as well as lettering catalogs and the like, from which you can select. I repeat my original injunction: Pick a simple alphabet, at least initially. Gothic and flowery lettering is not designed for the carver but for the penman and illustrator, and most woods won't take the detail, even if your eyes and tools will. And incise your lettering, unless you have endless time and patience. Incised letters can be tinted easily for legibility, by simply putting on a stop coat of varnish and flowing a paint or stain into the lettering then wiping off the excess as a scrimshander does on ivory. (If the surface of the piece is tinted by the coloring, it can be lightly sanded to clean it up, but you can't do that with raised lettering!)

Because thin plastic sheet can be molded to almost any form and will pick up even surface roughness and grain lines, some carvers have had commissions to produce patterns for such work. These patterns are often in woods that will display a decided grain, like oak, particularly with a little sandblasting after carving. Sign carvers also make use of this characteristic of wood, sandblasting their lettering after completion to give it a weathered look. It is also quite common to batter the sign a bit with a chain or other flexible but hard object to add to the weathering, as well as to do some scorching with a blowtorch (which incidentally removes burrs and feather edges, and makes sanding unnecessary).

The "MDA 7" shown here (Fig. 136) is in this category. It was produced in white pine with raised and serifed lettering to serve as a pattern in clay or Plasticine. Because it was to be applied directly to the material, which had to read correctly, the pattern had to be in reverse and also had to have slightly sloping sides so it could be withdrawn after it was pressed into the material.

Another problem that you may face on occasion is to produce a monogram. This is usually composed of three letters, but may be two or four, or even more in the case of a company or an individual who carries a "Junior" or "III," for example. The simplest approach is to make the letter of the Christian name dominant, with the other two laced over it. Because so many letters in the English alphabet have vertical and horizontal lines, this is relatively easy. A dominant circular letter like c or o can enclose the others, or one with a space at top and/or bottom, like m, n, or w, can do the same.

Sometimes one letter can serve to complete another, as in the initials AGA, in which the G can tie together the two A's, one over the other, by forming the crossbars as it cuts through both. Of course, modern printers avoid the entire problem by putting the letters in order, vertically, horizontally or diagonally, but the calligrapher interlocks them in one way or another, even if he or she must modify the letter form to do it.

Fig. 134. Dog 1¼ × 9 × 10 in (3.2 × 23 × 25 cm) is set on a base 4½ × 13 in (11 × 33 cm), with forward bevel that reads: "Lord, help me this day to keep my nose out of other people's business."

486

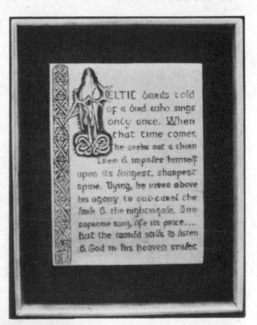

Fig. 135 (right). Panel in English syca-more (harewood), about 12 × 16 in (30 × 41 cm), has incised lettering com-bined with a trenched low-relief of a bird impaled on a thorn, which also provides an initial letter C. Thorn grows from a Celtic interlaced potted-tree design forming the left border. The alphabet is Celtic, with some additions to make it understandable today.

Fig. 136 (left). Serifed and weighted letters provide a pattern for clay impressions. Letters must have sloping sides to pull from the clay. Wood is white pine, and overall size is 2 × 7½ in (5.1 × 19 cm).

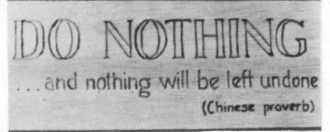

Fig. 137. Simple incised and serifed lettering, with weighted verticals, forms the first line of this desk block. Second and third lines are simple incising. All lines are filled with pig-ment, after which the surface is sanded (as in scrimshaw) and then matte-varnished.

487

CHAPTER XVII
Lettering an Award Panel

Carved elements appliqued, caption data incised

AWARDS OF ONE KIND OR ANOTHER lend themselves particularly to wood-carving, and can range from a simple shaped plaque for a background to something that includes likenesses. Almost always, however, unless the award incorporates an engraved plate, some lettering will be required, and some research will be necessary.

This example (Fig. 141) is one of the more elaborate panels I've done, presented to a man on his 55th birthday. The client suggested the general form: an indication of the subject's college background, indicated by initial letters and mascots, and his professional life to date.

The first step in designing such a panel is to do the research. In this case, I had to find out the shape of the Princeton letter P, the Columbia letter C, and the New York University letter forms as well as its symbol. All involved telephone calls to the college offices. To simplify the design, I decided to use only the heads of the Princeton tiger and the Columbia lion, and only the torch from the circa-1952 NYU symbol, an Olympic runner carrying a torch. (NYU and Prudential now use stylized symbols, but the torch I carved, as well as the Prudential Insurance Rock of Gibralter, are both older designs—and were in use at the time my subject was there.)

An essential in the design of an award, unless the overall shape is to be symbolic, is the shape and size of the plaque, because other elements must be fitted to it. I had in mind a rectangle of fairly conventional proportions, and was fortunate to have saved the top of a small stand. It was glued up of 1-in (2.54-cm) maple, 13 × 17½ in (33 × 45 cm), with rounded corners and fluted edges, so it required only top sanding to be ready for use. I planned to incise the lettering with a V-tool, and trials on the back of the top showed that it could be carved with a good, clean line, providing, as always, that the V-tool was sharp.

The next step was to lay out the plaque and size the elements. The principal employer of the subject turned out to be Bear, Stearns & Co., which immediately suggested another symbol in rebus form—a back view of the three bears and their visitor, Goldilocks. In an animal anatomy book, I found a head-on view of a Malay tiger and a practically tail-on view of a bear. My family crest is a lion head with tongue out, and this seemed appropriate to the occasion because the subject had attended Columbia, but was forced to leave after a few months (as a result of his father's death), so did not earn his intended law degree there. (Hence the lightning bolt and the displaced final letters of LLB.)

A phone call to the nearest Prudential Insurance man brought several folders, one of which showed the old symbol of the Rock. I designed my own Goldilocks and had all the elements. The arrangement worked out quite simply: three colleges along the top row, three employers along the bottom. However, because the subject had worked for the first two while he was studying nights at NYU, it seemed preferable to place that unit directly beneath the NYU one and connect them with more rebus symbols—a moon for the night study at NYU, and a sun shining on the Rock for the day work, with a two-way arrow connecting them. Thus the major employer could occupy major space at the lower left. (The alternative would be a conventional left-to-right arrangement of each line.)

To lay out the bear group involved drawing silhouettes of the bear pose in three sizes and shuffling them one over the other to get a shape that fit the space and still emphasized the "bear sterns." Goldilocks was sized to fit.

To get contrast with the maple, I decided to make parts of the units three-dimensional. This would avoid a confusing welter of incised lines and lend some depth to the panel. Also, I could use a contrasting color of wood—in this case mahogany scraps—except for Goldilocks, who wouln't really have been appropriate in a dark wood. She is of pine. The heads, bear group, torch and Goldilocks were blanked out with a coping saw, then whittled.

Lettering was laid out as simple unserifed letters, except for the subject's name and the college initials, which conform to *their* style. Incising serifs is troublesome, particularly when the lettering is only ¼ in (6.4 mm) tall. Also, all lettering was done in capitals, to get maximum size for carving. Letter carving was done with the V-tool and a light mallet; this gives much better control than carving by hand. It was necessary in some instances, such as periods and short lines running with the grain, to make stop cuts with the knife, and in a few instances to finish an angular meeting point with the knife, but, in general, lettering could be done quite rapidly by this method.

489

When lettering was completed, the panel was fine-sanded to remove burrs, then given two good sprayed coats of satin varnish. This provides both a surface finish and a stop for the "antiquing," which is done by brushing in a dark stain and wiping it off the surface, as would be done with scrimshaw. It is very important that the lettering be fully varnished, or the stain will run into the grain at the sides and discolor the surface. (I had this problem in one or two places, which later required scraping of the surface in those areas and respraying.) I used, incidentally, a German Beiz sal-ammoniac, water-based stain, walnut in color.

Once all this is done, the emblems, separately spray-varnished, are glued in place, the assembly given a third coat of varnish, then two coats of wax or clear shoe polish. Sign it, add ring hangers on the back, and it's ready to go.

Fig. 138 (left). Templates were cut from heavy paper to size elements and test their locations. This was particularly important in posing the three bears and Goldilocks, and in checking that the torch was not so large as to obscure the lettering.

Fig. 139. Finished emblems ready to be glued into place.

490

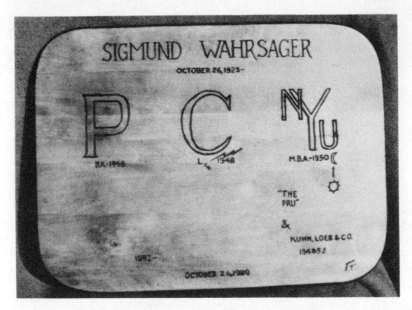

Fig. 140 (above). Lettering was incised with a V-tool on this maple panel, which was then sprayed with two coats of matte varnish. The varnish acted as a stop when stain was put over the surface and then wiped off, as is done in scrimshaw. Fig. 141 (below). Finished panel, showing elements glued in their proper locations. All but Goldilocks are mahogany; she is pine. Finish is matte varnish and wax.

CHAPTER XVIII

Finishing Suggestions

Including gold-leafing, antiquing, metal inlay

THERE ARE A GREAT MANY WAYS TO FINISH relief carvings, of course. Outdoor signs, and panels, usually in pine, basswood or possibly oak, will be painted in most cases, and may even be "antiqued" on an instant basis by beating with chains, scorching slightly with a blowtorch or sandblasting to take off sharp edges. (Some carvers start with old boards to get authenticity; in that case the poorer the finish the more authentic. Poor finish goes with splintered ends and rotten spots—and poor carving. I've known of carvers who buried their products for a week or two to give them antiquity—or dealers who did it after them.) If an outdoor panel is not painted, it should probably be marine-varnished—which means high gloss; matte and satin finishes simply will not hold up in the weather.

With the above exceptions, I prefer a good wood and a natural finish, with low gloss. You can obtain this on good hardwoods simply by oiling and waxing. I have found processed oils such as Danish finish and tung-oil finish to be better than boiled linseed, though more expensive; they're all that's needed on teak, for example, even for constant exposure. Teak will retain its color and finish with such oiling semiannually. And instead of the familiar waxes, which are preferable for something that will be touched or handled frequently, I use Kiwi® neutral shoe polish. It does not turn white or grey in crevices, nor build up with subsequent polishing. (Kiwi is the "wax finish" used in such divergent places as Bali and Sri Lanka.)

Panel carvings can often be improved by antiquing, the application of a slightly darker stain and immediate rub-off, so the darker color is retained only in crevices. This is what happens anyway as a panel ages—dirt collects in crevices and darkens them, thus giving the panel color contrast and greater

492

apparent depth. If you plan to antique, give the panel a couple of coats of spray matte varnish first; it helps seal the pores and prevent instant absorption of the darker stain in cross-grain areas. I have also found very useful the so-called Beiz finishes, based on sal-ammoniac instead of oil, incorporating a wax and apparently obtainable only in Germany. These finishes, like American Minwax®, provide color and polish in a single coat—particularly on soft woods—and can be applied one over the other for special effects and toning.

Signs, nameplates and liturgical carvings are quite common in relief carving, and may require gilding or gold-leafing of anything from lettering to the entire surface. Gilding is actually just another kind of lacquering, and the technique is detailed on the container. Bronzing, coppering and silvering are similar. All can be applied in many tints with spray cans—with a spray-can result. I have done better with rub-on compounds, particularly for various shades of gold. These are apparently gilt in a wax, so careful application with the fingertips and rubbing in improves the finish. Paints, brush or spray, tend to pile up in crevices and show brush marks. They are not durable when exposed to the weather and somehow look synthetic. If used, they must be covered with some sort of finish, such as a polyurethane varnish.

The ultimate in such work is to apply gold leaf, which is ridiculously expensive today. Real gold leaf is about one three-hundredth as thick as a human hair! There is, of course, imitation gold leaf just as there is silver leaf, also an imitation. Imitation gold is readily available in paint and hobby stores, comes in packets containing 5.2 sq ft (.468 sq m) as 25 leaves, each 5½ in (14 cm) square. The imitation gold is thicker than the real thing, harder to pick up, handle and cover an area with, and usually comes in loose sheets separated by thin paper. Imitation gold must be protected or it will tarnish, particularly out of doors. Real gold, these days mostly from West Germany, comes in packets of 25 leaves, 3¼ in square (21 sq cm) totalling 284 sq in (1,832 sq cm). It is actually quite hard to find. It can range from 13½ to 23 karats in purity; real gold is 24 K but has a tendency to split when worked. Woodcarvers use 22 to 23 K gold leaf. Real gold leaf comes either in loose or transfer sheets, the latter held to the backing tissues by jeweller's rouge. The transfer gold is easier to use because it is applied just like a decal, the tissue peeled off after it is applied. It avoids a great deal of fussing with brushes and specialized transfer devices, but is somewhat less economical because parts of sheets may be lost or incorrectly applied.

If you plan to use real gold leaf, the carving should be suited to it. This means selecting a wood that is not too coarse in grain—basswood is ideal—and without undercuts or extremely complex or difficult-to-reach areas. The gold may bridge over such areas or not adhere properly.

The traditional process of applying gold leaf to surfaces, including wood-carvings, is described in exhaustive detail in *Wood Carving*, by Wheeler & Hayward (Sterling), in which the process occupies two entire chapters. Included are meticulous descriptions of how one mixes a special gesso and a special boles, selects proper brushes and knives and how many preparatory coats are to be applied before the gold leaf. Further, there is the necessity of selecting between oil and water application of the leaf, the use of special brushes for free leaves and so on. Actually, the method can be much simpler. Suppliers of gold leaf can provide it, or it can be done as explained to me by Gardner Wood, who has gold-leafed many temple carvings over the past fifteen or more years.

Gardner Wood advises beginning with a relatively dense wood, such as basswood, that requires no filler (oak is obviously a bad choice). If filling is necessary, use a lacquer sealer like Prime®, following the directions on the can. When it dries, sand lightly with very fine or worn sandpaper to get rid of any raised wood fibres. Then cover the surface with gold size, available from the gold-leaf supplier and most paint stores. It is a slow-drying, oil-base size (one brand is Swift's®), and should be brushed on in a thin coat and left overnight. The surface is ready for application of the leaf when tacky—when a dry finger touched to it comes away with a pinging sound, and without picking up any size. (The surface will stay in this state for a day or more under normal conditions.) The gold leaf is simply laid over this tacky surface and pressed down with dry fingertips. Transfer sheets have a blank corner, so the sheet can be picked up without touching the gold. When rubbed down, the transfer tissue can then be readily lifted off. Inevitably, some gold will be wasted, and some missed areas will have to be filled in. To prevent gold adhesion in unwanted areas, dust them with a little talcum powder; to remedy it, just use an ordinary ink eraser.

When covered, the surface must be burnished to remove jeweller's rouge that held the gold to the transfer sheet and to seal it. This is best done with balls of combed cotton rubbed over the surface in a circular polishing motion. If done properly, the surface will immediately show a higher gloss. Following burnishing, any areas that are likely to be abraded—such as the shank of a candlestick or the pushing surface on a door—should be protected. A finish like McClosky® Heirloom varnish will do the job nicely.

494

A gold-leafed surface is basically ultra-smooth, though it may sometimes be desirable to have a textured surface. Mr. Wood achieves the latter by using a product called Liquid Steel, basically an epoxy containing powdered steel, which can be brushed on the wood surface before gold-leafing. This creates a black surface that can be raked, combed or otherwise textured as desired. It is lightly sanded when dry. Because of the texturing, it is obvious that the application of gold leaf would cause bridging and holes that would show the black surface. To avoid this, the textured surface is sprayed with bronze or another tone. Then gold leaf is applied, rubbed in and burnished. It will leave some voids because of the texturing, but these create an antiqued look.

Gold leaf alone tends to be flat and uniform, so it may be desirable to antique it to bring out depths and shadows. There is available a heavy paste called Rub'n Buff® (American Art Clay Co., Inc., PO Box 68163, Indianapolis, Indiana 46286) available in many art-supply stores in 18 tones of brass, bronze, copper and gold. The paste will stick to any surface, and can be applied by rubbing or by thinning with turpentine and using a brush in difficult areas. Various tones can be applied one over the other to get special effects. It is particularly effective over textured areas, and the more the surface is rubbed the better it gets. The virtue of such texturing is that the surface color can range from a yellow gold to a green in recessed areas. As before, the treated surface should be protected with a good polyurethane varnish if subjected to frequent handling or other unusual wear. Otherwise, gold leaf will stand years of atmospheric wear, requiring only occasional washing with water and a mild soap to remove smog and grime deposits.

On old gunstocks you will find a form of inlay that could be more widely used because it is relatively simple to do. It can be done with silver, brass or copper flat wire or strip, or combinations, and usually takes the form of long cyma curves or scrolls—sometimes with added accents produced by endwise inlay of "spots" of round wire. In India, it was common to decorate small stylized figures of horses, elephants and the like with brass inlay in this way (Figs. 142 and 143), and examination indicates that the brass was formed to desired shapes, simply driven into a wood such as teak, then sanded off until the crushed fibres of wood at the surface and any projecting brass were removed. The entering edge of the brass was slightly wedge-shaped for penetration.

The conventional method of inserting silver and gold is more considerate of the wood. The desired design is laid out on the surface or transferred to

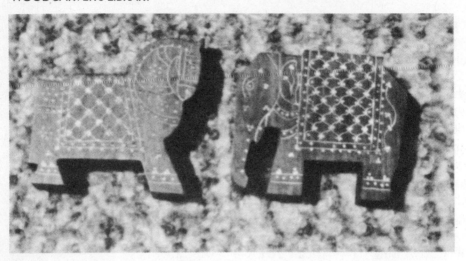

Fig. 142 (above). Horse and elephant are of teak, decorated with brass inserts. The horse, for example, is ¾ × 3 × 3 in (1.9 × 7.6 × 7.6 cm), and wire inserts are $\frac{1}{64}$ × $\frac{1}{32}$-in (.40 × .79-mm) ribbon. Even the larger spots are made from bits of the same wire, curled up. Fig. 143 (below). Camel and two bullocks are also of teak with brass inserts. Pieces such as these, as well as those in Fig. 142, were made in India years ago, but are probably too costly to produce at today's tourist prices.

it after all but final sanding has been done (so metal dust sanded off later will not penetrate surface crevices). Then a narrow trench is produced along the lines of the design by driving in a thin blade sharpened from both sides like a firmer. These can be made from any thin tempered steel, such as straight X-acto® chisel blades. Blade widths can vary from ¼ in (6.4 mm) down to $\frac{1}{16}$ in (1.6 mm), the latter for following curves. These blades should be driven into a depth corresponding with wire or strip width and leave a V-shaped groove as wide at the top as the metal is thick. The metal ribbon is then cut off, formed to shape and driven in progressively, using a light hammer and a dowel. The wire should be just about level with the surface, so light sanding will smoothe it at surface level. If the wire buckles during driving, cut out and replace the buckled portion, since flattening out buckled ribbon and attempting to redrive it usually results in failure and added complication from enlargement of the trench.

In woods such as walnut and teak, the sides of the trench will close in and grip the wire with no problems; but you can use thinned glue in the slot to make sure, or rough the side of the wire ribbon slightly with a file. Make sure that any two pieces of wire that butt together are a good joint, because any gap will be very visible when the work is finished. It may be helpful to file the end of the ribbon at a slight angle in such a case, so the upper portion actually wedges in place as it is driven down. Once the wire is in place, the surface is final-sanded, metal filings brushed and dusted away and the piece is ready for finishing. And any finish will include some moisture that will cause the sides of the trench to swell back and grip the insert tightly.

APPENDIX A

Sharpening Hints

THERE ARE FOUR STEPS TO SHARPENING A TOOL, of which the first, grinding, will probably have been taken by the tool supplier. You should not have to grind a tool unless you break it, nick it badly or resharpen it so often that you wear down the basic included angle. Grinding on modern high-speed wheels is fast but dangerous; you're almost certain to burn the tool end, thus drawing the temper and spoiling the tool.

Whetting and honing are hand operations, done on progressively finer-grained stones, either natural or manufactured. Whetting is done on Washita, a yellowish or greyish stone, or on medium-coarse artificial stone. Honing is done on Arkansas, a white, very hard stone from which "slips" are also made. Slips are the small, shaped stones for taking the feather edge off the inner edge of tools, particularly gouges and V-tools, as well as delivering a final polish to a firmer. Makers and sellers of these stones provide detailed instructions for their use.

Stropping is the final operation, and is exactly like what a barber does on a straight razor. It is done on a leather strop or on a board with strop leather glued to its face. Some small boards have two differing smoothnesses of leather, one with oil and a very fine abrasive such as crocus or tripoli, and the other often with oil alone. While whetting and honing are done edge-first, stropping is done with edge last so the tiny saw teeth on the edge of the blade are aligned. In normal use, stropping is fairly frequent, honing less so and whetting only periodic, depending upon wood hardness, frequency of tool use and your own habits in handling.

Many carvers have recently turned to buffing to replace all three final sharpening operations, using buffing wheels shaped to the tools and a series of buffing compounds such as rouge or tin oxide. This has a tendency to round or shorten the actual cutting edge, and may make it wear longer. Some carvers also prefer hollow-grinding as done with a razor, which tends to thin the blade angle (normally 30 degrees) at the cutting edge, making it cut faster in soft woods but probably require more frequent sharpening.

The typical movements in hand sharpening and stropping are shown (Figs. 144–145). It is important to spread the wear over the stones and strop to prevent their being worn hollow. Stones should be kept lubricated with thin machine oil, or even a 50-50 mixture of machine oil and kerosene. They should be wiped off and the oil replaced when it turns grey from metal inclusions and dust. Periodically, stones can be washed with benzine or gasoline. Natural stones can be boiled in water with a little baking soda to remove oil and grit. Manufactured stones should not be boiled but rather warmed in an oven.

Note that I use a circular or oval motion in stoning a knife, making certain I get the tip—where most dulling usually occurs in detail carving. Stoning is sketched in *A*, stropping in *C*. Edge sharpness can be tested as in *D* by trying it on the edge of a piece of paper or on the thumbnail; it should cut paper and "stick" on the nail, indicating cutting. To test tip sharpness, try it on a scrap of soft wood. Similar suggestions for sharpening chisels are sketched in *E* and *F*, the use of a slip in *G*. Getting the almost microscopic inner bevel on gouges shown in *G* helps maintain sharpness. Gouges can be sharpened like firmers, but this is tricky because the tool must be rotated at uniform speed while being pushed on the stone; over-rotation will round off corners, while under-rotation will leave them dull. On a gouge, a major dull area can be spotted as a line of light on the tip, *B*. Trickiest to sharpen is the V-tool, because a misshapen edge is easy to get and hard to use. Too thick a

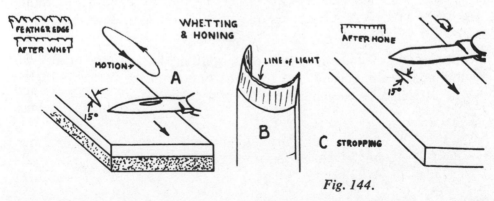

Fig. 144.

499

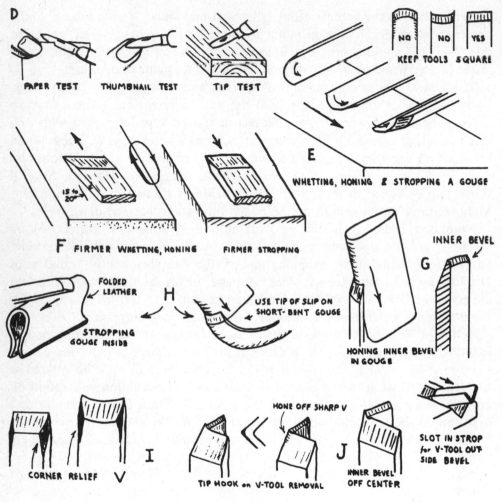

D

PAPER TEST   THUMBNAIL TEST   TIP TEST

NO NO YES
KEEP TOOLS SQUARE

E
WHETTING, HONING & STROPPING A GOUGE

15 to 20°

F FIRMER WHETTING, HONING   FIRMER STROPPING

INNER BEVEL

G

FOLDED LEATHER

H

USE TIP OF SLIP ON SHORT-BENT GOUGE

STROPPING GOUGE INSIDE

HONING INNER BEVEL IN GOUGE

CORNER RELIEF V   I

HONE OFF SHARP V

TIP HOOK on V-TOOL REMOVAL

INNER BEVEL OFF CENTER

J

SLOT IN STROP for V-TOOL OUT SIDE BEVEL

Fig. 145.

tip will tear the wood and may even cause splitting, but too thin an edge will crumble and, again, not cut. Relieving the bottom of the "V" very slightly may be helpful, as is bevelling the edges of a gouge (I).

APPENDIX B

How to Change Size

AVAILABLE DESIGNS ARE OFTEN TOO SMALL, or may not fit the wood you choose. If you can take a good photo of the design or of the subject, it can be projected onto the wood or a ·piece of paper in the desired enlargement and traced. You can then use elements from several transparencies together. Or you can have prints made to the desired size. Failing these, you can take the original drawing or photo to an art studio and ask them to make a suitably sized photostat (ordinary copiers won't do it: they copy only same size in most cases).

I have used all of these methods, but I usually am working without a negative, so I use one of two methods to get a pattern. The first is the method of squares (Fig. 146). I have a grid of ⅛-in (3.2-mm) inked squares on transparent plastic that I place over the original—say a drawing in this book. If I am doubling size, I draw a similar grid of ¼-in (6.4-mm) squares on paper or the board. If I'm tripling, it's ⅜-in (9.5-mm) squares; if I'm enlarging to 1½ times, it's ³⁄₁₆-in (4.8-mm) squares. Then I copy the design square by square. This is easy, but I become confused among the squares on occasion.

The other method I call point-to-point (Fig. 147) because it resembles the puzzles that children do by drawing a line from number to number. I establish base lines at the side and bottom (or top) of the original, either by drawing them in or putting a square over the original and anchoring it in place. I draw similar base lines on paper or on the panel. Then I locate prominent points, one by one, by getting the horizontal and vertical dimensions of each from the base lines, multiplying each dimension by the multiplying factor and plotting it on the new sketch. To double, I multiply each dimension by two, and so on. This method gets a bit hairy if you want to enlarge 50 percent and have to multiply 1⅞ in (4.8 cm) by 1½ (3.8 cm), but it works well for me since I am reasonably fast and accurate at simple mental arithmetic. When key points are located, simply draw the design between them and fair them in. I find this best for working from a photo or book illustration, on which outlines may not be clear enough for the method of squares.

Fig. 146.

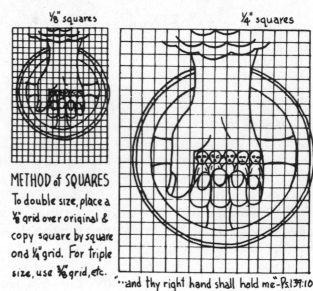

⅛" squares   ¼" squares

METHOD of SQUARES
To double size, place a ⅛" grid over original & copy square by square ond ¼" grid. For triple size, use ⅜" grid, etc.

"...and thy right hand shall hold me"-Ps.139:10

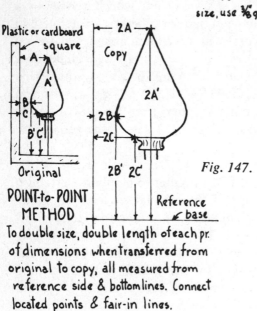

Plastic or cardboard square

A

Original

Copy

2A

2A'

2B

2C

2B' 2C'

Reference base

Fig. 147.

POINT-to-POINT METHOD
To double size, double length of each pr. of dimensions when transferred from original to copy, all measured from reference side & bottom lines. Connect located points & fair-in lines.

Index